BEHOLD THE SON

A Study of the Gospel of John

J. Randolph Turpin, Jr.

Declaration Press

Behold the Son

Third Edition

Contents

And truly Jesus did many other miraculous signs
in the sight of his disciples that are not written in this book.
But these are written that you might believe
that Jesus is the Christ, the Son of God,
and that by believing you may have life in his name.
(John 20:30-31)

PREFACE

There came a point in the mid 1990's when my heart's yearning to go deeper with God became so intense that I cried out, "Lord, I want to be as close to you as it is humanly possible for a man to be close to you. I want to be as close to you as John was close to you."

He instantly responded, "Then walk with me as John walked with me."

I was drawn into further reflection on John's life. I cherished the words that he wrote—three epistles, the *Apocalypse* and the Gospel that bears his name. I thought of others throughout history who shared my longing for the presence and glory of God: Enoch, who walked with God and crossed the boundary between heaven and earth; Noah, who found favor in the eyes of the Lord, knew his voice and was led by that voice to rescue the human race from total annihilation; Abraham, who was called "the friend of God" and followed his heavenly Friend, even when he had no idea where he was taking him; Moses, whose sense of absolute need for God's presence caused him to cry out, "Show me your glory!"; David, the worshiping warrior king who became what he was by being "a man after God's own heart"; and Paul, who already knew Jesus deeply and yet expressed his own insatiable hunger for increased intimacy with Christ, saying, "I want to know him!"

Like Moses, I too was crying out, "Lord, show me your glory!" And here was John—a man who reports, "We beheld his glory."[1] This man claims to have seen what I have longed to see. I wanted to learn from him; I wanted to

[1] See 1:14.

hear everything this man has to say. This Gospel has become a place that I often revisit to renew my gaze upon the reality of who Jesus truly is.

The volume in hand has been prepared as a resource for personal study and as a tool for teachers walking their students through a survey of this Gospel. The occasion that prompted the production of the first edition was a fourteen-week series that I prepared for the church where I was serving at the time—Royal Ridge Church of God (Scarborough, Maine). As the class worked through the text, additional insights were recorded, and the original manuscript was revised and refined.

The second edition was prepared specifically for use in my Gospel of John class at Valor Christian College (Columbus, Ohio). As I taught the class, I fine-tuned the manuscript on the basis of insights gained from student feedback and the use of the material in the course. I am especially grateful for the contributions of Frances Luzynski, Yvonne R. Navedo, Holly Barnett, Teofilo Ponce, LaNancia Martin and Heather Crawford. These Valor students approached the study with a passion for knowing the heart of Jesus.

While engaged in the editorial process for this third edition, Pastor Rod Parsley invited me to conduct a month-long series on the Gospel of John at both campuses of World Harvest Church (Columbus, Ohio and Elkhart, Indiana). Preparation for that series motivated the completion of this edition. The receptivity of the World Harvest congregation has greatly blessed me, and I feel both humbled and honored by the favor God has given me with Pastor Parsley—a great apostolic leader.

In these pages you will find the complete text of the Gospel According to John. The translation is the result of two processes: my own work at converting the words and expressions of the King James Version into contemporary English and a small amount of work translating from the Greek text. The King James Version was selected because of its familiarity and because of its availability in the public domain. Occasional reference has also been made to the New International Version in the footnotes.

Limited attention will be given to defending the authorship of this Gospel. I am personally convinced that John, the son of Zebedee, recorded this account. Some reputable scholars have proposed that it was a different John who penned these words. Most agree that the author must have been an eyewitness to the events detailed in the narrative.

The commentary in the footnotes features technical notes, cross references, material from sermons I have preached on this Gospel and personal reflections. To further assist in the study, tables have been inserted providing a harmony of the Gospels in those places where such information might prove relevant and helpful. Occasional opportunities for personal reflection are also inserted in the body. To facilitate note-taking, the text has been formatted with wide margins—lots of white space.

Preparing this material has been a great spiritual journey—a worshipful experience. At moments it has seemed as though the veil has been parted, allowing me to behold some aspect of Jesus that I have never seen before. May *you* behold the Son of God with every turn of the page, with every word that you ponder, and with every prayer that you pray in response to the message of this amazing Gospel.

J. Randolph Turpin, Jr.
Columbus, Ohio
February 2, 2016

INTRODUCTION

Cerinthus was in the bath house! As soon as the Apostle John learned that Cerinthus was there, he jumped up and stormed out yelling, "Let us flee, lest the building fall down! Cerinthus, the enemy of the truth, is inside!"[2] So goes the story as told by Polycarp—a disciple of the Apostle John.

Who was this man named Cerinthus, and why was he so disliked by John—the apostle most remembered for his exhortations to love? Cerinthus was a Christian heretic.[3] The commotion associated with him was at its peak in Ephesus around 100 A.D. Among other false doctrines, he taught that the world was created by angels; that Jesus—a mere man—was the biological son of Joseph; that Jesus received "Christ" at baptism and that "Christ" departed from him as he approached the cross-death; that Jesus will be raised from the dead at the last day, and that all men will rise with him; and that salvation is obtained by obedience to the Jewish law. The only New Testament writing that Cerinthus accepted was a mutilated collection of passages that roughly resembled the Gospel of Matthew. Having formulated

---

[2] A paraphrase of Irenaeus quoting Polycarp in *Against Heresies*, III.3.4. John's behavior in this bath house incident is a reminder of his thunderous traits. Whether it was for his loud voice, his boldness or his tendency to strike out rashly, Jesus had named John and his brother James the "Sons of Thunder." See Mark 3:14-17; 10:35-41; and Luke 9:49-50, 51-56.

[3] Cerinthus is also believed to have been an Egyptian Jew who practiced his own perverted version of Judaism.

a "Gospel" of his own making, he founded a school in Asia Minor and gathered his own disciples.[4] It was in response to this heretical movement that the Apostle wrote what we now recognize as 1 John and 2 John.

As false teaching continued to cloud the truth regarding the personhood of Jesus, church leaders in Asia Minor approached the aging Apostle John, requesting that he write a "spiritual Gospel" in response.[5] John was the last surviving eyewitness from Jesus' inner circle; his testimony could put an end to the confusion over Jesus' nature, person and deity. Mark, Matthew and Luke had already written their accounts of the life and ministry of Jesus, but to confront the heresies at hand, something more was needed to counter the heretical claims of Cerinthus and others like him.

John wrote his Gospel from Ephesus. When he was finished, his completed work did more than just silence the voice of error. He provided a window into some of the most intimate times that Jesus spent with his disciples. He provided a view deep into the heart of the Lord. He provided a way for readers in generations to come to truly know the Son of God. Regarding this Gospel, Warren W. Wiersbe has written, "Please come to this book with the heart and mind of a worshiper… And, remember, you are not studying a book—you are seeing a Person."[6]

---

[4] "Cerinthus" in the *Encyclopedia Britannica*, accessed September 4, 2012, http:// www.britannica.com/ EBchecked/ topic/ 103530/ Cerinthus and "Cerinthus" in *Catholic Encyclopedia*, accessed September 4, 2012, http:// www.newadvent.org/ cathen/ 03539a.htm.

[5] Irenaeus, *Against Heresies*, III.11.

[6] Warren W. Wiersbe, *Be Alive* (Wheaton, Illinois: Victor Books, 1989), 7.

Date and Authorship

Both internal and external evidence point to John the son of Zebedee[7] as the author. The date of writing was probably between A.D. 80 and 95. John was one of the original Twelve, and he was part of Jesus' inner circle, along with James (his brother) and Peter.

External evidence. A number of external evidences support the position that the Apostle John was the author of this Gospel:

1. Clement of Alexandria noted that in John's latter years, church leaders in Asia Minor asked him to write a *spiritual* Gospel to counter heretical teachings regarding the personhood of Christ.
2. Theophilus of Antioch (about A.D. 170) mentioned that John was the author.
3. Ignatius and Tatian also quoted from the Fourth Gospel, with the assumption that John was the author.
4. Irenaeus (a disciple of Polycarp who was a disciple of John) quoted this Gospel as John's work.[8]

Internal evidence. Nowhere in this Gospel is John mentioned by name. However, the writer does drop a number of hints that he is in fact the Apostle John. Internal evidences of John's authorship may be condensed as follows:

1. The author was a Jew—as is clearly reflected in writing style and Jewish understandings.
2. He was an eyewitness—as is evidenced by the author's many detailed descriptions of places, people and time.[9]

---

[7] The sons of Zebedee are referenced in 21:2.

[8] The preceding list of evidences is based on William MacDonald, *Believer's Bible Commentary: New Testament* (Nashville, Tennessee: Thomas Nelson Publishers, 1990), 279.

[9] See 4:46; 5:14; 6:59; 12:21; 13:1; 14:5, 8; 18:6; and 19:31.

3. He was an apostle and was intimately familiar with the life of Jesus' inner circle.[10]

4. The writer repeatedly refers to an anonymous "disciple whom Jesus loved"[11] while he seems to have no problem referring to the other disciples by name. After awhile it becomes clear that the disciple being referenced was John. In a sense, it appears as though the writer was going out of his way to not draw attention to himself by name.[12]

5. Other noteworthy passages related to the eyewitness character of the author are 1:14; 19:35; and 21:24.[13]

Purpose

John's stated purpose is found toward the end of his book. In John 20:31, he writes, "But these[14] are written that you might believe that Jesus is the Christ, the Son of God, and that by believing you may have life in his name." In one sense, this Gospel was written to introduce and establish seekers in faith in the Son of God. In another sense, with the threat of the heresies of John's day, this Gospel was written so that believers might confidently continue in their faith, having received a more substantial testimony to the reality of who Jesus truly is. The writer works with an obvious focus on his stated purpose, and that focus is reflected in the features and structure of the book.

---

[10] See 6:19, 60, 61; 12:16; 13:22, 28; and 16:19.

[11] In reference to "the disciple whom Jesus loved," see 13:23; 19:26; 20:2; and 21:7, 20.

[12] See 13:23; 19:26; 20:2; and 21:7, 20.

[13] The preceding list of evidences is based on William MacDonald, *Believer's Bible Commentary: New Testament* (Nashville, Tennessee: Thomas Nelson Publishers, 1990), 280.

[14] In 20:31, "these" is a reference to the "miraculous signs" mentioned in the preceding verse.

Special Features and Structure

Attention should be given to the special features and structure of this book distinguishing it from the other Gospels.

Details of ministry in Judea and Jerusalem. One of the most notable features is that John provides many details of Jesus' ministry in Judea and Jerusalem that are not mentioned in the other three Gospels. He also reveals aspects of Jesus' personhood that were not given as much attention by Matthew, Mark or Luke. On the other hand, John omits huge blocks of information that the other Gospel writers are careful to record. Why are there so many omissions? The answer is two-fold:

1. The church already possessed the works of Matthew, Mark and Luke, and a rewriting of details covered so excellently in their Gospels was not necessary.
2. John was very focused on his purpose to refute the heresies of his day, and to attempt a writing of a comprehensive Gospel narrative had the potential of distracting from that purpose.

Evidences that Jesus Was Messiah. John carefully selected evidences that Jesus was the Messiah, and he arranged them in the text in a masterful way. His supporting evidences are presented in the following manner:

Seven miraculous signs:

1. Turning the water into wine (2:1-11)
2. Healing the nobleman's son (4:46-54)
3. Healing the crippled man at the pool of Bethesda (5:2-18)
4. Feeding the five thousand (6:1-15)
5. Walking on the water (6:16-21)
6. Healing the man blind from birth (9:1-41)
7. Raising Lazarus from the dead (11:1-46)

Seven discourses:

1. The new birth and new life (3:1-21)
2. The water of life (4:4-42)

3. The deity and sonship of Christ (5:19-47)
4. The bread of life (6:22-59)
5. The life-giving Spirit (7:37-44)
6. The light of the world (8:12-30)
7. The Good Shepherd (10:1-21)

Seven "I am" statements:[15]

1. "I am the Bread of life" (6:35, 41, 48, and 51).
2. "I am the Light of the world" (8:12; 9:5).
3. "I am the Gate" (10:7, 9).
4. "I am the Good Shepherd" (10:11, 14).
5. "I am the Resurrection and the Life" (11:25).
6. "I am the Way, the Truth, and the Life" (14:6).
7. "I am the Vine" (15:1, 5).

This Gospel is structured around the seven miraculous signs. The final and most climatic miraculous evidence not noted in the above list was Jesus' own bodily resurrection from the dead—the ultimate sign that he is the Christ, the Son of God.[16]

Other prominent themes. Many other themes stand out in this Gospel:

- Jesus as "the Son of God"
- The word "believe" (occurring 98 times)
- The concept of "eternal life"[17]
- The ministry of the Holy Spirit
- The concept of truth and its embodiment in the Son, the Spirit and the Word

---

[15] There are a few additional "I am" statements that do not have a predicate: 4:26; 6:20; 8:24, 28, 58; 13:19; and 18:5, 8.

[16] See 20:1 – 21:25.

[17] See 3:15-16, 36; 4:14, 36; 5:24, 39; 6:27, 40, 47, 54, 68; 10:28; 12:25, 50; and 17:2.

- The prominence of the number seven
- The prominence of these words: "Father," "word," "light," "flesh," "love," "witness," "testify," "know," "darkness" and "world."

Potential Impact of this Study

The potential impact of this study is closely tied to this Gospel's stated purpose. In John's stated purpose in 20:31, he says, "These are written that you might believe that Jesus is the Christ, the Son of God, and that by believing you may have life in his name." This study has the potential (1) to cause people who have not previously believed to start believing the reality of who Jesus truly is, (2) to strengthen the faith of those who already believe, and (3) to bring those who believe into eternal life in Jesus' name.

The profound significance of these words is amplified by Church of God preacher, Ronnie Luke, who said, "The world is dying from lack of knowledge of the truth of who this man really is."[18] This study is likely to ignite a fire for evangelism in those who will receive it.

While the igniting of an evangelistic fervor is an expected outcome of studying this book, the intended outcome was to both establish *and* strengthen faith (i.e., "believing") in Jesus as the "one of a kind" Son of God. With that strengthening of faith comes increased spiritual vision. With such strengthened faith comes an elevated confidence in the reality of God's indescribable and incomparable love. However, in the final analysis it must be said that the ultimate anticipated result of hearing this message is that those who receive and believe will have "life in his name"[19]—a life that is

---

[18] Ronnie Luke, notes from sermon by Ronnie Luke, Northern New England Church of God Camp Meeting, late 1990's (Scarborough, Maine).

[19] John 20:31.

nothing less than the life of the eternal realm, and a life that can only be defined in terms of knowing the Son of God deeply.[20]

Suggestions for Group Study

One could spend a lifetime studying this Gospel, but conducting a group study with an indefinite stopping point is not usually sustainable. For that reason, a fourteen session study is suggested here, with the first session being an introduction and the other thirteen sessions covering the twenty-one chapters of the book. The following fourteen session schedule is based roughly on an outline proposed by Warren W. Wiersbe in *The Bible Expository Commentary*.[21]

A Fourteen Session Group Study Schedule		
Session 1		An Introduction to the Gospel of John
Session 2	1:1-14	Prologue
	1:15-34	The Testimony of John the Baptist
Opportunity (1:35 – 6:71)		***Jesus presents himself to...***
Session 3	1:35 - 2:12	His Disciples
Session 4	2:13 - 3:36	The Jews
Session 5	4:1-54	The Samaritans
Session 6	5:1-47	The Jewish Leaders
Session 7	6:1-71	The Multitudes
Opposition (7:1 -12:50)		***There is conflict with the Jewish leaders over...***
Session 8	7:1 – 8:11	Moses
	8:12-59	Abraham
Session 9	9:1 – 10:42	Who Messiah Is
Session 10	11:1 – 12:36	His Miraculous Power
	12:37-50	They Would Not Believe on Him

[20] See John 17:3.

[21] Warren W. Wiersbe, *The Bible Expository Commentary*, 6 volumes (Colorado Springs, Colorado: David C. Cook, 2004).

Outcome (13:1 -21:25)		
Session 11	13:1 - 17:26	The Faith of the Disciples (Part 1)
Session 12	13:1 - 17:26	The Faith of the Disciples (Part 2)
Session 13	18:1 - 19:42	The Unbelief of the Jews
Session 14	20:1 - 21:25	The Victory of Christ

CHAPTER 1

Prologue (1:1-14)

In the beginning[22] the Word[23] already existed,[24] and the Word was with God,[25] and the Word was God.[26]

---

[22] **1:1. *"In the beginning."*** These words echo the first words of the first book of the Hebrew Scriptures (Genesis 1:1). Consideration of origins is a gateway to comprehending meaning and purpose. Here and elsewhere in this Gospel, the writer uses Old Testament truth as a springboard for presenting the revelation of the Son of God.

[23] **1:1. *"The Word."*** The *logos,* translated "the Word," is the eternal Son of God. The word, *logos,* is used three times in 1:1 and one time in 1:14, and with no explanation. When a term appears with no explanation, it can be assumed that the original recipients did not need it explained—to them it was obvious what it meant.

The concept of *logos* was significant to both Jewish and Greek readers. To the Jew, the *logos* was God revealing himself. See Hebrews 1:1-3. In Greek philosophy, the *logos* was the intelligent mind of the universe that brought order out of that which would have otherwise been in chaos.

[24] **1:1. *"Already existed."*** The KJV translates, "In the beginning was the Word." The verb, "was," is the imperfect of *eimi,* signifying that which continuously "was" in the past. Consider Christ's pre-existence in Colossians 1:17 (NIV): "He is before all things, and in him all things hold together."

2 He was with God in the beginning.[27]

---

[25] **1:1. *"The Word was with God."*** Whereas "the Word already existed" speaks of his pre-existence, "the Word was with God" speaks of his co-existence. The words, *pros ton Theon,* translated "with God" in the KJV, more literally read, "toward the God." The suggestion here is that in the beginning, the Word was in face-to-face personal communion with God. He pre-existed in fellowship with his Father. In 17:5, Jesus' prayer suggests his anticipation for a return to this fellowship.

[26] **1:1. *"The Word was God."*** God was being revealed in Jesus. When Jesus walked the earth and people listened to him, they were hearing God. When they looked at him, they were seeing God. The Word did not *become* God; in the beginning the Word *already existed* as God. The Word was and is eternally God. See Colossians 1:15-17; 2:9.

The deity of Jesus is the consistent message through the Gospel of John. Jesus claimed to be God. Consider all of his "I Am" statements in this Gospel. (See 6:35 and its notes.) He said things like, "I and my Father are one" (10:30) and "He who has seen me has seen the Father" (14:9). Thomas cried out, "My Lord and my God" (20:28), yet Jesus did not rebuke him for speaking those words. Titles were given to Jesus that belong only to God: e.g., the eternal Judge, the holy One, the Alpha and the Omega, the Lord of the Sabbath, the Savior, Mighty God, Lord of lords, the Lord of glory and the Redeemer. He possessed the attributes of God: he was and is eternal, omnipresent, omniscient and omnipotent. He performed works that only God can do: he raised the dead, overpowered Satan, conquered the kingdom of darkness and forgave sins. Finally, he received worship. Angels and men refused worship, but Jesus accepted, knowing that only God should be worshiped.

[27] **1:2. *"He was with God in the beginning."*** These words can also be rendered, "The Word was already in face-to-face fellowship with God in the beginning." The repetition of this truth already expressed in 1:1 suggests that the *relationship* between God the Father and God the Son is an important theme in this Gospel.

What was this face-to-face fellowship like? The Father's words in Luke 3:22 (NIV) provide a hint: "You are my Son, whom I love; with you I am well pleased." The Word was eternally loved by the Father before the creation of the world, and

3 All things came into being through him,[28] and apart
from him not even one thing came into existence that
has come to be.[29]
4 In him was life,[30] and the life was the light of men.[31]
5 And the light keeps shining in the darkness, and the
darkness has not overpowered it.[32]

---

the Father did not esteem him as another god or a lesser god. The Word existed in intimate perfect communion with the Father in perfect love.

[28] **1:3. *"All things came into being through him."*** The Word is Creator. Someone has rightly stated, "Creatorship implies ownership, and ownership implies priority of claim." The fingerprints of the eternal Word are on every molecule of the universe. He is the Creator and Lord of all.

[29] **1:3. *"Apart from him not even one thing came into existence that has come to be."*** The phrases, "came into being," "came into existence" and "has come to be" are all derivatives of the Greek word, *ginomai* (to become). The Gospel writer uses the word three times in this one verse, impressing upon the reader the truth regarding the origin of all things. The emphasis suggested by this repetition counters the error of Cerinthus who taught that the world was created by angels. The three occurrences of *ginomai* in 1:3 also stand in contrast to the four occurrences of the imperfect of *eimi* in 1:1-2, signifying that which continuously "was" in the past. The point is that the Word continuously "was" (1:1) before anything in creation ever "became" or "came into existence" (1:2). The Creator-Word stands in contrast to his creation; he is not part of the created order, and he was never created.

[30] **1:4. *"In him was life."*** Scientists search the universe for the origin of life, but the search ends here. Jesus is the origin of life. The life that people long for and need can only be found in him. All who are apart from Jesus remain in the realm of death.

[31] **1:4. *"The life was the light of men."*** The "life" was the "light." Light is used here as a metaphor to depict the power of this life. The life that is in the Word has the power to overtake all of the spiritual darkness that is in man.

Harmony of the Gospels[33]			
	Matthew	**Mark**	**Luke**
Preface			1:1-4
John the Baptist 's Birth Foretold			1:5-25
Jesus' Birth Foretold			1:26-38
Mary Visits Elizabeth			1:39-56
Birth of John the Baptist			1:57-80
Genealogies	1:1-17		3:23-38
Jesus' Birth	1:18-25		2:1-7
Extended Birth Narrative			2:8-20
Circumcision and Presentation in Temple			2:21-38
Magi from the East	2:1-12		
Flight to Egypt and Return to Nazareth	2:13-23		2:39
Jesus at the Temple at Twelve Years of Age			2:40-52

---

[32] **1:5. *"The darkness has not overpowered it."*** In other words, "the darkness cannot put out the light." These words occurring in association with "the beginning" (1:1) call to mind the contrast between darkness and light in the creation narrative (Genesis 1:1-5). Drawing upon that contrast, John 1:1-5 provokes deep thought. The destiny of every person rests upon the truths contained in these five verses.

[33] **Harmony of the Gospels.** This Harmony of the Gospels is based in part on the work of Alfred Nevin as presented in "Harmony of the Gospels," *Blue Letter Bible,* accessed August 11, 2012, http:// www.blueletterbible.org/ study /harmony/ index.cfm.

6 ¶ There was a man sent from God,[34] whose name was
John.[35]
7 This man came as a witness—to bear witness[36] of the
Light, so that through this Light all people might
believe.[37]

---

[34] **1:6. *"There was a man sent from God."*** The portrait of John the Baptist that is to follow serves as an example of what believers in Jesus are called to become. May every follower of Jesus come to the place where they hear the call of God—the call that sends them to their respective stations in life and places in this world. There in each place to which they have been sent, they are authorized to represent and bear witness of the Light—Jesus.

[35] **1:6. *"John."*** This John is John the Baptist and not John, the writer of this Gospel. A number of factors in John the Baptist's spiritual formation undoubtedly influenced him toward becoming this prophet in the wilderness, but ultimately the compelling force behind his ministry and conduct was the fact that he was one who had been "sent from God."

[36] **1:7. *"This man came as a witness—to bear witness."*** The writer speaks of John the Baptist coming to "bear witness" regarding the person of Jesus. A major feature of this Gospel is its collection of witnesses and testimonies confirming that Jesus is in fact the Son of God—even God in the flesh.

[37] **1:7. *"So that through this Light all people might believe."*** John the Baptist's objective resonates with this Gospel's purpose as stated in John 20:31: "But these are written that you might believe that Jesus is the Christ, the Son of God, and that by believing you may have life in his name." John the Baptist's example speaks to all who are sent to bear witness of the Light. The hope in the heart of one sent by God is that "all people" ("all men" in the KJV) might believe.

At first glance, one might think that *believing* is the prerequisite for this Light to effectively illuminate the human heart. Look more carefully at the passage. It says that John the Baptist came to bear witness so that "*through this Light* all people might believe." Faith is *not* the prerequisite for the Light to have impact. Faith is the *result* of the Light having impact. Herein is encouragement for those who have been sent to bear witness of the Light. We must not concern ourselves with whether or not

> 8 He was not that Light, but he was sent to bear witness of that Light[38]—
> 9 the true Light that illuminates every person who comes into the world.[39]
> 10 He was in the world, and the world was made by him, and the world did not know him.[40]
> 11 He came unto his own,[41] and his own did not receive him.[42]
> 12 But whoever did receive him,[43] to them he gave the authority[44] to become the children of God,[45] even to them who believe on his name—

---

faith pre-exists in the hearts of the people we would desire to reach. We are to simply bear witness of the Light. As we make him—the Light—known, he will cause faith to arise in those who see and hear our testimony of him.

[38] **1:8.** ***"He was sent to bear witness of that Light."*** Those who bear witness to the Light are reminded that they are to never seek the preeminence. The mission is never about them. Their mission is solely for the purpose of bearing witness to the Light.

[39] **1:9.** ***"The true Light that illuminates every person who comes into the world."*** Although many may not receive the Light, it is God's intention that every person who comes into this world may be illuminated by this Light.

[40] **1:10.** ***"The world did not know him."*** Creation did not recognize its Creator.

[41] **1:11.** ***"He came unto his own."*** On one hand, "his own" is best understood as a reference to his own people—the Jews. On the other hand, all of humanity was rightfully "his own," for he is the Creator of all things, and all creation belongs to him.

[42] **1:11.** ***"His own did not receive him."*** All of Jesus' original followers were Jews—his own people. However, as a whole, the Jews as a people group did reject him.

[43] **1:12.** ***"Whoever did receive him."*** How does one *receive* him? As this verse states, one *receives* him by *believing* on his name.

13 children born, not of blood, nor of the will of the
flesh, nor of the will of man, but of God.[46]
14 And the Word[47] was made flesh[48] and dwelled[49]
among us,[50] and we beheld[51] his glory,[52] the glory of the
only begotten[53] of[54] the Father, full of grace[55] and truth.[56]

---

[44] **1:12. *"Authority."*** *Exousia,* the word translated "authority," can also be translated "power" or "right."

[45] **1:12. *"The authority to become the children of God."*** These words speak of the privilege and honor bestowed upon the believer to appear on the stage of history as a child of God, with all the rights associated with sonship.

[46] **1:13. *"Born... of God."*** A person cannot cause himself or herself to become a child of God. Jesus is received by faith. In that moment of receptivity the believer experiences the new birth and becomes one who has been born of God. See John 3:1ff for further teaching on the new birth.

[47] **1:14. *"The Word."*** The word, *logos,* is used three times in 1:1 and one time here. See the notes for 1:1.

[48] **1:14. *"The Word was made flesh."*** These words are sometimes translated "the Word became flesh." The very reason that John wrote this Gospel was to get this truth across: Jesus is God, and Jesus is God in human flesh. This is the doctrine of the incarnation: the Word became a human being. He is Emmanuel, meaning, "God is with us" (Matthew 1:23).

[49] **1:14. *"Dwelled."*** The Greek word for "dwelled" carries the idea of living in a tabernacle or a tent.

[50] **1:14. *"Dwelled among us."*** Jesus' humanity was not an illusion. He really did take on humanity and live among other human beings. "Dwelled among us" calls to mind Hebrews 2:14 which says, "He shared in their humanity." See Colossians 2:9.

Jesus, the Word, dwelled among us so that we could know God. If there is ever any doubt as to who God is or what He is like, or if you question the motives or intentions of God in the Old Testament, look *to* Jesus, and look *through* Jesus. As Bill Johnson has said in multiple places and on multiple occasions, Jesus is the lens through which we should see God. He is perfect theology. Look through Jesus to see God the Father. Jesus lived among us to make the Father known.

[51] **1:14.** ***"Beheld."*** The word, "beheld" (also translated, "gazed upon"), introduces the theme of spiritual vision and attentiveness. This theme will appear repeatedly throughout the Gospel of John.

[52] **1:14.** ***"We beheld his glory."*** When the Gospel writer says, "we beheld his glory" or "we gazed upon his glory," he may be reflecting on his experience of seeing the glorified Jesus in Matthew 17:1–9; Mark 9:2-8; and Luke 9:28–36.

The writer's testimony, "We beheld his glory," is an invitation to the reader to also behold his glory. Like Moses, my heart's cry is, "Lord, show me your glory!" (Exodus 33:18). I want to be "transformed into his image with ever-increasing glory" as I fix my gaze upon his glory (2 Corinthians 3:18). We have all fallen short of his glory (Romans 3:23), and it is his glory that we need. The writer, John, claims, "We have seen his glory!" (1:14). I want to hear what this man has to say. I am on a quest for what this man has seen. He has been where I want to be.

[53] **1:14.** ***"Only begotten."*** This expression translates from *monogenous*—a form of *monogenes,* meaning most literally, "the only one to become." It might be better understood as, "the only one of its/his kind to appear in history or come into existence." See also 1:18 and 3:16.

[54] **1:14.** ***"Of."*** The word, *para,* translated "of" in the KJV, can also be translated "from" or "beside." The emphasis here is on the proximity of the only begotten one to the Father.

[55] **1:14.** ***"Full of grace."*** What is grace? Broadly considered, grace is an attitude that God has toward us. It is an attitude of favor—favor that we do not deserve. Grace is a state in which we live as believers. Grace is an event—an event of God's movement toward us. He is moving toward you today. That is grace. Grace is an actual gift given. Grace is the power of God. It is a power that is superior to sin. It is a power that enables all that God would ever require or ask of us. Grace is a demand upon our lives—a demand that requires compliance.

In the context of the passage at hand, grace is God's goodwill—his favor or his disposition to do good. It is essential to the nature of God. The use of the word

The Testimony of John the Baptist (1:15-34)

15 ¶ John testified of him, and spoke with a loud voice,
saying, "This is the one of whom I said, 'He who comes

"grace" in the New Testament often carries a sense of empowerment for those who are the recipients of God's goodwill. In non-religious contexts, grace is understood as that which brings joy, pleasure, delight, sweetness, charm and loveliness. John's testimony regarding the Word is that he was full of God's goodwill, and with that revelation of God's heart, he empowers those who fix their gaze upon him.

[56] **1:14.** ***"Full of grace and truth."*** Concerning "grace," see the previous note for "full of grace" (1:14).

"Truth" is a reoccurring theme in John's Gospel. Here and in 1:17, Jesus is presented as one who is full of "grace and truth." Jesus said that "he who practices truth comes toward the light" (3:21). He said that the Father is searching for people who will worship in "spirit and truth" (4:23-24). He affirmed that John the Baptist had borne witness to the truth (5:33). Jesus said, "You will know the truth, and the truth will set you free" (8:32). He continually revealed the truth through his spoken word (8:40, 45-46). He taught that "the devil did not abide in the truth because there is no truth in him" (8:44). Jesus said, "I am the way, the truth and the life" (14:6). He spoke of the Holy Spirit as the "Spirit of truth" (14:17, 26; 16:13) who would guide believers "into all the truth" (16:13). Jesus prayed for his disciples to be sanctified through his Father's truth. Then he said concerning the word of his Father, "your word is truth" (17:17). Jesus came to "bear witness to the truth," and he said that everyone who is of the truth hears his voice (18:37). Finally, Pilate asked of Jesus the question that we too are left to ponder: "What is truth?" (18:38)

1:1-14. Compare 1:1-14 and 1 John 1:1-4. The similar emphases of these two passages suggest that John may be confronting the same heretical issues in both contexts.

> after me is preferred before me,[57] for he was before me.'"[58]
> 16 Out of his fullness, we have all received, even grace upon grace.[59]

---

[57] **1:15.** ***"'He who comes after me is preferred before me.'"*** John the Baptist uses a play on words, most literally saying, "He who is coming behind me has come to be in front of me." It is a way of saying, "He is coming after me, but at the same time, he has already passed me up! He is far greater than me, and he deserves the preeminence."

[58] **1:15.** ***"'He was before me.'"*** John the Baptist stated regarding Jesus, "He was before me." Jesus was born *after* John the Baptist, not *before* him. Jesus started his public ministry *after* John the Baptist, not *before* him. What does John mean then when he says that Jesus was *before* him? Here John the Baptist's words speak of the eternal *pre-existence* of the Son of God.

[59] **1:16.** ***"Grace upon grace."*** The NIV translates, "one blessing after another." The meaning of "grace upon grace" is "grace heaped upon grace" or "grace in place of grace already given."

Here we are met with the generous heart of God. Imagine that you have been invited to my house for ice cream. You come to the table, and I dish out to you one single teaspoon of ice cream and say, "Here's your ice cream. Enjoy it, but while you are eating it, remember that you don't deserve it." I think that experience would drain the joy out of the whole occasion, and you certainly would not find my heart toward you to be very gracious.

Imagine a different scenario. You come to my table, and I give you the largest bowl that I can find. Then I start heaping scoop after scoop of ice cream into that bowl—more than you could ever eat! Then I joyfully say to you, "Here's your ice cream! Enjoy it! And if you want more, come back; there is plenty where that came from!" That would convey an entirely different kind of heart.

Although none of us deserve grace, God does not hold our unworthiness over our heads. Rather, he generously and joyfully heaps empowering grace upon us—

17 For the law[60] was given by Moses,[61] but grace and truth[62] came by Jesus Christ.[63]
18 No man has seen God at any time;[64] the only begotten Son, the one who is close to the Father's heart,[65] he has made him known.[66]

---

more than we feel that we need. If we do feel that we are running low on grace, we can always come back to the table; there is always more.

[60] **1:17.** ***"The law."*** The "law" revealed the will of God, but the law never had power to enable man to fulfill what it required.

[61] **1:17.** ***"The law was given by Moses."*** In subtle ways, the writer confronts the heresy of Cerinthus and others like him who taught that salvation could only come through obedience to Jewish law. The author is careful to honor Moses' rightful place in the history of redemption, while elevating the fullness of salvation as manifested in and through Jesus. See 1:45; 7:19; 7:23 and 8:5.

[62] **1:17.** ***"Grace and truth."*** These words should be understood as "grace and a true view of God" or "grace and the reality of God." Some have wrongly depicted "grace" as the *kind* side of God and "truth" as the more *severe* or demanding side of God. They erroneously think of "grace" and "truth" as two counter weights that are necessary for the sake of "balance." They think, "Moses gave us the law, but Jesus gave us grace and law (i.e., truth)." Such a conclusion is inaccurate. In a sense, "grace and truth" is a way of saying, "grace, even truth" or "grace, even the reality of God himself."

"Truth." See the note for "full of grace and truth" in 1:14.

[63] **1:17.** ***"The law was given by Moses, but grace and truth came by Jesus Christ."*** While God's requirements for humanity were revealed through the law, his disposition toward humanity is revealed through Jesus.

[64] **1:18.** ***"No man has seen God at any time."*** Biblical usage of the word "God" may reference the entire Godhead or it may reference any particular member of the Godhead. Here the reference is to a particular member of the Godhead—God the Father. The meaning is that no man in the flesh has ever seen God *the Father.* However, there are numerous Old Testament references to people seeing the Angel

19 ¶ This is the record of John,[67] when the Jews[68] sent
priests and Levites from Jerusalem to ask him, "Who
are you?"[69]
20 He confessed and did not deny, saying, "I am not
the Christ."[70]

---

of the Lord—the pre-incarnate Son of God, who is God. Old Testament incidents of people seeing God may have been encounters with the pre-incarnate Son of God. Also see 6:46.

[65] **1:18.** ***"Close to the Father's heart."*** These words are translated "in the bosom of the Father" in the KJV. The "bosom" is the front of the body between the arms. The idea conveyed here is that the Father embraces his Son, holding him close to his chest.

[66] **1:18.** ***"He has made him known."*** The word translated "made him known" is translated "declared" by others, and it carries the idea of unfolding or making known.

Colossians 1:19 (NIV) says, "For God was pleased to have all his fullness dwell in him." Colossians 2:9 (NIV) says, "For in Christ all the fullness of the Deity lives in bodily form." Hebrews 1:3 (NIV) states, "The Son is the radiance of God's glory and the exact representation of his being." If a person wants to know what God the Father is like, the beholding of God's Son is the only way to gain such knowledge.

[67] **1:19.** ***"John."*** This John is John the Baptist.

[68] **1:19.** ***"The Jews."*** According to 1:24, these Jews were Pharisees.

[69] **1:19.** ***"The Jews sent priests and Levites from Jerusalem to ask him, 'Who are you?'"*** Seeing that John was the son of a priest (Luke 1:5-25, 57-80), his identity was probably already known to the priests and Levites sent from Jerusalem. Their concern was over who John might claim to be, in light of his large following and the unusual nature of his ministry. It was their legitimate responsibility to investigate in this manner.

[70] **1:20.** ***"'Christ.'"*** The word means Anointed One, and it is the equivalent of the Hebrew concept of Messiah.

21 They asked him, "What then? Are you Elijah?"[71]
And he said, "I am not."[72]
"Are you the prophet?"[73]
And he answered, "No."
22 Then they said to him, "Who are you? Tell us that
we may give an answer to them that sent us. What do
you say of yourself?"
23 He said, "I am the voice of one crying in the
wilderness, 'Prepare the way of the Lord!'[74] as the
prophet Isaiah said."
24 They who were sent were from the Pharisees.[75]

---

[71] **1:21.** ***"'Are you Elijah?'"*** Regarding the Jewish expectation for the coming of Elijah, see Malachi 4:5-6.

[72] **1:21.** ***"And he said, 'I am not.'"*** In Matthew 17:12, Jesus suggests that John the Baptist was in fact Elijah, meaning that he had come in the spirit and anointing of the prophet Elijah. Why then did John the Baptist deny being Elijah? In all likelihood, he was probably not fully aware of who he was. Jesus, on the other hand, had perfect understanding of John's significant role in God's redemptive plan.

[73] **1:21.** ***"'Are you the prophet?'"*** "The prophet" refers back to a prophecy in Deuteronomy 18:15-18 stating that one day a prophet similar to Moses would appear.

[74] **1:23.** ***"'Prepare the way of the Lord!'"*** These words may also be translated, "Make straight the way of the Lord!" or "Make level the way of the Lord!" This is the cry of a forerunner: "Prepare the way! The Lord is coming!" See Isaiah 40:3 within the context of chapter 40 to grasp the significance of John the Baptist's prophetic ministry.

[75] **1:24.** ***"Pharisees."*** The Pharisees were a sect noted for their strict observance of Jewish practices, adherence to oral laws and traditions, belief in an afterlife and

> 25 And they asked him and said to him, "Why do you
> baptize then, if you are not the Christ, neither Elijah
> nor the prophet?"[76]
> 26 John answered them, saying, "I baptize with water,
> but among you stands one whom you do not know.[77]
> 27 He is the one, who coming after me is preferred
> before me, whose sandal strap I am not worthy to
> loosen."[78]
> 28 These things were done in Bethabara[79] beyond the
> Jordan[80] where John was baptizing.

---

the coming of Messiah. They are mentioned in 1:24; 3:1; 4:1; 7:32, 45, 47, 48; 8:3, 13; 9:13, 15, 16, 40; 11:46, 47, 57; 12:19, 42; 18:3.

[76] **1:25.** See notes for 1:20-21.

[77] **1:26.** ***"'One whom you do not know.'"*** Jesus remained hidden until his appointed time to be revealed.

[78] **1:27.** ***"'The one, who coming after me is preferred before me, whose sandal strap I am not worthy to loosen.'"*** John the Baptist is referring back to his own words in 1:15. Here in 1:27, he is in effect saying, "I am not even worthy to be his servant."

[79] **1:28.** ***"Bethabara."*** The word means "house of the ford," signifying that it was commonly a place where people crossed the river. Bethabara is probably the place to which Jesus escaped when the Jews tried to capture him later in 10:39-40.

[80] **1:28.** ***"Beyond the Jordan."*** "The Jordan" is a reference to the Jordan River. "Beyond the Jordan" might also be translated, "on the other side of the Jordan." "Beyond Jordan" may suggest that this baptismal site was not actually on the Jordan River; rather, it might have been on one of the tributaries flowing into the Jordan.

29 ¶ The next day John saw Jesus coming toward him,
and he said, "Behold, the Lamb of God[81] who
takes away the sin of the world![82]
30 This is he of whom I said, 'After me comes a man
who is preferred before me, for he was before me.'[83]
31 I was not aware of his true identity,[84] but the reason
I came baptizing with water was that he should be
made known to Israel."[85]

---

[81] **1:29.** ***"'The Lamb of God.'"*** John the Baptist declares Jesus to be the God-ordained sacrificial offering. See 1:36.

[82] **1:29.** ***"'Takes away the sin of the world.'"*** The words, "takes away," speak of picking up and carrying away. The expression, when used for the concept of taking away sin, means that the one taking away the sin becomes chargeable with the guilt of that sin. This understanding of taking away sin is also found in Hebrews 9:28.

In 1:29, ***"'The sin.'"*** This expression is presented in the singular and not the plural. The thought here is that the singular collective burden of the whole world's sin would be transferred to the Lamb of God.

Isaiah 53:6 says, "The Lord has laid on him the iniquity of us all." (See Isaiah 53:6-12.) Paul refers to Christ as our Paschal Lamb (1 Corinthians 5:7). Peter also refers to Jesus as the Lamb (1 Peter 1:19). Paul further states in 2 Corinthians 5:21, "God made him who had no sin to be sin for us, so that in him we might become the righteousness of God."

From our vantage point many generations after the declaration of John the Baptist, we can easily grasp the concept of Jesus as the sacrificial Paschal Lamb. However, in the Baptist's day, the idea of a suffering Messiah was foreign to the Jewish Messianic expectation. This understanding of Jesus as the sacrificial Lamb could have only come to John the Baptist by prophetic revelation.

[83] **1:30.** See 1:15 and 1:27.

[84] **1:31.** ***"'I was not aware of his true identity.'"*** These words can also be translated, "I did not know him." John and Jesus were cousins, and obviously they

Harmony of the Gospels			
	Matthew	**Mark**	**Luke**
John the Baptist's Ministry	3:1-12	1:1-8	3:1-18
Jesus' Baptism	3:13-17	1:9-11	3:21-22
The Temptation of Christ	4:1-11	1:12-13	4:1-13

32 John testified, saying, "I saw the Spirit[86] descending
from heaven like a dove, and it remained on him.
33 I was not aware of his true identity,[87] but the one
who sent me to baptize with water said to me, 'The

---

would have known one another in the flesh. However, John did not know who Jesus was in spirit (i.e., His true identity as the Messiah) until the revelation came to him.

[85] **1:31.** ***"'The reason I came baptizing with water was that he should be made known to Israel.'"*** John the Baptist recognized that there was something taking place through his baptisms that went far beyond his own understanding. Even when he did not know who the Messiah was, his ministry served to make the Messiah known. Those who serve in Christian ministry should be encouraged to know that often their labors accomplish significant purposes far beyond what is immediately understood.

[86] **1:32.** ***"'I saw the Spirit.'"*** The word, *tetheamai* (from *theaomai*), is translated, "I saw," but it more precisely means, "I have gazed upon" or "I have viewed attentively."

John the Baptist said, "I saw the Spirit." John saw the un-seeable; he saw the Holy Spirit. These words set the tone; this is all about spiritual vision. The theme of spiritual vision will be reflected again in 1:34 and reoccurs throughout this Gospel.

[87] **1:33.** ***"'I was not aware of his true identity.'"*** See note for 1:31.

man on whom you see the Spirit descend and remain,
he is the one[88] who baptizes in the Holy Spirit.'[89]
34 And I have seen[90] and have testified that this is the
Son of God."[91]

---

[88] **1:33.** ***"'The man on whom you see the Sprit descend and remain, he is the one.'"*** Throughout biblical history, many had experienced the Spirit coming upon them momentarily or for the fulfillment of specific tasks, but here something unique is occurring. The Spirit came upon Jesus and *remained* upon him.

Jesus' relationship with the Holy Spirit serves as a foreshadowing of the relationship we are promised with the Holy Spirit. Jesus promised that once the Holy Spirit would come upon us, he would abide with us forever (John 14:16).

Regarding the sign of the descent of the Spirit upon Jesus, John the Baptist in essence stated, "Had it not been for God giving me this sign, I would not have known that Jesus was the Anointed One. In fact, I wouldn't have even thought of him. He and I are cousins. We used to play together when we were kids. This knowledge could only come by revelation."

[89] **1:33.** ***"'The one who baptizes in the Holy Spirit.'"*** Baptism *in* the Holy Spirit and baptism *by* the Holy Spirit are two separate events in the life of the believer. When a person is baptized *by* the Holy Spirit (1 Corinthians 12:13), the Holy Spirit baptizes the believer into Christ and into the Body of Christ. When a person is baptized *in* or *with* the Holy Spirit (Luke 3:16; John 1:33 and Acts 2:33), Christ baptizes the believer into the Holy Spirit.

[90] **1:34.** ***"'I have seen.'"*** These words continue the theme of spiritual vision. Beyond this point in the text, it is interesting to observe the revelatory ministry of the Holy Spirit at work.

[91] **1:34.** ***"'This is the Son of God.'"*** Here is the first open declaration of Jesus' identity as the Son of God. John the Baptist did not need a prolonged season to verify Jesus' identity. Later the Baptist may have doubted (Matthew 11:2-3; Luke 7:18-19), but at this early point in the Gospel narrative, he was thoroughly convinced on the basis of prophetic revelation alone.

Jesus Presents Himself to His Disciples (1:35 – 2:12)

35 ¶ Again the next day John[92] and two of his disciples[93]
stood.
36 And looking[94] upon Jesus as he walked, he said,
"Behold, the Lamb of God!"[95]
37 The two disciples heard what he said, and they
followed Jesus.[96]
38 Then Jesus turned[97] and saw them following,[98] and
he said to them, "What are you seeking?"[99]

---

[92] **1:35. *"John."*** The reference is to John the Baptist.

[93] **1:35. *"Two of his disciples."*** The "two of his disciples" were Andrew and John—the eventual writer of this Gospel account. The fact that they were disciples of John the Baptist says that they were seeking what he was seeking. They had set their lives apart as he had set his apart.

[94] **1:36. *"Looking."*** The emphasis on spiritual vision continues.

[95] **1:36. *"'Behold, the Lamb of God!'"*** A transition is taking place. In essence, John the Baptist is saying, "Eyes off of me! Fix your eyes on the Lamb of God!" Earlier in 1:29, John the Baptist said, "Behold, the Lamb of God who carries away the sin of the world!"

[96] **1:37. *"They followed Jesus."*** A change of masters is taking place. Good-by to former revelations; everyone should now be turning to the new. To follow Jesus implied departure from lesser pursuits. They followed Jesus, but it was too early for them to understand the full ramifications of their decision.

[97] **1:38. *"Then Jesus turned."*** Here is a suggested pattern:

1. They heard the truth: Jesus is "the Lamb of God who takes away the sin of the world."
2. They acted on what they heard: "they followed."

They said to him, "Rabbi, (which by interpretation means Master[100]) where are you staying?"[101]

---

3. "Then Jesus turned...." The point here is that Jesus turns to those whose hearts pursue him in response to truth.

[98] **1:38.** ***"Jesus... saw them following."*** Can you imagine how Jesus felt? He must have been thinking, "It now begins." As the preincarnate Word, he had waited for centuries for this moment. The first of Adam's race were now coming, driven by an internal desire that they did not yet understand. These men were in pursuit of truth—the promise. These men were seekers. Jesus' heart must have been pounding.

If you will listen carefully, you should be able to hear an encouraging message between the lines of this text: "He sees your desire—your desire for him." Here is hope for the one asking, "Does he see how much I want him?" Yes, he does; and he turns toward you and sees you in your passion to come after him.

[99] **1:38.** ***"'What are you seeking?'"*** These were Jesus' first words in John's Gospel. The fact that this was the first time that he spoke elevates the importance of the question that he asked: "What are you seeking?" Jesus opened the door, inviting these curious men to express *their* heart's desire. He knew better than they what they were seeking. It was for their sake that he asked, "What is your heart longing for?" How would they answer? Would they dare say, "We are seeking you"? Perhaps they wondered, "Will he accept us?"

Again this account offers encouragement for those who have a seeking heart. It provides hope for the one wondering, "Doesn't he see how much I want him?" It is for the one wondering, "Is this going anywhere in my life? Is my spiritual passion accomplishing anything? Does my praying really make a difference?" Jesus is indeed drawn to such heart-longings. Jesus saw the desire of these two disciples. Jesus sees your desire for him. This is the first in a series of three encouraging observations or messages that can be gleaned from this portion of Scripture. The other two messages are found in 1:42 and 1:48.

[100] **1:38.** ***"'Master.'"*** This word can also be translated, "Teacher."

[101] **1:38.** ***"'Where are you staying?'"*** This is the question asked by the two who had set out to follow Jesus. With their question they were actually making a

39 He said to them, "Come[102] and see."[103] They came
and saw where he was staying and remained with him
that day, for it was about the tenth hour.[104]
40 One of the two who heard John speak and followed
him was Andrew, Simon Peter's brother.
41 He first found his own brother Simon and said to
him, "We have found the Messiah,"[105] which when
translated means, "the Christ."

---

statement in response to Jesus' question, "What are you seeking?" They wanted to be with the Lamb. In essence, these earliest of disciples were saying, "We want to see where you live and how you live. We want to breathe what you breathe and eat what you eat, just like we did with John the Baptist. Where are you staying? Wherever that place might be, that is where we want to be. We want to be with you."

[102] **1:39.** ***"'Come.'"*** The invitation was given. Their seeking hearts brought him joy. He longed to be with them. They were not yet at the point where they would forsake all other things to follow him; that would come later by the Sea of Galilee. Someone has said, "In our walk with Jesus, we come to many points of departure where we forsake things that are old to pursue that which is new."

[103] **1:39.** ***"'Come and see.'"*** Jesus was saying, "Respond to my call, and then you will see what your hearts long to see. You *will* see where I dwell." This is the Lord's response to the one whose heart-cry is, "Lord, I just want to be where you are!" The invitation to "come and see," will appear again in 1:46 with Philip's response to Nathanael and yet again in 4:29 when a Samaritan returned to her community to tell the people about Jesus.

[104] **1:39.** ***"It was about the tenth hour."*** The writer of this Gospel used Roman time references. It was about 10:00 a.m. From that hour onward, these men spent the rest of the day with Jesus.

[105] **1:41.** ***"He first found his own brother Simon and said to him, 'We have found the Messiah.'"*** Good news cannot be held back. Andrew seemingly could not wait to tell somebody. Here is the first instance of one person seeking to lead another

42 He brought him to Jesus, and when Jesus fixed his
eyes upon him,[106] he said, "You are Simon the son of
Jonah; you shall be called Cephas," which when
translated means, "a stone."[107]

---

person to Jesus. In John's Gospel, every time Andrew appeared, he brought someone to Jesus:

1. In the text at hand, he brought his brother, Simon.
2. In 6:8 he brought the boy with the loaves and fishes.
3. In 12:20-22 he brought the Greeks who wanted to see Jesus.

Andrew began with someone who was close to him: his own brother. The text says that he "found" him. Andrew's message to Simon was this: "We have found the Messiah!" They had devoted their lives to that quest—the search and wait for the Messiah. That is why they followed John the Baptist. The search had now come to an end. See Jeremiah 29:13.

[106] **1:42. *"Jesus fixed his eyes upon him."*** The KJV translates, "Jesus beheld him." Jesus "fixed his eyes on" Simon. These were not ordinary encounters. These are the eyes of Creator meeting the created. These are all-knowing and all-seeing eyes penetrating the depths of a man's soul.

[107] **1:42. *"'You are Simon the son of Jonah; you shall be called Cephas,' which when translated means, 'a stone.'"*** Jesus was saying, "This is what you are: just a man. This is what you shall be: solid as a rock." In this passage, Jesus was prophesying. See the gift of prophecy in 1 Corinthians 12:10.

Jesus sees your destiny. There is hope for the one asking, "Am I significant in his eyes? Is my life going anywhere?" This is the second in a series of encouraging observations or messages in this section. The first in this series is found in 1:38: "He sees your desire." The third is found in 1:48.

43 ¶ The following day Jesus decided to go into Galilee,
found Philip[108] and said to him, "Follow me."[109]
44 Philip was of Bethsaida, the city of Andrew and
Peter.
45 Philip found Nathanael[110] and said to him, "We have
found him[111] of whom Moses (in the law)[112] and the

---

[108] **1:43.** ***"Jesus decided to go into Galilee, found Philip..."*** Jesus' actions were not random or by chance. He was intentional. He purposefully directed his attention to a specific region—Galilee. Then having entered Galilee, he purposefully sought for those who would follow him, and after going after them, he found each of them.

[109] **1:43.** ***"'Follow me.'"*** Jesus was not saying, "Here are three steps." He was not saying, "Here is a program—a method." He was not saying, "Go to this seminar." He was not saying, "Read this book." He was saying, "Be with me; know me; and follow me." Jesus was summoning Philip and others like him to forsake all other quests and to align with him. This was a moment of departure from all that preceded; something new was beginning.

[110] **1:45.** ***"Philip found Nathanael."*** Here Nathanael, also known as Bartholomew, was introduced. Nathanael was from Cana of Galilee (21:2).

Do not miss the significance of one newly found person finding another person in need of being found. Most often God ventures into humanity to seek and save the lost by working through humanity. He finds people by working through us to do the finding.

[111] **1:45.** ***"'We have found him.'"*** Philip had been a seeker. He had sought the Messiah in the law. He had sought the Messiah in the prophets. Now he had been found *by* the Messiah! The one whom he had sought had now found him!

[112] **1:45.** ***"Moses (in the law)."*** In subtle ways, the writer confronts the heresy of Cerinthus and others like him who taught that salvation could only come through obedience to Jewish law. The author is careful to honor Moses' rightful place in the history of redemption, while elevating the fullness of salvation as manifested in and

> prophets did write—Jesus of Nazareth, the son of Joseph.[113]
> 46 And Nathanael said to him, "Can anything good come out of Nazareth?"[114]
> Philip said to him, "Come and see."[115]

---

through Jesus. Here, through the words of Philip, the writer demonstrates that even Moses through the law testified of Christ. See 1:17; 7:19; 7:23 and 8:5.

[113] **1:45.** ***"'Jesus of Nazareth, Son of Joseph.'"*** Philip referred to Jesus as "the son of Joseph." Philip's understanding of Jesus' identity was still in an elementary phase; one would not expect at this point for Philip to have a fully developed Christology. To many, Jesus would have been known as "the son of Joseph." At this point the idea that Joseph was only Jesus' foster father was not openly known, and the fact that Jesus was the only begotten Son of God had only been revealed to a few.

[114] **1:46.** ***"'Can anything good come out of Nazareth?'"*** Nazareth was a tiny frontier community that was not known for anything important. Craig S. Keener notes that members of the Judean elite were especially unimpressed with Jesus' rural Galilean origins (7:41-42, 52). Even the reference to Nazareth in the inscription on Jesus' cross, "Jesus of Nazareth, the King of the Jews," was intended by Pilate to be a mockery (19:19). On one hand, Jesus came from that which was unimportant—Nazareth. On the other hand, he came from God; he came as the Lamb of God (1:36). Craig S. Keener, "Can Anything Good Come out of Nazareth?" *Bible Odyssey,* accessed January 5, 2016, http:// www.bibleodyssey.org/ places/ related-articles/ can-anything-good-come-out-of-nazareth.aspx.

[115] **1:46.** ***"'Come and see.'"*** Philip answered with these words in response to Nathanael. These were the same words that Jesus used when two of the Baptist's disciples asked Jesus where he was staying (1:39). Rather than argue, defend, debate, or give a logical presentation, Philip simply said, "Come and see." What a simple yet powerful witness.

In John 4:29, the woman at the well will say the same thing to her neighbors: "Come and see!" These words speak of the simplicity of the Christian witness.

Pause and Reflect

1. What does 1:35-46 teach us about introducing others to Jesus?
2. Pray for a revival of *passion* for Jesus and *compassion* for others that would result in many being introduced to the Son of God.

47 Jesus saw Nathanael coming to him[116] and said of
him, "Behold, a true Israelite in whom is no deceit!"[117]
48 Nathanael said to him, "Where do you know me
from?"
Jesus answered and said to him, "Before Philip called
you, when you were under the fig tree, I saw you."[118]

Come and see what God is doing! Come and see what he is doing in lives! Come and see *my* life!

On another note, many would prefer that the call be, "See and come." They would be more comfortable with seeing and understanding all that is being asked of them before taking a step of faith. But that is not the way that it usually works in the kingdom. It is when we "come"—depart from where we have been for the sake of going to where we are being called—that we will then "see" the glorious things that God has in store for those who believe.

[116] **1:47. *"Jesus saw Nathanael coming to him."*** Again the eyes of the one who seeks the created was upon one who seeks the Creator. He saw Nathaniel "coming to him." What joy must have been in Jesus' heart each time he saw another one "coming to him"!

[117] **1:47. *"'Behold, a true Israelite in whom is no deceit!'"*** The KJV translates, "guile." On one hand, Jesus was speaking of the sincerity of Nathanael's heart, but he may have also been saying, "Here is a true seeker of righteousness who won't *accept* anything false or deceitful." In this passage, Jesus discerned the spirit of Nathaniel. See the gift of the discerning of spirits in 1 Corinthians 12:10.

49 Nathanael answered and said to him, "Rabbi, you
are the Son of God; you are the King of Israel!"[119]
50 Jesus answered and said to him, "Because I said to
you, 'I saw you under the fig tree,' you believe. You
will see greater things than that."[120]
51 And he said to him, "I tell you the truth,[121] from now
on you will see heaven open, and the angels of God
ascending and descending upon the Son of man."[122]

---

[118] **1:48. *"'When you were under the fig tree, I saw you.'"*** In this passage, Jesus told of a word of knowledge he had received. See the gift of the word of knowledge in 1 Corinthians 12:8.

"'Under the fig tree.'" In that day, the shade of a fig tree was regarded as a place of prayer and meditation. Could it be that Jesus saw Nathanael in the place of his praying and seeking? Here is a good place to make personal application. Yes, he sees your desire (1:38); he sees your destiny (1:42); and—the third in a series of three messages of encouragement—He sees your devotion (1:48). There is hope for the one asking, "Does my praying really make a difference?"

[119] **1:49. *"'Rabbi, you are the Son of God; you are the King of Israel!'"*** Take note of what springs up when Nathanael realizes Jesus' eye had been on him: in that moment, *faith* arises! When a person comes into an awareness that Jesus actually sees him or her, it changes the way that person sees or perceives the Son of God.

[120] **1:50. *"'Because I said to you, 'I saw you under the fig tree,' you believe. You will see greater things than that.'"*** Note the progression: "Because I said... you believe." More specifically, "Because I said, 'I saw you...,' you believe." In essence, "You believe because you now know that I see you!" The progression goes further. Because "you believe," "you will see." More specifically, because "you believe," "you will see greater things than that." This promise that believing disciples will see greater things than the things Jesus had been doing appears again in 14:12. Faith in Jesus at one level of revelation is preparation to experience more revelation.

[121] **1:51. *"'I tell you the truth.'"*** The KJV translates, "Verily, verily." The Greek words here are a transliteration of the Hebrew expression, "Amen, amen." The

---

double "amen" is an expression similar to the medieval cry, "Hear ye! Hear ye!" It was a way of saying, "What I am about to say is very important!" The expression also conveys, "You can be certain of what I am about to tell you."

[122] **1:51.** ***"'From now on you will see heaven open, and the angels of God ascending and descending upon the Son of man.'"*** In this passage, Jesus prophesied Nathaniel's future. See the gift of prophecy in 1 Corinthians 12:10. An expanded paraphrase might read, "From this point forward, you will have spiritual vision. You are about to witness the unveiling of the kingdom of heaven. You will see heavenly realities. You will see the Son of man glorified."

"'The angels of God ascending and descending.'" Jesus' words call to mind the angels of God ascending and descending on Jacob's ladder between heaven and earth in Genesis 28:12. Here Jesus compares himself with that ladder. Jesus is the bridge between heaven and earth. Craig S. Keener.

"'Son of man.'" The expression, "son of man," brings emphasis to the humanity of Jesus. Some also consider it a Messianic reference to Daniel 7:13-14:

> In my vision at night I looked, and there before me was one like a son of man, coming with the clouds of heaven. He approached the Ancient of Days and was led into his presence. He was given authority, glory and sovereign power; all nations and peoples of every language worshiped him. His dominion is an everlasting dominion that will not pass away, and his kingdom is one that will never be destroyed.

See 3:13-14; 5:27; 6:27, 53, 62; 8:28; 12:23, 34 and 13:31.

CHAPTER 2

The First Sign:
Turning Water into Wine (2:1-11)

On the third day[123] there was a wedding[124] in Cana of Galilee, and the mother of Jesus was there.[125]

2 And Jesus and his disciples were invited to the wedding.

---

[123] **2:1.** ***"The third day."*** This term may refer to the end of a three-day journey from Judea to the Galilee region, or it may refer to the third day of the Jewish week. The setting for the story about to be told is a wedding feast. According to John Lightfoot and others, Jewish law stated that virgins were to be married on the fourth day of the week. If such is the intended meaning of "the third day" in this text, then the feast described in this narrative would have occurred on the day prior to the marriage. John Lightfoot, "John 2," *Bible Study Tools*, accessed January 1, 2013, http:// www.biblestudytools.com/ commentaries/ lightfoot-new-testament/ john/2.html.

[124] **2:1.** ***"There was a wedding."*** There was a lot going on here symbolic of the Lamb's marriage to the people of God—the bride.

[125] **2:1.** ***"The mother of Jesus was there."*** Mary, the mother of Jesus, is a key character in this story. Note that Joseph was not mentioned. Many commentators think that Joseph had been dead for years and that Jesus, being the older child, had stayed home to take care of the family.

3 When they were running out of wine, the mother of Jesus said to him, "They have no wine."[126]

---

[126] **2:3. *"'They have no wine.'"*** From a first century viewpoint, something was about to go terribly wrong on this festive occasion. In that culture, to run out of wine at a wedding feast would not have been good.

Jesus' mother knew that the joy of the occasion was about to be dampened. Think of how a little girl dreams of her wedding day for years prior to her marriage. As she is growing up, she attends the weddings of relatives and friends thinking, "Someday *I* will have a wedding like this!" Then that little girl grows up, and it is time for *her* wedding. Years of dreaming now converge on this single week of celebration. Every detail has been envisioned. Do you get the picture? Jesus' mother no doubt wanted this marriage feast to be the "picture perfect" occasion that the bride, groom and their families had dreamed it would be. It was Mary's desire to see the fulfillment of joyful expectation.

Mary may have also been concerned that the host of the feast was about to be embarrassed because of the shortage; some have even proposed that his reputation was at stake. It was going to look like the family was either lacking in resources or that they had mismanaged the arrangements. Jesus' mother may have wanted to save a reputation on this day.

This story presents a powerful example of intercession. As the next verse will make clear, Jesus knew that Mary's statement, "they have no wine," was actually a request. She was implying, "They have no wine, and you have the power to do something about it!" (This is also an example of the significant role that parents often play in nudging their children toward the fulfilling of their destinies.) She had been pondering the reality of his divine identity for a long time. She had been pondering his mission. She had good reason to believe that Jesus would act. She had received a promise. In 2:3, she was praying on the basis of that promise—Luke 1:32ff: "He will be great and will be called the Son of the Most High. The Lord God will give him the throne of his father David, and he will reign over the house of Jacob forever; his kingdom will never end."

It was not yet the time for the full manifestation of Jesus' divine identity, yet Mary longed for him to be manifested. So she interceded: "They have no wine." Her

> 4 Jesus said to her, "Dear woman,[127] do you realize the significance of this matter to me and to you?[128] My hour[129] is not yet come." [130]

---

implied question was, "Will you manifest yourself in this hour?" He answered her yearning—not fully, but at least in part.

"Wine." Applying this account figuratively, wine often represented joy or the Holy Spirit. This story can speak to those who are in need of joy—those who are in need of the presence of the Holy Spirit in their lives.

[127] **2:4.** ***"'Dear woman.'"*** Jesus addresses his mother as "woman" and not as "mother." In that culture, to address a female as "woman" was to address her with great respect. It was almost like saying, "My lady." Jesus' mother had been accustomed to approaching him on the basis of the mother-son relationship. Now she sees that something is different: the Holy Spirit's anointing was upon him, and he was entering into his mission. There was now a new basis for her relationship with him; he is here revealed as her Lord.

[128] **2:4.** ***"'Do you realize the significance of this matter to me and to you?'"*** The question in 2:4 is not just part of the story; it is presented for the reader to ponder. The KJV translates, "Woman, what have I to do with you?" The NIV translates, "Dear woman, why do you involve me?" A more literal rendering from the Greek, *ti emoi kai soi,* would be, "What is it to me and to you?" The meaning could be, "What concern is this matter to either of us?" However, it seems that the paraphrase given in the body of this text may better represent the Greek text and the context of what is going on in the narrative. When Jesus said, "Do you realize the significance of this matter to me and to you? My hour is not yet come," he was in effect saying this:

> "Do you understand the ramifications of what you are suggesting? It will affect both you and me; life will no longer be business as usual. Are you really ready for that? This miracle will reveal my glory, and it will initiate aspects of my mission and a chain of events that may be premature. It will start the countdown leading to 'my hour'—my death."

[129] **2:4.** ***"'Hour.'"*** The word translated "hour" is *hora,* meaning "any definite time, point of time, moment." "*hora,*" *Thayer's Greek Lexicon, Blue Letter Bible,* accessed January 10, 2016, https:// www.blueletterbible.org/ lang/ lexicon/ lexicon.cfm?t=

---

kjv&strongs= g5610. In this Gospel, when referring to the approaching hour or time for Jesus to face the crucifixion, John seems to use *hora* (2:4; 7:30; 8:20; 12:23, 27; 13:1; and 17:1) and *kairos* (7:6-8) interchangeably with little intended differentiation of meaning.

[130] **2:4. *"'My hour is not yet come.'"*** Jesus frequently familiarized his followers with the phrase "My hour." His "hour" was to become a constant symbol of his death. See John 7:30; John 8:20; John 12:23-28; Matthew 26:18; John 13:1; John 17:1; and Matthew 26:45. The public revelation of Jesus' divine identity at this point on the timeline could set in motion a sequence of events that would lead quickly to his death. This was not the time for that countdown to begin.

However, consider the power of one person's intercession. Bill Johnson has an interesting insight into what is going on here. We learn later that Jesus only did those things that he saw his Father doing (5:19). With Jesus saying, "My hour is not yet come" (implying that it was premature to start performing miracles), we know he did not perceive that his Father wanted to turn water into wine on this day; but Mary stepped in. She interceded, and suddenly Jesus started turning water into wine. What happened? If Jesus only did what he saw his Father doing, then evidently his Father changed directions in response to Mary's faith and intercession. If Jesus was turning water into wine, that meant that the Father was at work in the unseen realm turning water into wine. That which had been previously reserved for a future time—the public working of miracles—was drawn into the present by one person's intercession.

God is hoping that we will become bolder in our faith and in our intercession. Sometimes he wants us to press beyond what I call "his *apparent* refusal to respond" to ask him to do it anyway. Such faith demonstrates our confidence in his nature, his character and his word. He loves it when we believe he is who he says he is. He loves it when we believe he will do what he says he will do. He loves it when we believe that he really loves us enough to do extraordinary things in our life situations. The fulfillment of dreams and promises may seem to be postponed, delayed and reserved for some distant future time, but maybe all it would take is one person taking the risk to ask, believe and act. That is what Mary did.

5 His mother said to the servants,[131] "Whatever he says
to you, do it."[132]
6 There were set there six waterpots[133] of stone,
according to purification customs of the Jews,[134]
containing twenty to thirty gallons[135] each.

---

[131] **2:5. *"His mother said to the servants."*** When some people tell this story, they make it sound like Jesus' mother totally ignored what he said about it not being his hour. On the contrary, the exact opposite may be taking place. It could be that Mary involved the servants in order to keep Jesus inconspicuous, having respect for what he said about it not being his hour. As the story progresses, it appears that Jesus remained in the background while the miracle was taking place; it is possible that only Jesus, his mother, the disciples and a few servants actually witnessed the transformation of substance that follows in the narrative. Not even the table master knew what was going on (2:9). Everyone immediately benefited from the miracle, but only a few were initially aware that supernatural things were happening.

[132] **2:5. *"'Whatever he says to you, do it.'"*** Mary's confidence was that whatever Jesus' words would be to these servants, it would be sufficient. She did not know what he would do, but she knew that once the matter was committed to him, the situation would be resolved.

In application, a key concept rests in the statement, "Whatever he says to you, do it." What has he been saying to *you*? Others may expect us to do certain things, but if we are not doing what *he* says, we may miss the miracles that he wants to accomplish through our lives.

[133] **2:6. *"Six waterpots."*** Could there be some symbolism intended here? At this point, it appears that Jesus only had six disciples. Six waterpots were about to be filled with water, but something inside would need to change. Something in man was about to change.

[134] **2:6. *"Purification customs of the Jews."*** The purification customs in view here pertain to the cleansing of the bride in preparation for her marriage to the bridegroom. The water pots were there for cleansing, but the miracle that Jesus would work would represent much more than just cleansing from defilement and sin.

> 7 Jesus said to them, "Fill the waterpots with water," and they filled them up to the brim.[136]
> 8 Then he said to them, "Draw out now, and take some to the table master,"[137] and they took it to him.[138]

For those who feel that their entire Christian life is all about being repeatedly cleansed of sin, here is good news. God want us to come to the point where we are no longer preoccupied with getting rid of sin. Yes, let us receive cleansing when cleansing is needed, but let us also move on from there. There comes a point when our experience with God is no longer just about cleansing. There comes a point where there is supposed to be some joy in this life. The water of cleansing does turn into the wine of *joy*! God wants all who belong to him to be filled with the Holy Spirit continually and overflowing with joy. Let Jesus turn the water into wine!

[135] **2:6.** ***"Twenty to thirty gallons."*** The words *metreias duo e treis* are translated "two or three firkins" in the KJV. One *metretes* (a Greek measurement) was equal to roughly nine or ten gallons; some calculate it to precisely 9.9 gallons while others say that it is a little less than nine gallons. The six waterpots combined could hold between 120 and 180 gallons of water.

[136] **2:7.** ***"'Fill the waterpots with water.' And they filled them up to the brim."*** The servants obeyed his instruction precisely, taking what he said literally. He said, "Fill the waterpots," and the servants "filled them up to the brim." They may have even overdone it. Jesus was obeyed, and everyone was about to experience his creative power and be fully satisfied. The Bible says much to commend those who heed the Lord's commands. See Matthew 7:21; John 14:21; 1 John 2:17; and Matthew 7:24-25.

[137] **2:8.** ***"'Table master.'"*** The table master was in charge of making sure the dining room furnishings and the food items were set up and arranged properly, he was to also taste the food and wine beforehand.

[138] **2:7-8.** ***"Jesus said... And they...."*** Take note that it was the servants who filled the waterpots with water. It was the servants who drew it out, and it was the servants who took it to the governor of the feast. Not once did Jesus' hands touch the water or the waterpots. Not once did he touch the dipper that drew out the water or the cup that was carried to the governor of the feast. Jesus did not even

9 When the table master had tasted the water that was
made wine, he did not know from where it came,[139] but
the servants who drew the water knew. The table
master called the bridegroom
10 and said to him, "Every man serves[140] the good wine
first, and then, when the guests should be getting
drunk,[141] the inferior wine is served; but you have kept
the good wine until now."[142]

---

give a pronouncement, declaring, "Water, I command you to become wine!" The entire miracle took place in the hands of the servants! The things that Jesus contributed to the working of this miracle were his presence and the sound of his voice, saying, "Fill the waterpots with water," and "Draw out now, and take it to the governor of the feast." The only thing that the servants contributed to the working of this miracle was obedience to what Jesus said. Their faithful response was a key factor in what took place. The water turned into wine because the servants cooperated with Jesus and obeyed his commands. Never underestimate what God might do with the most mundane tasks assigned to you. He may just use it to bring about a miracle!

[139] **2:9.** ***"The table master... did not know from where it came."*** Jesus had obviously been inconspicuous in the performing of this miracle (see note on 2:5). Not even the table master knew what he had done.

[140] **2:10.** ***"'Serves.'"*** The Greek word translated here as "serves" is derived from *tithemi,* meaning "to set" or "to place."

[141] **2:10.** ***"'When the guests should be getting drunk.'"*** These words are a translation of *hotan methusthosin.*

[142] **2:10.** ***"'You have kept the good wine until now.'"*** This statement may be symbolic of the quality of life in the new covenant.

11 This beginning of miracles[143] Jesus did in Cana of
Galilee. He manifested his glory,[144] and his disciples
believed on him.[145]

12 ¶ After this he went down to Capernaum[146] with his
mother, his brothers[147] and his disciples. They remained
there a few days.[148]

---

[143] **2:11.** ***"This beginning of miracles."*** This was the first public miracle that Jesus performed. Yet this expression, "this beginning of miracles," did not just mean that this was miracle number one in a series of miracles. This was the initiation. This was the miracle that set everything that followed into motion. More was on the way.

If one miracle happens in your life, God does not intend that miracle to be a stand-alone event. That miracle is like a springboard or a launching pad for the next miracle, and the next, and the next! There is more to come.

[144] **2:11.** ***"He manifested his glory."*** Both here and in 11:4, 40, the manifestation of Jesus' "glory" is associated with him working miracles. This miracle in Cana demonstrated his very purpose for coming to earth: to reveal the creative power of God. He had the power to create and produce what was needed to meet man's need.

[145] **2:11.** ***"His disciples believed on him."*** What was the significance of this miracle to his first six disciples? This occasion marked the point where they started placing their faith in him. The manifestation of Jesus' glory through the demonstration of his miraculous power is one of the ways that faith is ignited in human hearts.

Supernatural ministry affects the hearts and minds of people, causing them to believe upon Jesus. See 2:23; 4:48, 53; 7:31; 10:37-38; 11:15, 45, 48; 12:11; 14:11; and 20:30-31. However, some see his miracles and still do not believe. See 6:36; 7:5; and 12:37.

[146] **2:12.** ***"Down to Capernaum."*** Sometimes people say "up" when they mean "north," and they say "down" when they mean "south." In the Bible, "up" and "down" are references to elevation and not directions related to points on the

Jesus Presents Himself to the Jews (2:13 – 3:36)

13 ¶ The Jews' Passover[149] was imminent, and Jesus
went up to Jerusalem.[150]
14 He found in the temple those who sold oxen, sheep
and doves,[151] and the money-changers[152] sitting.

---

compass. After being in Cana at approximately 900 feet *above* sea level, Jesus dropped in elevation to Capernaum located at 680 feet *below* sea level. Capernaum is positioned over 16 aerial miles to the *northeast* of Cana. See "up to Jerusalem" in 2:13. Also see 4:49; 5:1; 6:16; 7:8, 10, 14; 11:55; and 12:20.

[147] **2:12. *"His brothers."*** The brothers of Jesus were named James, Joseph (Joses), Judas (Jude or Judah) and Simon (Mark 6:3). His brothers are also mentioned in 7:3, 5, and 10.

[148] **2:12. *"A few days."*** A more literal translation would be "not many days," as reflected in the KJV.

[149] **2:13. *"The Jews' Passover."*** John's repeated reference to the Passover highlights the significance that it held for the telling of the Gospel story. See 2:23; 6:4; 11:55; 12:1; 13:1; 18:28, 39; and 19:14. He called it the *"Jews'"* Passover so that Gentile readers unfamiliar with Jewish customs would understand that he was talking about a Jewish celebration. The association of particular feasts with Jewish tradition is also made in 7:2 and 11:55.

[150] **2:13. *"Up to Jerusalem."*** See notes for "down to Capernaum" in 2:12. "Up" and "down" are references to elevation and not points on the compass. Jerusalem is located almost eighty aerial miles south of Capernaum—a direction that westerners in the twenty-first century would not normally think of as "up." However, a journey from Capernaum at 680 feet below sea level to Jerusalem at about 2,400 feet above sea level would take the traveler "up" to a higher elevation. See 4:49; 5:1; 6:16; 7:8, 10, 14; 11:55; and 12:20.

[151] **2:14. *"Oxen, sheep and doves."*** These animals were sold to be offered in sacrifice at the temple.

15 And[153] when he had made a whip of small cords, he drove them all out of the temple,[154] including the sheep and the oxen.[155] And he poured out the changers' money and overthrew the tables.
16 And said to them that sold doves, "Take these away from here;[156] do not make my Father's[157] house a marketplace."[158]

---

[152] **2:14.** ***"Money-changers."*** The money-changers provided a needed service, converting the foreign currency of pilgrims to the local currency of the Jews.

[153] **2:15.** ***"And."*** In twenty-first century English writing, beginning a sentence with the conjunction "and" is typically avoided. However, in John's writing, he frequently began sentences with the conjunction, *kai* (translated "and"). His use of the conjunction gives a sense of continual and often swift movement from one thing to another. Certainly the scene described in these verses was filled with such action; thus, in this translation, the conjunction at the beginning of these verses has been retained in a number of places.

[154] **2:15.** ***"He drove them all out of the temple."*** "All" refers to "those who sold oxen, sheep and doves, and the money-changers" (2:14). This is the first of two incidents in which Jesus drove the vendors and their livestock out of the temple. The second took place in Jesus' final week before his death, and that account is documented in Mark 11:15–19; Matthew 21:12–17; and Luke 19:45–48. In the second incident, Jesus' purpose in cleansing the temple is seen more clearly.

[155] **2:15.** ***"Including the sheep and the oxen."*** People *and* animals went running out of the temple court. The "doves" are not mentioned here; however, they are mentioned in the next verse and seem to have been handled differently.

[156] **2:16.** ***"'Take these away from here.'"*** "These" refers to the doves. It appears that Jesus did not physically and forcibly drive out the doves. Rather, he *told* those who were selling the doves to carry them outside of the temple area.

[157] **2:16.** ***"'My Father's.'"*** Jesus openly referenced God the Father as his Father, affirming his identity as the Son of God. See also 5:17, 43; 6:32, 65; 8:19, 28, 38, 49, 54;

17 And his disciples remembered that it was written,
"The zeal of your house has consumed me."[159]

Pause and Reflect

The area of the temple that Jesus cleansed is believed to have been the outer court reserved as a place where non-Jews could worship and pray. The Jews must have lost their sense of hospitality toward people who were not Jews, for the absence of Gentiles left a void that had been filled in by other things. The absence of worship and prayer invited distraction.

Jesus overturned the tables, removing the busyness that had replaced consideration toward other people. He overturned the tables, removing the distractions that replaced prayer and had robbed God of the worship he was worthy of receiving. He rearranged the furniture to restore the place to what it had been designed to be.

What tables need to be overturned in your life to make room for the things that are important to God? Once you become aware of those things, invite Jesus to come in and rearrange the furniture of your life.

18 ¶ Then the Jews answered and said to him, "What
sign do you have to show to us, [160] seeing that you do
these things?"

10:17-18, 25, 29, 30, 32, 37; 12:26-27; 14:2, 7, 12, 20-21, 23, 28; 15:1, 8, 10, 15, 23-24; 16:10; 18:11; 20:17, and 21.

[158] **2:16.** ***"Do not make my Father's house a marketplace."*** The temple was intended to be a place to worship and encounter God, but other things and other activities had detracted from that design. By cleansing the temple, Jesus restored it to its original purpose.

[159] **2:17.** ***"The zeal of your house has consumed me."*** See Psalm 69:9.

> 19 Jesus answered and said to them, "Destroy this
> temple,[161] and in three days, I will raise it up."[162]
> 20 Then the Jews said, "It took forty-six years to build
> this temple,[163] and will you raise it up in three days?"
> 21 But he spoke of the temple of his body.
> 22 When he was risen from the dead, his disciples
> remembered that he had said this to them, and they
> believed the scripture[164] and the word that Jesus had
> said.[165]

---

[160] **2:18.** ***"'What sign do you have to show us...?'"*** By inquiring about a sign, the Jews were essentially asking for Jesus to show them his credentials, or his "temple cleansing permit." Only a person with divine authority could legitimately act as Jesus had acted. If Jesus was going to act like someone with divine authority, then in their thinking, he must quickly produce proof of his divine authorization.

[161] **2:19.** ***"'Destroy this temple.'"*** The temple of which Jesus spoke is the temple of his body (2:21). These words are a foreshadowing of his crucifixion (19:1-42).

[162] **2:19.** ***"'In three days, I will raise it up.'"*** These words are a foreshadowing of Jesus' resurrection (20:1-18).

[163] **2:20.** ***"'It took forty-six years to build this temple.'"*** Some hold that the stated number of years, "forty-six," does not accurately represent how long it had taken to build or renovate the temple under Herod. If the number is not correct, it is important to remember that it is not the writer, John, who is claiming that it took forty-six years. These words are being spoken by emotional anger-driven Jews who might have been exaggerating the number. John faithfully records the words just as he heard them on that day.

[164] **2:22.** ***"They believed the scripture."*** When Jesus rose from the dead, it may have been Psalm 16:10 or Hosea 6:2 that his disciples believed.

[165] **2:22.** ***"The word that Jesus had said."*** Later in the days preceding his death and resurrection, Jesus would speak to his disciples plainly about his resurrection. See Matthew 16:21; 17:23; 20:19.

23 ¶ While he was in Jerusalem at the Passover Feast, [166]
many believed in his name when they saw the miracles
that he did.[167]
24 But Jesus did not entrust himself to them, because
he knew all men.[168]
25 He did not need anyone to testify regarding man,
for he knew what was in man.[169]

---

[166] **2:23.** ***"Passover Feast."*** John's repeated reference to the Passover highlights the significance that it held for the telling of the Gospel story. See 2:13; 6:4; 11:55; 12:1; 13:1; 18:28, 39; and 19:14.

[167] **2:23.** ***"Many believed in his name when they saw the miracles that he did."*** Supernatural ministry affects the hearts and minds of people, causing them to believe upon Jesus. See 2:11; 4:48, 53; 7:31; 10:37-38; 11:15, 45, 48; 12:11; 14:11; and 20:30-31. However, some see his miracles and still do not believe. See 6:36; 7:5; and 12:37.

[168] **2:24.** ***"Jesus did not entrust himself to them, because he knew all men."*** Jesus was conservative in his estimation of the faith of those who believed on him at this point in time. He knew the hearts of all people. He could already perceive that in the face of sacrifice and suffering, these might not be so quick to believe in him. Their fickle nature caused him to be cautious.

[169] **2:25.** ***"He knew what was in man."*** The central thought that began in 2:24 goes deeper in 2:25. Jesus knows all people, but he also knows what is *in* all people—their innermost thoughts, affections, needs and desires. See note for 2:24.

The writer may have more in mind than Jesus' knowledge of the nature of man in general. John may also be referring to Jesus' prophetic ability to discern the hearts and minds of individuals. In the power of the Spirit, Jesus functioned in a way that resembles how believers operating in the charismatic gift of the discerning of spirits would later function (1 Corinthians 12:10).

CHAPTER 3

The First Discourse: New Birth and New Life (3:1-21)

There was a man of the Pharisees[170] named Nicodemus,[171] a ruler of the Jews.

2 He came to Jesus by night[172] and said to him, "Rabbi, we have perceived[173] that you are a teacher who has come from God, for no man can do[174] these miracles that you do, except God be with him."[175]

---

[170] **3:1. *"Pharisees."*** The Pharisees were a sect noted for their strict observance of Jewish practices, adherence to oral laws and traditions, belief in an afterlife and the coming of Messiah. They are mentioned in 1:24; 3:1; 4:1; 7:32, 45, 47, 48; 8:3, 13; 9:13, 15, 16, 40; 11:46, 47, 57; 12:19, 42; 18:3.

[171] **3:1. *"Nicodemus."*** Here Nicodemus appears the first time in this Gospel. He appeared a total of three times in John's Gospel: 3:1-21; 7:45-51; and 19:39-42.

[172] **3:2. *"He came to Jesus by night."*** Some have speculated that Nicodemus may have come to Jesus at night to prevent being seen by other Jewish rulers. His standing among them could have been threatened had they known he was considering becoming a follower of Jesus.

[173] **3:2. *"'We have perceived.'"*** Nicodemus spoke in the first person plural. He was not the only Pharisee who recognized that Jesus was a teacher who had come from God.

> 3 Jesus answered and said to him, "I tell you the truth,[176] unless a man be born again,[177] he cannot see[178] the kingdom of God."[179]

---

[174] **3:2.** ***"No man can do."*** Here we are struck with the inability of man as the contrasting backdrop for the ability of God.

[175] **3:2.** ***"We have perceived that you are a teacher who has come from God, for no man can do these miracles that you do, except God be with him."*** John's inclusion of these words lends support toward the defense of the personhood of Jesus, the Son of God. However, as 3:3 will show, even an acknowledgment of these truths is not enough to grant Nicodemus a full perception of or entrance into the kingdom of God.

[176] **3:3.** ***"I tell you the truth."*** The KJV translates, "Verily, verily." The Greek words here are a transliteration of the Hebrew expression, "Amen, amen." It was a way of saying, "You can be certain of what I am about to tell you."

[177] **3:3.** ***"Born again."*** These words can also be translated, "born from above." In 2 Corinthians 5:17, Paul speaks of the believer becoming a "new creation"—another way of expressing the concept of the new birth. See also 1 Peter 1:3-4. Birth is a family concept. Hints that Jesus was creating a new spiritual family are found in 3:3, 7; 20:17; and 21:23.

[178] **3:3.** ***"He cannot see."*** Until people are born again, they are blind. They are incapable of perceiving or experiencing the kingdom of God. The word translated, "see," might also be translated, "experience." Jesus' words here emphasize perceiving and encountering the kingdom. In 3:5 he speaks of "entering" the kingdom. "Experiencing" and "entering" the kingdom are two aspects of the same spiritual encounter.

[179] **3:3.** ***"Unless a man be born again, he cannot see the kingdom of God."*** It is as though Jesus were saying, "Nicodemus, the human dilemma is much worse than you realize. Not only is man unable to do miraculous works without being born again (3:2), but he also cannot see or enter (as 3:5 will indicate) the realm of God's reign and authority."

4 Nicodemus said to him, "How can a man be born when he is old? Can he enter the second time into his mother's womb and be born?"[180]

5 Jesus answered, "I tell you the truth, unless a man be born of water[181] and of the Spirit,[182] he is not able[183] to enter[184] into the kingdom of God.[185]

---

180 **3:4.** ***"'Can he enter the second time into his mother's womb and be born?'"*** In all likelihood, Nicodemus realized that Jesus was speaking metaphorically. It could be that he knew Jesus was referring to a major life transition similar to what a proselyte to Judaism might experience. If he did in fact know that Jesus was speaking metaphorically, then here in 3:4 he too was speaking metaphorically, saying in effect, "How can a man like me make such a major change in his life at such an old age? That would be like climbing back into my mother's womb and trying to start all over. At my age, that just seems impossible."

181 **3:5.** ***"'Born of water.'"*** These words may be a reference to a baptism that was practiced with proselytes into Judaism. In this baptism, the baptismal candidate promised to renounce idolatry, to receive the God of Israel as his God, and to conform his life to God's law.

182 **3:5.** ***"'Born... of the Spirit.'"*** Being "born of the Spirit" is foreshadowed by the act of being "born of water." The water used in Jewish proselyte baptisms was only a symbol of the Holy Spirit. Here Jesus reminded Nicodemus that it has always been about what God's Spirit would do. See Ezekiel 36:25.

183 **3:5.** ***"'He is not able.'"*** The concept of man's inability stated in 3:3 continues here. The Greek words, *ou dunatai,* translated here as "is not able," is translated "cannot" in the KJV. The emphasis here does not seem to be as much on prohibition as it is on inability.

184 **3:5.** ***"'To enter.'"*** Jesus speaks of *entering* the kingdom, in contrast to his emphasis on *seeing* or *experiencing* it in 3:3.

185 **3:3-5.** ***"'He is not able to enter into the kingdom of God.'"*** Nicodemus knew that man was unable to do such *miracles* as Jesus did without God's favor (3:2). Jesus told him that man is also unable to *enter* God's kingdom apart from a new birth.

> 6 That which is born of the flesh is flesh, and that
> which is born of the Spirit is spirit.[186]
> 7 Do not marvel[187] that I said to you, 'You must be born
> again.'
> 8 The wind[188] blows wherever it pleases,[189] and you
> hear its sound,[190] but you cannot see[191] from where it

To see and enter the kingdom of God is beyond human ability, apart from being born again. We cannot even come close to achieving what needs to be done. We are nowhere near to what we need to be. We even lack the capacity to perceive or understand the kingdom; we cannot see it. It is impossible to remedy our own fallen condition. There is only one solution. We must be born from above—from heaven.

Consider now the positive side of Jesus' negative statement. When a person *is* born from the kingdom of heaven ("from above" in 3:3) he is then enabled to see and enter into the kingdom of heaven.

[186] **3:6. *"'That which is born of the flesh is flesh, and that which is born of the Spirit is spirit.'"*** The works of the flesh or natural man produce nothing but fleshly or natural results. It is the work of the Spirit that produces spiritual results.

[187] **3:7. *"'Do not marvel.'"*** Jesus is suggesting that Nicodemus should not be surprised regarding the mysterious nature of what he is talking about.

[188] **3:8. *"'The wind.'"*** Jesus uses a play on words. The word here, *pneuma,* can be translated as either "spirit" or "wind." It can also be translated as "breath."

[189] **3:8. *"'The wind blows wherever it pleases.'"*** The movements of the wind are a metaphor for the sovereign movements of the Holy Spirit. The wind's power can be harnessed for the purpose of propelling things such as windmills, kites and sailboats; but the wind cannot be controlled. The wind does whatever the wind wants to do.

[190] **3:8. *"'You hear its sound.'"*** May we train ourselves to hear the sound of the wind—the Holy Spirit.

[191] **3:8. *"'See.'"*** Or "perceive."

comes and where it is going. So is every one born of the
Spirit."[192]
9 Nicodemus answered and said to him, "How can
these things be?"
10 Jesus answered and said to him, "Are you the
teacher of Israel and do not know these things?[193]
11 I tell you the truth, we speak what we know, and we
testify to what we have seen;[194] and you do not
receive[195] our testimony.[196]

---

[192] **3:8.** ***"'So is everyone born of the Spirit.'"*** Being born again is just as mysterious and wonderful as the movements of the wind. As the wind moves, so is the movement of anything that gets caught up in it. Things that yield to the wind, such as fallen leaves on an autumn day, are carried wherever the wind goes.

Similarly, as the Spirit moves, so is the movement of the Spirit-born person who gets caught up in the presence of the Spirit. That person will go wherever the Spirit is going and will move as the Spirit is moving. The Holy Spirit cannot be controlled, but the Spirit-born person can access and be influenced by his presence, power, movement and leading.

[193] **3:10.** ***"'Are you the teacher of Israel and do not know these things?'"*** Jesus is not rebuking Nicodemus as much as he is helping him to acknowledge the limitations of his own knowledge. Nicodemus needs to realize that his religious understandings had been incomplete. In 1 Corinthians 2:14, Paul teaches that without the Holy Spirit, a person cannot accept or understand the things that come from the Spirit, for they are spiritually discerned.

[194] **3:11.** ***"'We speak what we know, and we testify to what we have seen.'"*** Jesus has first-hand knowledge of what he is talking about. He is not making this up.

[195] **3:11.** ***"'You do not receive.'"*** The "you" is plural. Jesus was not saying that Nicodemus as an individual was not receiving; he was saying that the Jews whom Nicodemus represented were not receiving.

> 12 If I have told you earthly things, and you do not believe, how shall you believe, if I tell you of heavenly things?[197]
> 13 No man has ascended up to heaven, but he that came down from heaven, even the Son of man[198] who is in heaven.[199]

---

[196] **3:11.** *"'Testimony.'"* See 3:32-33; 5:31, 34, 36; 8:13-14, 17; 12:18; 19:35 and 21:24.

[197] **3:12.** ***"'If I have told you earthly things, and you do not believe, how shall you believe, if I tell you of heavenly things?'"*** If true faith *is* present, even vague figures of speech based on earthly symbols will adequately convey spiritual realities, and the heart of a person will receive. If faith is *not* present and if unbelief is ruling the heart, even precise explanations of heavenly realities will not help. Unbelief is unbelief. The unbelief that hinders when symbolic language is used is the same unbelief that will hinder when clear revelation is given.

Jesus was tutoring his followers by speaking of spiritual truths in earthly terms. It was important for them to respond in faith, because he was preparing them for greater revelations. In keeping with Bill Johnson's understanding of this passage, Jesus' desire was to ultimately reveal to them heavenly things for which there was no earthly parallel.

[198] **3:13.** ***"'Son of man.'"*** The expression, "son of man," brings emphasis to the humanity of Jesus. Some also consider it a Messianic reference to Daniel 7:13-14: "In my vision at night I looked, and there before me was one like a son of man, coming with the clouds of heaven. He approached the Ancient of Days and was led into his presence. He was given authority, glory and sovereign power; all nations and peoples of every language worshiped him. His dominion is an everlasting dominion that will not pass away, and his kingdom is one that will never be destroyed." See 1:51; 3:13-14; 5:27; 6:27, 53, 62; 8:28; 12:23, 34 and 13:31.

[199] **3:13.** ***"'Even the Son of man who is in heaven.'"*** Jesus began to speak plainly to Nicodemus, revealing who he really is. When Jesus said, "even the Son of man who is in heaven," he may have been suggesting that while he was physically on

14 ¶ "And as Moses lifted up the serpent in the
wilderness,[200] even so must the Son of man[201] be lifted
up,[202]
15 that whoever believes[203] in him should not perish,[204]
but have eternal life.[205]

---

earth, he was yet spiritually in the presence of his Father in heaven. In similar fashion, later in Ephesians 2:6 Paul speaks of believers on earth as those who are simultaneously seated in heavenly places in Christ.

In another sense, when Jesus said, "even the Son of man who is in heaven," could it be that Jesus was speaking from a vantage point outside of the limitations of time? Admittedly it requires a stretch in the imagination, but if allowable within the framework of his mission, Jesus may have in this moment positioned himself in spirit at a place outside of time prior to his incarnation or at a point after his ascension, and from that vantage point he could have spoken of himself as being presently in heaven. If this interpretation is a possibility, it is not the only place in John's Gospel where Jesus presents himself in this manner. See notes for 16:33; 17:4, 11, 12, 22 and 24.

[200] **3:14.** ***"'As Moses lifted up the serpent in the wilderness.'"*** The lifting of the serpent in the wilderness was for the healing of the people (Numbers 21:5-9), but it was also a sign showing that the one on the pole was accursed for the sake of those who would be healed. See John 12:32 and Galatians 3:13.

[201] **3:14.** ***"'Son of man.'"*** See 3:13 note.

[202] **3:14.** ***"'Even so must the Son of man be lifted up.'"*** Regarding Jesus being "lifted up," also see 8:28 and 12:32-34.

[203] **3:15.** ***"'Whoever believes.'"*** These words may also be translated, "all who believe."

[204] **3:15.** ***"'Should not perish.'"*** These words may also be translated, "should not be destroyed." In this life, separation from God leaves a person in a deteriorating condition, subject to the one who steals, kills and destroys (10:10) and subject to the destructive power of sin (James 1:15). Beyond this life, the final state of those who

16 ¶ "For God so loved[206] the world,[207] that he gave[208] his only begotten Son,[209] that whoever believes in him[210] should not perish,[211] but have eternal life.[212]

---

do not believe is described in Daniel 12:2; Matthew 13:41, 50; 25:41, 46; John 3:36; Hebrews 9:27; Revelation 20:11-15 and 21:8.

[205] **3:15. *"'Eternal life.'"*** The words may also be translated "everlasting life." See the footnote to 3:16 related to eternal or everlasting life. For additional references to eternal life in John's Gospel, see 3:16, 36; 4:14, 36; 5:24, 39; 6:27, 40, 47, 54, 68; 10:28; 12:25, 50; and 17:2.

[206] **3:16. *"'God so loved.'"*** God *is* love (1 John 4:8), and no one will ever love as greatly as he. Some have erroneously looked at the judgments of God in the Old Testament and thought that they have found evidence of a mean-spirited God who is void of love. I have even heard it expressed that "God, the Son, had to come to save us from God, the Father." Nothing could be further from the truth. Throughout the pages of the Hebrew Scriptures, God moved toward mankind with compassion, working to redeem man, caring for the weak, delivering the afflicted, correcting injustices and sending prophets to warn of impending dangers and judgments. Those who encountered God and knew him pressed the limits of human language to express his boundless love and mercies. Consider how the Psalms declare the extravagance of God's love. A representative list of other scriptures would also include Deuteronomy 4:37; 7:7; Isaiah 66:13; Jeremiah 31.3; Hosea 11:1; 14:5; and Zephaniah 3.17.

[207] **3:16. *"'For God so loved the world.'"*** Yes, God loved the *kosmos*—the created world and all that is in it; but when we hear that "God *so* loved the world," we somehow feel the longing of his heart for the world of *humanity* in particular—those who had drifted so far from him. His passion was to restore fellowship with the world of humanity.

[208] **3:16. *"'He gave.'"*** Our God is a giving God. He has never been anything other than a giving God. He not only created the world with its wonders, but he gave it all to us for our provision and enjoyment. Throughout human history, our God has demonstrated his goodness by giving again and again. Even when his

generosity has been rejected, his heart has always been to give again. Here in this text we are met with the ultimate gift—the sacrificial offering of his son.

209 **3:16. *"'Only begotten Son.'"*** "Only begotten" translates from *monogenous*—a form of *monogenes*, meaning most literally, "the only one to become." It might be better understood as, "the only one of its/his kind to appear in history or come into existence." See also 1:14 and 1:18.

Sin was separating the sons and daughters of Adam from the God who loved them so much, and it would ultimately plunge them into eternal death and damnation. God did not want the world of men to so perish, yet the wages of sin is death (Romans 6:23). Justice required that someone had to pay for sin. Who would pay for the sins of the whole world? Who *could* even pay for the sins of the whole world? It would require a perfect and blameless sacrifice. It would require a blood sacrifice.

From the beginning, God knew that only One could take away the sin that was separating humanity from his presence. So God took on the form of human flesh, and he lived here among the fallen descendants of Adam. Then while remaining sinless, he took upon himself the blame, the guilt, the pain, the torment and the punishment for the sins of the whole world. It was not an easy thing to do.

210 **3:16. *"'Whoever believes in him.'"*** Everyone is included in this promise. None are excluded from the invitation to salvation. The promise is for all.

The essence of belief as presented in this text is two-fold: to be convinced and to trust. Any person who is convinced of the truth concerning Jesus and who places their trust in him will be saved.

211 **3:16. *"'Should not perish.'"*** See 3:15 note.

212 **3:16. *"'Eternal life.'"*** The King James Version translates these words as "everlasting life," rightly conveying the idea of "life without end." However, something more than a quantitative measure of life may be intended here. The words "eternal life" retain the qualitative aspect of the concept. It is a *kind* of life that is *without beginning or end*. In other words, Jesus is speaking of "the life of heaven" or "the life of the eternal realm." For cross reference, see 15:13. For

17 For God did not send his Son into the world to condemn the world, but that the world through him might be saved.[213]

18 ¶ "He who believes on him is not condemned, but he who does not believe is condemned already,[214] because he has not believed in the name of the only begotten Son of God.[215]
19 This is the condemnation: that light has come into the world, and men loved darkness rather than light,[216] because their deeds were evil.

---

additional references to eternal life in John's Gospel, see 3:15, 36; 4:14, 36; 5:24, 39; 6:27, 40, 47, 54, 68; 10:28; 12:25, 50; and 17:2.

213 **3:17.** ***"'God did not send his Son into the world to condemn the world, but that the world through him might be saved.'"*** The reader is reminded that the mission of Christ is not one of condemnation, but salvation. The church would do well to keep these words in mind as it considers its redemptive relationship with the world. See also 5:45 and 12:47.

214 **3:18.** ***"'He who believes on him is not condemned, but he who does not believe is condemned already.'"*** The world was condemned before Jesus came. Romans 1:18 speaks a similar truth, showing that "the wrath of God" is already revealed from heaven against sin. In Jesus, God's mission was to redeem man and save him from judgment.

215 **3:18.** ***"'He who does not believe is condemned already, because he has not believed in the name of the only begotten Son of God.'"*** See 3:36.

216 **3:19.** ***"'Men loved darkness rather than light.'"*** The responsibility for the condemnation of man rests upon man. People are condemned because of their choice to love darkness—life apart from God's light.

20 For everyone who does evil hates the light, neither
comes to the light, in order to avoid having their deeds
exposed.[217]
21 But he who practices truth[218] comes toward the
light,[219] that his deeds may be made manifest,[220]
showing that they have been carried out in God."[221]

22 ¶ After these things Jesus and his disciples came
into the land of Judea, and there he spent time with
them and baptized.

---

[217] **3:20.** ***"'In order to avoid having their deeds exposed.'"*** The KJV reads, "lest his deeds should be reproved," giving emphasis to God's disapproval and the corrective power of the light.

[218] **3:21.** ***"'Truth.'"*** See the note for "full of grace and truth" in 1:14.

[219] **3:21.** ***"'He who practices truth comes toward the light.'"*** Each action of one's life in accordance with truth is a movement "toward the light." Those who conduct their lives in alignment with truth have no need to hide. In fact, once they have experienced the liberating power of truth, they desire more of it, and they desire to be as close to truth and light as they possibly can be.

[220] **3:21.** ***"'That his deeds may be made manifest.'"*** The closer that a person gets to the light, the more that the genuineness of his or her life shines forth.

[221] **3:21.** ***"'Showing that they have been carried out in God.'"*** The thought concerning deeds carried out "in God" may include works accomplished according to God's will and with his approval or works accomplished under God's influence and with his assistance.

23 ¶ John was also baptizing in Aenon near to Salim,[222]
because there was much water there, and the people
came and were baptized,
24 for John was not yet cast into prison.[223]

25 ¶ Then a question arose between some of John's
disciples and the Jews about cleansing.[224]
26 They came to John and said to him, "Rabbi, the man
who was with you on the other side of the Jordan,[225] the
one you have testified about, behold[226] what is
happening. He is baptizing, and everyone is coming to
him."[227]

---

[222] **3:23. *"Aenon near to Salim."*** Aenon was located north of Jericho on the west side of the Jordan River. It was a place known for its springs.

[223] **3:24. *"John was not yet cast into prison."*** The imprisonment of John the Baptist is noted in Matthew 4:12; 14:3; Mark 1:14; 4:17; and Luke 3:19-20.

[224] **3:25. *"Cleansing."*** The context suggests that the discussion about cleansing or purification pertained to baptism.

[225] **3:26. *"The Jordan."*** The reference is to the Jordan River that runs from north to south, flowing from the Sea of Galilee and emptying into the Dead Sea.

[226] **3:26. *"'Behold.'"*** The words "look at" would also be appropriate, but here the KJV word, "behold," has been retained to reinforce the idea that the Jews wanted the Baptist to consider this matter seriously.

[227] **3:26. *"'Everyone is coming to him.'"*** The perception here is that "everyone is following him." See 12:19.

27 John answered and said, "A man can receive
nothing, except it be given him from heaven.[228]
28 You yourselves have witnessed that I said, 'I am not
the Christ,' but that I am sent before him.[229]
29 He who has the bride is the bridegroom, but the
friend of the bridegroom, who stands and hears him,
rejoices greatly because of the bridegroom's voice.[230]
This then is my joy, and it has been fulfilled.[231]

---

[228] **3:27.** ***"'A man can receive nothing, except it be given him from heaven.'"*** John the Baptist is in essence saying, "If Jesus is gaining more followers than me, it is only because those people have been given to him by the Father in heaven."

[229] **3:28.** ***"'You yourselves have witnessed that I said, 'I am not the Christ,' but that I am sent before him.'"*** In effect, John the Baptist was saying, "This has never been about me. It has always been about him. I am not the Christ; I was sent to prepare the way for the Christ."

[230] **3:29.** ***"'He who has the bride is the bridegroom, but the friend of the bridegroom, who stands and hears him, rejoices greatly because of the bridegroom's voice.'"*** John the Baptist used terms reminiscent of the bridal theme found in various places throughout the Bible. In ancient times, after a man proposed to his wife-to-be, he would return home to prepare a place where he and his bride would live. However, before returning home, he would entrust the care of the bride to attendants, known as "friends of the bridegroom." The friends of the bridegroom were very loyal to the bridegroom; they were careful to not even remotely consider winning the affections of the bride for themselves.

Once the bridegroom returned for his bride, the friends of the bridegroom and others would line the streets as the couple made their way toward their new home. At some point in the procession, the bridegroom would begin to converse with the bride. Often this conversation would be the first time that the two had ever spoken to one another. At the sound of the bridegroom's voice, the friends of the bridegroom would begin to rejoice. The friends rejoiced because their share of work for the wedding had resulted in the successful uniting of the couple.

30 He must increase, but I must decrease.[232]
31 He who comes from above[233] is above all. He who is of the earth[234] is earthly and speaks of the earth. He who comes from heaven is above all.
32 What he has seen and heard, that he testifies, and no man receives his testimony.[235]
33 He who has received his testimony has certified[236] that God is true.
34 For he whom God has sent speaks the words of God, for God does not give the Spirit by measure unto him.[237]

---

231 **3:29. *"'This then is my joy, and it has been fulfilled.'"*** In application of the aforementioned, John the Baptist was careful to not think of the multitudes as belonging to him. They all belonged to the bridegroom—Jesus. The sound of Jesus' voice as he spoke to his growing circle of followers brought joy to John the Baptist, not jealousy. The time for the long-awaited uniting of the heavenly bridegroom with his bride had begun.

232 **3:30. *"'He must increase, but I must decrease.'"*** John the Baptist's "decrease" related to two developments. First, his personal God-given mission to prepare the bride for the bridegroom was drawing to a close. Second, John the Baptist was the last of the old covenant prophets, and the old covenant was soon to give way to the new.

233 **3:31. *"'He who comes from above.'"*** John the Baptist is referring to Jesus, speaking of his place of origin—"above."

234 **3:31. *"'He who is of the earth.'"*** John the Baptist identified himself as "he who is of the earth," in contrast to Jesus who is "He who comes from above."

235 **3:32. *"'Testimony.'"*** See 3:11, 3:32-33; 5:31, 34, 36; 8:13-14, 17; 12:18; 19:35 and 21:24.

236 **3:33. *"'Has certified.'"*** The KJV translates, "hath set to his seal."

35 The Father loves the Son and has given all things
into his hand.[238]
36 He who believes on the Son has eternal life,[239] and he
who does not believe the Son will not see life,[240] but the
wrath of God[241] remains on him."

Pause and Reflect

1. If you have placed your faith in the Son of God, pause right now to give thanks to God for the joy of knowing Jesus and for the gift of eternal life.
2. Believing on the Son is a heaven or hell issue (3:36). If a person does not place their faith in the Son of God, that person will not see life. If you have not yet placed your faith in the Son of God, pause right now and pray, "Jesus, I believe that you are the Son of God. Forgive me for my

---

[237] **3:34.** ***"'God does not give the Spirit by measure unto him.'"*** There is no limit and no end to the possibilities of what the Father will do through the Spirit through Jesus.

[238] **3:35.** ***"'The Father loves the Son and has given all things into his hand.'"*** The expression, "the Father loves the Son," occurs again in 5:20, where Jesus said, "For the Father loves the Son and shows him all things that he is doing." In both instances, the Father's love for the Son has ramifications for what the Father has entrusted to his Son.

[239] **3:36.** ***"'Eternal life.'"*** See also 3:15-16; 4:14, 36; 5:24, 39; 6:27, 40, 47, 54, 68; 10:28; 12:25, 50; and 17:2.

[240] **3:36.** ***"'He who believes on the Son has eternal life, and he who does not believe the Son will not see life.'"*** The reader is faced with the reality that believing in Jesus is "a matter of life and death."

[241] **3:36.** ***"'The wrath of God.'"*** This expression calls to mind the words that Jesus spoke earlier in 3:18. Also see Romans 1:18.

sins, wash me from my sins, and come into my life. I want to be born again. I want to follow you."

3. Do you know someone who has not yet placed their faith in the Son of God? You probably know many who have not taken this critical step in life. Pause right now with at least one person's name in mind, and pray for that person's salvation.

Chapter 4

Jesus Presents Himself to the Samaritans (4:1-54)

When the Lord learned that the Pharisees[242]
had heard he[243] was making and baptizing
more disciples than John,
2 (although Jesus himself did not baptize; rather, it was
his disciples,)
3 He left Judea, and departed again into Galilee.[244]

---

[242] **4:1. *"Pharisees."*** The Pharisees were a sect noted for their strict observance of Jewish practices, adherence to oral laws and traditions, belief in an afterlife and the coming of Messiah. They are mentioned in 1:24; 3:1; 4:1; 7:32, 45, 47, 48; 8:3, 13; 9:13, 15, 16, 40; 11:46, 47, 57; 12:19, 42; 18:3.

[243] **4:1. *"He."*** The word is "Jesus" in the original text. The pronoun is preferred in this translation to avoid awkward syntax.

[244] **4:3. *"He left Judea, and departed again into Galilee."*** If Jesus had remained in Judea, the Pharisees would have become too preoccupied with monitoring his activities. Such attention at this point in Jesus' ministry could have potentially set into motion a sequence of events that would have prematurely taken Jesus to the cross.

The Second Discourse:
The Water of Life (4:4-42)

4 And it was necessary[245] for him to go through Samaria.

5 Then he came to a city of Samaria, which is called Sychar, near to the parcel of ground that Jacob gave to his son, Joseph.

6 Jacob's well was there. Then Jesus, being wearied with his journey, sat on the well,[246] and it was about the sixth hour.[247]

7 There came a woman of Samaria to draw water.[248] Jesus said to her, "Give me to drink."

---

[245] **4:4.** ***"It was necessary."*** The KJV translates, "must needs." The idea of the expression is that circumstances have dictated the necessity of the action. He may have been moved by the Spirit and a compelling compassion to reach the Samaritans—a people estranged from Israel. Jesus had a vision for this harvest.

[246] **4:6.** ***"Jacob's well was there. Then Jesus, being wearied with his journey, sat on the well."*** "Sat on the well" is translated in the KJV as "sat thus [meaning 'in this manner'] on the well."

The image of the eternal Son of God sitting on Jacob's well is somewhat dramatic—even poetic. It is a scene of contrasts, and it represents a major shift. Jacob's well (Israel's well) would not satisfy the thirst—the true need—of the woman who is about to appear in this narrative, but Jesus would satisfy that thirst.

[247] **4:6.** ***"The sixth hour."*** The time would have been about 6:00 a.m., seeing that in this Gospel the writer used Roman time and not Jewish time. Consideration of the time of day adds to the understanding of why Jesus was so weary from the journey. Evidently, he had traveled on foot through at least a portion of the night and arrived at the well not only tired but also deprived of sleep.

[248] **4:7.** ***"Water."*** For readers living with an abundance of good water readily available at water fountains, household faucets and plastic containers, the intended

8 (His disciples were gone away into the city to buy
meat.)
9 Then the woman of Samaria said to him, "How is it
that you, being a Jew, are asking drink of me—a
woman of Samaria?[249] The Jews have no dealings with
the Samaritans."[250]
10 Jesus answered and said to her, "If you knew the
gift of God and who it is that said to you, 'Give me to

---

impact of the water metaphor in this story may be missed. In this first century Middle Eastern setting, pure drinkable water was precious and even rare in some places.

[249] **4:9.** ***"'How is it that you, being a Jew, are asking drink of me—a woman of Samaria?'"*** In John 4:9, the woman rightly questions how Jesus could be asking water from her, seeing that He was a Jew, and she was a Samaritan woman. Not only was it considered inappropriate for Jews and Samaritans to interact in such a manner, but it was also considered inappropriate for a man to approach a woman in such a manner alone. John 4:27 also implies what was perceived as the cultural inappropriateness of this interaction.

[250] **4:9.** ***"'The Jews have no dealings with the Samaritans.'"*** After the Assyrians took into captivity most of the people of the northern kingdom of Israel in 722 B.C., Gentiles were brought into the region of Samaria to resettle the land. The remaining Jews intermarried with the Gentiles. As a result, the Samaritans of Jesus' day were an ethnic mix of Babylonians, Assyrians, Jews and peoples from other places. From a Jewish perspective, this mix meant that these Samaritans were an impure race with a distorted religion only slightly resembling the faith of the Jews. These compromises combined with an ancient history of stressed relationships between the northern and southern kingdoms created a wall of bitterness between the two people groups.

drink,' you would have asked of him, and he would
have given you living water."[251]
11 The woman said to him, "Sir, you have nothing to
draw with, and the well is deep. Where will you get
your living water?[252]
12 Are you greater than our father Jacob,[253] who gave
us the well[254] and drank from it himself, and his
children and his cattle?"
13 Jesus answered and said to her, "Whoever drinks of
this water will thirst again,
14 but whoever drinks of the water that I give will
never thirst.[255] But the water that I give will be in him a
well of water[256] springing up into eternal life."[257]

---

[251] **4:10.** ***"'Living water.'"*** In a literal sense, "living water" may mean water that is moving, as opposed to water that is still or even stagnant. Figuratively speaking, "living water" is water that has life-giving qualities. Looking at the verse as a whole, it is as though Jesus were saying, "If you knew God's heart for you, and if you could catch a glimpse of who I really am—the full expression of God's heart, then you would be drawn into that revelation of love and would not hold back from asking for the living water that I bring." Jesus' words are full of grace.

[252] **4:11.** ***"'Where will you get your living water?'"*** These words are more literally translated, "From where then do you have that living water?"

[253] **4:12.** ***"'Are you greater than our father Jacob...?'"*** The woman's question to Jesus was a question for Jewish readers to ponder. Jesus was in fact far greater than the religious heritage of both the Jewish and Samaritan people.

[254] **4:12.** ***"'Are you greater than our father Jacob, who gave us the well.'"*** The woman refers to the well as a gift to her people from their father, Jacob. These people were very aware of their Jewish origins and still claimed full rights to their inheritance.

15 The woman said to him, "Sir,[258] give me this water,
that I may not be thirsty and have to keep coming to
this place to draw water."[259]
16 Jesus said to her, "Go, call your husband, and come
back."[260]

---

[255] **4:14. *"'Whoever drinks of the water that I give will never thirst.'"*** Is there any other life-sustaining substance, whether figurative or literal, for which this claim can be made? The thirst of man's soul may be satisfied through some temporal means in one moment, but in a short time, dissatisfaction returns. Here Jesus promises to permanently satisfy the thirst of the human soul.

[256] **4:14. *"'The water that I give will be in him a well of water.'"*** Even devoted Christians can sometimes feel spiritually dry; however, they have been given unending access to an internal resource. It is "a well of water" from which they may draw refreshment and strength at any time. See 7:38.

[257] **4:14. *"'Eternal life.'"*** See also 3:15-16, 36; 4:36; 5:24, 39; 6:27, 40, 47, 54, 68; 10:28; 12:25, 50; and 17:2.

[258] **4:15. *"'Sir.'"*** The word rendered as "Sir" is actually *kurie* (from *kurios*), meaning, "Lord." The woman was not yet at the point where she would have recognized the lordship of Jesus or anything divine about him; therefore, her word choice should be understood as a matter of good etiquette (i.e., addressing a stranger with a respectful salutation) and not as an expression of faith or worship.

[259] **4:15. *"'Sir, give me this water, that I may not be thirsty and have to keep coming to this place to draw water.'"*** A more literal rendering of the woman's request would read, "Lord, be giving me this water that I may not be thirsting and not be coming to this place to be drawing."

[260] **4:16. *"'Go, call your husband, and come back.'"*** On the surface, it appears as though Jesus ignored the woman's request. On the contrary, Jesus' instruction to her should be understood as a direct response to her request for living water. How is that so? With these words, Jesus began to speak prophetically into her life, thus initiating the life-giving flow. Prophecy is life-giving.

17 The woman answered and said, "I have no
husband."
Jesus said to her, "You have spoken well, saying, 'I
have no husband,'
18 for you have had five husbands, and the man you
now have is not your husband.[261] In this you have
spoken truthfully."
19 The woman said to him, "Sir, I perceive that you are
a prophet.[262]
20 Our fathers worshipped in this mountain,[263] and you
say that in Jerusalem is the place where men ought to
worship."[264]

---

[261] **4:18.** ***"'You have had five husbands, and the man you now have is not your husband.'"*** Jesus was supernaturally functioning in that which would be the equivalent to the charismatic gift known as a "word of knowledge" in 1 Corinthians 12:8. This is the first of two miracles Jesus performed after coming out of Judea into Galilee. The second is referenced in 4:54.

[262] **4:19.** ***"'Sir, I perceive that you are a prophet.'"*** The precision of Jesus' word of knowledge in 4:18 convinced the woman that he was a prophet.

[263] **4:20.** ***"'Our fathers worshipped in this mountain.'"*** The woman referred to the Samaritan belief that God had chosen Mount Gerizim as the place of worship and not Jerusalem.

[264] **4:20.** ***"'Our fathers worshipped in this mountain, and you say that in Jerusalem is the place where men ought to worship.'"*** With her sins having now been brought to light, it appears that the woman wanted to change the subject. Often when people sense that a Christian's witness may be getting too close to the important issues of the heart, they will want to shift the conversation toward something religious in an attempt to demonstrate that they are not totally void of spiritual understanding.

21 Jesus said to her, "Woman, believe me, the hour is
coming when you shall neither in this mountain nor
yet at Jerusalem worship the Father.[265]
22 You do not know what you worship; we do know
what we worship, for salvation is of the Jews.[266]
23 But the hour is coming, and the hour has already
come,[267] when the true worshippers shall worship the

When the woman said, "Our fathers worshipped in this mountain," she was referring to the Samaritan belief that God had chosen Mount Gerizim as the place of worship and not Jerusalem. Why did they choose Mount Gerizim? Even the non-Jews who settled in the region of Samaria eventually adopted part of the Jewish religion. However, after the return of the Jews from Babylonian captivity, the Jews in Jerusalem refused to allow the people of the region of Samaria to participate in the rebuilding of the temple. This distancing contributed to the hostility between the two groups. The people of Samaria built a rival temple on Mount Gerizim, which was eventually destroyed by a Jewish king in B.C. 130. Another temple was built to take its place at Shechem. Thus it can be seen why it said in John 4:9 that the "Jews have no dealings with the Samaritans."

[265] **4:21.** ***"'The hour is coming when you shall neither in this mountain nor yet at Jerusalem worship the Father.'"*** These words were a foreshadowing of a time when worship would no longer be limited to particular places. Following the cross-death, resurrection and ascension of Jesus, the Holy Spirit would be poured out upon all flesh, and by the blood of Jesus, a way would be opened for all peoples to approach God. Jesus' words also suggested that he foresaw the Roman destruction of Jerusalem in 70 A.D., thus removing it as a place of worship.

[266] **4:22.** ***"'You do not know what you worship; we do know what we worship, for salvation is of the Jews.'"*** Jesus' words are not spoken in arrogance; these words are a statement of truth. The entire body of revelation pertaining to salvation had been entrusted to the Jews. The Samaritans held the Pentateuch as sacred, but they did not have the same regard for the remainder of the Hebrew Scriptures. Consequently, from Jesus' perspective, their understanding of worship and salvation was incomplete.

> Father in spirit and truth,[268] for the Father seeks such to worship him.[269]
> 24 God is Spirit, and they that worship him must worship him in spirit and truth."[270]

---

[267] **4:23. *"'The hour is coming, and the hour has already come.'"*** Here is an expression that will appear again in 5:25. Jesus spoke of a time that was coming, but he also spoke as though that time had already come. These words feature the "already, but not yet" nature of God's kingdom. It is both present and future. When Jesus spoke these words, a time was coming when the Holy Spirit would be given, thus enabling the worship of God in spirit and in truth. But in another sense, the time had already come for the woman to worship in spirit and truth, for the object of her worship—Jesus—was sitting in front of her; she was already in his presence.

[268] **4:23. *"'The true worshippers shall worship the Father in spirit and truth.'"*** Worship "in spirit and truth" is highlighted as the mode of worship the Father desires and seeks. Some view "spirit and truth" as a way to bring *"balance"* in worship. Their view is that the spontaneous and emotional nature of worship "in spirit" must be balanced with worship "in truth"—in essence, worship guided by the Scriptures. However, "spirit" and "truth" are not contrary to one another. Rather, "truth" is a word that further defines what worship in "spirit" is; worship "in spirit" is in fact worship in "truth" or "reality." The expression can actually be translated, "in spirit, even truth." In short, the meaning is that worship in "spirit" is real worship.

"'Truth.'" See the note for "full of grace and truth" in 1:14.

[269] **4:23. *"'The Father seeks such to worship him.'"*** Here the Father is not seeking worship; he is seeking *worshippers*—those who will acknowledge him and who will center their lives upon his presence. The realization that the Father is *seeking* lovers of his presence stirs the heart to value and steward his presence.

[270] **4:24. *"'God is Spirit, and they that worship him must worship him in spirit and truth.'"*** Knowing that God is Spirit and that he must be approached and worshiped in spirit and truth causes one to desire a life that is deeply spiritual—a life that is rightly aligned with the revelation of who God is and the realization of what he is really like.

25 The woman said to him, "I know that Messiah is
coming—the one called Christ. When he comes,[271] he
will tell us all things."[272]
26 Jesus said to her, "I that speak unto you am he."[273]

27 ¶ At that moment, his disciples came and
wondered[274] why he was talking with the woman,[275] yet
no one said, "What are you looking for?" or, "Why are
you talking with her?"[276]

---

[271] **4:25.** ***"'When he comes.'"*** More precisely, the text could read, "Whenever he may be coming."

[272] **4:25.** ***"'He will tell us all things.'"*** The woman expressed her belief that when the Messiah comes, he will tell "all things." Only moments later, she would suddenly realize that this man—Jesus—had in fact told her "all things" about herself. In her own words, she would soon testify, "Come and see a man who told me everything that I have ever done. Isn't this the Christ?" (4:29)

[273] **4:26.** ***"'I that speak unto you am he.'"*** There was no doubt about it. Here Jesus said it plainly: "I am the Messiah."

[274] **4:27.** ***"Wondered."*** The KJV translates, "marveled."

[275] **4:27.** ***"Why he was talking with the woman."*** Three objections could have been raised regarding Jesus conversing with this woman:

1. She was a Samaritan.
2. She was a woman.
3. She was an immoral woman.

[276] **4:27.** ***"No one said, 'What are you looking for?' or, 'Why are you talking with her?'"*** The implication is that the disciples wanted to ask those questions, but did not dare to do so. As far as their mission was concerned, they wanted to have nothing to do with these Samaritans. They would have preferred to move on to some other place where they could reach their own kind. They did not have a vision for this portion of the harvest.

28 The woman then left her water pot,[277] went her way
into the city and said to the people,
29 "Come and see[278] a man who told me everything
that I have ever done. Isn't this the Christ?"[279]
30 Then they went out of the city and came to him.[280]

---

277 **4:28.** ***"The woman then left her water pot."*** The fact that the woman left her water pot at the well carries two practical implications and one symbolic implication:

1. Practically, she became so excited about meeting the Messiah that she ran off, forgetting about her water pot and unknowingly leaving it behind, or
2. she ran off with the intent to bring others back to meet Jesus, thus leaving her water pot only because she would be returning for it.
3. Symbolically, leaving her water pot behind represented leaving her old way of life behind her.

278 **4:29.** ***"'Come and see.'"*** These words speak of the simplicity of the Christian witness. Come and see for yourself! Come and see what God is doing! Come and see what he is doing in lives! Come and see *my* life!

Many would prefer that the call be, "See and come;" they would be more comfortable with seeing and understanding all that is being asked of them before taking a step of faith. But that is not the way that it usually works in the kingdom. It is when we "come"—depart from where we have been for the sake of going to where we are being called—that we will then "see" the glorious things that God has in store for those who believe. The invitation to "come and see" occurs three times in John's Gospel: 1:39, 46; and here in 4:29.

279 **4:29.** ***"'Come and see a man who told me everything that I have ever done. Isn't this the Christ?'"*** The woman's words are a reminder of what she said in 4:25, stating that when the Messiah would come, he would tell all things.

280 **4:30.** ***"Then they went out of the city and came to him."*** The woman's enthusiastic and convincing testimony stirred up curiosity, prompting an initial response from the people.

31 ¶ In the meantime, his disciples entreated him,
saying, "Rabbi, eat."
32 But he said to them, "I have food to eat that you do
not know about."
33 Then the disciples said to one another, "Has anyone
brought him something to eat?"
34 Jesus said to them, "My food is to do the will of him
that sent me and to finish his work.[281]
35 Are you not saying, 'There are still four months, and
then the harvest is coming'?[282] Behold, I say to you, lift
up your eyes and look on the fields, for they are
already white[283]—ready for the harvest.[284]

---

[281] **4:34.** ***"'My food is to do the will of him that sent me and to finish his work.'"*** Food is that for which men work, that for which men hunger, that which satisfies, and that which nourishes and gives strength. For Jesus, the thing for which he worked, the thing for which he hungered, and the one thing that satisfied his longing and gave him joy and strength was the doing of and completion of his Father's will. At this moment in the narrative, what was his Father's will? His Father's will was that the mass of Samaritans who were about to come their way be brought into the family of God. The gathering of this harvest was his food. Here Jesus has expressed his vision to his disciples. God's mission has always been to the whole world—all of humanity.

[282] **4:35.** ***"'There are still four months, and then the harvest is coming.'"*** Some commentators say that this reference places this episode in the month of Tevet (December-January). *Ellicott's Commentary for English Readers, Bible Hub,* accessed January 8, 2016, http://biblehub.com/commentaries/john/4-35.htm.

[283] **4:35.** ***"'White.'"*** White was the color of ripening grain.

[284] **4:35.** ***"'Behold, I say to you, lift up your eyes and look on the fields, for they are already white—ready for the harvest.'"*** Jesus directed his disciples to see the vision that he was seeing. What did these disciples see when they looked at the fields before them? The physical fields might have been brown, awaiting the harvest

> 36 Even now the reaper[285] is getting his reward[286] and is gathering fruit unto eternal life,[287] so that both the sower[288] and the reaper may rejoice together.[289]

---

that would come four months later. Jesus said, "Open your eyes..." or "Lift your eyes and look..." In effect he said, "Look beyond what natural eyes see. See what I see. See the vision. Look beyond what you are accustomed to seeing." In part, he was calling his disciples to shift to a cross-cultural perspective. They were Jews. The multitude that was to soon come their way—they were Samaritans! This is a call to look to the nations—the ethnic groups (*ethne*) of the world.

Jesus said, "Look at the fields. They are ripe. They are white for harvest." It has been said that the people of Sychar traditionally wore white garments. If that is the case, then at this very moment as the disciples lifted their eyes and looked at the brown fields, a multitude of people dressed in white were sweeping their way. Ready or not, the harvest was upon them! Harvest time is a window of opportunity. It will begin at a certain time, and it will end at a certain time. There is nothing that can be done to delay it, and there is nothing that can be done to speed it up. Like it or not, harvest is coming. Ready or not, here it comes. At this particular time in John 4, the harvest of Samaritans in Sychar was ready. They could not walk away from it. It was upon them.

The harvest is upon the church. Christians can turn their heads and pretend that it is not so, if they want to, but it does not change the fact that the grain in the fields is bent over heavy with the abundance, and the harvest must quickly be gathered. Wait too long, and the harvest will fall wasted to the ground. Others will come in and "satisfy" the spiritual hunger in the hearts of men with their false ideologies, and those souls will be eternally lost. The harvest is upon the church. If people do not think that it is a time to *harvest*, then at least they should do something to *prepare* for the time of harvest. At least plow, sow, cultivate and water. Do *something*. The harvest is today.

[285] **4:36. *"The reaper."*** The "reaper" is Jesus.

[286] **4:36. *"His reward."*** Jesus' "reward" is the harvest of souls. Using a different metaphor to describe the same thing, his "reward" is his bride.

37 Thus, the saying is true, 'One sows, and another
reaps.'
38 I commissioned you to reap[290] that which you have
not worked for; others have labored,[291] and you have
entered into their labors."[292]

39 ¶ Many of the Samaritans from that city believed in
him for the saying of the woman, who testified, "He
told me everything that I have ever done."[293]

---

[287] **4:36.** ***"'Eternal life.'"*** See also 3:15-16, 36; 4:14; 5:24, 39; 6:27, 40, 47, 54, 68; 10:28; 12:25, 50; and 17:2.

[288] **4:36.** ***"'The sower.'"*** Here "the sower" may be a reference to the Samaritan woman who ran into the city and sowed with her testimony.

[289] **4:36.** ***"'That both the sower and the reaper may rejoice together.'"*** Catch a glimpse of this scene. When the harvest is being reaped, both Jesus and those who have sown are caught up in a dance together! Hear the joyful sound—the shouts of joy in heaven and earth!

[290] **4:38.** ***"'I commissioned you to reap.'"*** The disciples are told that their commission involves them joining with him in the reaping of the harvest.

[291] **4:38.** ***"'Others have labored.'"*** These words may be a reference in part to the labor of the Samaritan woman whose labor consisted of the simple task of sharing her testimony.

[292] **4:38.** ***"'You have entered into their labors.'"*** What is going on here might be summarized in these words: The disciples had gone into Sychar, but they had no vision for the harvest of that city. They returned to Jesus bringing him physical food. In contrast, a Samaritan woman of ill repute had gone into Sychar with a testimony and with a vision—the hope that Jesus might give to others the same living water that he had given her. She returned to Jesus bringing him "food to eat" that his disciples did not know about (3:32)—a harvest of Samaritan souls. Now the disciples were called upon to enter into the labor of the Samaritan woman.

40 So when the Samaritans came to him, they asked
him to spend some time with them, and he stayed there
two days.[294]
41 Many more believed because of Jesus' own word,
42 and they said to the woman, "Now we believe, not
just because of what you have said. We have heard him
ourselves and know that this is indeed the Christ, the
Savior of the world."[295]

Harmony of the Gospels			
	Matthew	**Mark**	**Luke**
John the Baptist in Prison	4:12; 14:3	1:14; 4:17	3:19-20

---

[293] **4:39.** ***"Many of the Samaritans from that city believed in him for the saying of the woman, who testified, 'He told me everything that I have ever done.'"*** The Samaritans were not won by an anointed sermon or an elaborate evangelistic campaign. They were won by the testimony of an unlikely witness—a sinful woman whose heart had been kindly pierced by a prophetic word on the lips of God's Son.

[294] **4:40.** ***"When the Samaritans came to him, they asked him to spend some time with them, and he stayed there two days."*** The hunger of the Samaritan people serves as an example for all. Jesus responded to their desire and request for more.

[295] **4:39-42.** The progression of faith development is worthy of attention. There was an initial level of faith prompted in the hearts of the people by the woman's testimony; they heard *about* Jesus and believed. That faith grew and became more personal after actually meeting Jesus, spending time with him and listening to him teach; they had their own *encounter* with Jesus.

Not all Samaritan communities were equally receptive to Jesus. In Luke 9:51-56, a Samaritan village refused to receive him when they realized that he was heading toward Jerusalem to participate in a Jewish feast.

43 ¶ After two days, he departed from that place and
went into Galilee,
44 For Jesus testified that a prophet has no honor in his
own country.[296]
45 Then when he had arrived in Galilee, the Galileans
received him, having seen all the things that he did at
Jerusalem at the feast,[297] for they also went to the feast.

Harmony of the Gospels			
	Matthew	**Mark**	**Luke**
Jesus Returns to Galilee	4:12	1:14-15	4:14-15
The Synagogue at Nazareth			4:16-30
Calling of Andrew, Simon, James and John	4:13-22	1:16-20	5:1-11

The Second Sign: Healing of the Nobleman's Son (4:46-54)

46 So Jesus came again into Cana of Galilee, where he
had turned the water into wine. In Cana there was a
certain nobleman[298] whose son was sick at Capernaum.

---

[296] **4:44.** ***"Jesus testified that a prophet has no honor in his own country."*** The reference to a prophet not having honor in his own country suggests that Jesus chose to devote his efforts to areas outside of Nazareth—his hometown—due to the fact that the people of that city were reluctant to receive him as a prophet.

[297] **4:45.** ***"The Galileans received him, having seen all the things that he did at Jerusalem at the feast."*** The Galileans received Jesus because they had recently witnessed his miracles in Jerusalem: "While he was in Jerusalem at the Passover Feast, many believed in his name when they saw the miracles that he did" (2:23).

[298] **4:46.** ***"In Cana there was a certain nobleman."*** The word, "nobleman," suggests that this man was an officer serving the king.

> 47 When he heard that Jesus had come out of Judea into Galilee, he went to him[299] and asked him to come down[300] and heal his son, for he was at the point of death.
> 48 Then Jesus said to him, "Unless you see signs and wonders, you will not believe."[301]

---

[299] **4:47. *"When he heard that Jesus had come out of Judea into Galilee, he went to him."*** It is not stated whether or not the nobleman was already in Cana, but if he was not, then he made his way from Capernaum to Cana—a distance of about 16 miles. By horse, a person could make this trip in two hours. On foot this would have been about a six-hour journey. The time elements related to his return trip in 4:50-52 suggest that his journey required about a full day to complete. Thus it is highly likely that he was traveling on foot.

[300] **4:47. *"He went to him and asked him to come down."*** The nobleman's request was that Jesus come "down" to Capernaum. In biblical literature, directional terms such as "up" and "down" do not refer to north and south as is commonly the case in western language and literature. Rather, "up" and "down" are elevation references. If Jesus were to travel from Cana to Capernaum, he would be going "down" to a place of lower elevation.

[301] **4:48. *"'Unless you see signs and wonders, you will not believe.'"*** Although these words were spoken directly to the nobleman, Jesus may have been speaking for the benefit of others who were present. Jesus was citing a general principle, but this nobleman was about to respond with faith in a very unusual way (4:50). Generally, if it were not for the "signs and wonders," many would not have believed. They needed to see the proof of Jesus' claims manifested through supernatural works.

Supernatural ministry affects the hearts and minds of people, causing them to believe upon Jesus. See 2:11, 23; 4:53; 7:31; 10:37-38; 11:15, 45, 48; 12:11; 14:11; and 20:30-31. However, some see his miracles and still do not believe. See 6:36; 7:5; and 12:37.

49 The nobleman said to him, "Sir, come down[302] before
my child dies."
50 Jesus said to him, "Go your way; your son lives."[303]
And the man believed the word that Jesus had spoken
to him, and he went his way.[304]
51 As he was going down,[305] his servants met him and
reported, saying, "Your son lives."
52 Then he inquired of them the hour when he began
to get better. They said to him, "Yesterday at the
seventh hour[306] the fever left him."[307]

---

[302] **4:49.** ***"'Come down.'"*** "Up" and "down" are references to elevation and not points on the compass. See 2:12, 13; 5:1; 6:16; 7:8, 10, 14; 11:55; and 12:20.

[303] **4:50.** ***"'Go your way; your son lives.'"*** Jesus did not *pray* for the child to live; he *declared* that the nobleman's child lives. In light of 4:52, it is known that Jesus spoke these words at about 7:00 a.m.—the seventh hour.

[304] **4:50.** ***"The man believed the word that Jesus had spoken to him, and he went his way."*** It is interesting to note that even though Jesus had said to the nobleman, "Unless you see signs and wonders, you will not believe" (4:48), this nobleman believed without seeing a sign or a wonder! This man believed and acted solely on the basis of Jesus' word!

[305] **4:51.** ***"As he was going down."*** In light of 4:52, it is clear that the nobleman's journey back to Capernaum took place on the day following his encounter with Jesus.

[306] **4:52.** ***"'The seventh hour.'"*** In John's writing he uses Roman time and not Jewish time. The "seventh hour" would have been about 7:00 a.m., according to Roman time.

[307] **4:52.** ***"'The fever left him.'"*** This report demonstrates that Jesus was able to heal at a distance without being physically present with the afflicted person.

53 So the father knew that it was at the same hour in
which Jesus said to him, "Your son lives." And he and
his whole household believed.[308]
54 This is the second miracle[309] that Jesus did when he
came out of Judea into Galilee.

Harmony of the Gospels			
	Matthew	**Mark**	**Luke**
Deliverance in the Synagogue		1:21-28	4:31-37
Peter's Mother-in-law Healed	8:14-17	1:29-34	4:38-41
First Ministry Tour in Galilee	4:23-25	1:35-39	4:42-44
Healing of a Leper	8:1-4	1:40-45	5:12-16
Calming of a Storm	8:18-27	4:35-41	8:22-25
Deliverance in the Land of the Gadarenes	8:28-34	5:1-20	8:26-39
Jairus' Daughter Raised and a Woman Healed	9:18-26	5:21-43	8:40-56
Healing of Two Blind Men and a Deliverance	9:27-34		

---

[308] **4:53.** ***"He and his whole household believed."*** The nobleman and his entire household placed their faith in Jesus. In 4:50 the nobleman believed *for his son's healing* on the basis of Jesus' word. The faith seen here in 4:53 seems to be something more than faith for healing. The nobleman and his household placed their faith in *the person of Jesus.*

Supernatural ministry causes people to believe upon Jesus. See 2:11, 23; 4:48; 7:31; 10:37-38; 11:15, 45, 48; 12:11; 14:11; and 20:30-31. However, some see his miracles and still do not believe. See 6:36; 7:5; and 12:37.

[309] **4:54.** ***"The second miracle."*** The first miracle occurred in Jesus' prophetic encounter with the Samaritan woman at Jacob's well (4:16-18).

	Matthew	**Mark**	**Luke**
Healing of a Paralytic	9:1-8	2:1-12	5:17-26
Matthew the Publican	9:9-13	2:13-17	5:27-32
Question About Fasting	9:14-17	2:18-22	5:33-39

CHAPTER 5

Jesus Presents Himself to the Jewish Leaders (5:1-47)

The Third Sign: Healing of the Lame Man (5:1-18)

After this there was a feast of the Jews,[310] and
Jesus went up to Jerusalem.[311]
2 Now there is at Jerusalem by the sheep
market a pool, which is called in the Hebrew tongue
Bethesda,[312] having five porches.

---

310 **5:1.** ***"A feast of the Jews."*** Although the name of the feast is not given, it was probably the Feast of Purim because of its placement between the month of Tevet (December-January) in 4:35 and Passover in Nisan (March-April) in 6:4. The Feast of Purim was kept on the fourteenth day of Adar (March), and it commemorated the deliverance of the Jews from the plot of Haman in the Book of Esther. *Ellicott's Commentary for English Readers, Bible Hub,* accessed January 8, 2016, http:// biblehub.com/ commentaries/ john/5-1.htm.

311 **5:1.** ***"Up to Jerusalem."*** "Up" and "down" are references to elevation and not points on the compass. See 2:12, 13; 4:49; 6:16; 7:8, 10, 14; 11:55; and 12:20.

312 **5:2.** ***"Bethesda."*** Derived from the Hebrew or Aramaic, the word "Bethesda" means "house of mercy." Archaeologists propose that Bethesda was a place for Jewish ritual baths. "The Bethesda Pool, Site of One of Jesus' Miracles," *Bible History Daily* (Biblical Archaeology Society), updated June 1, 2015, accessed January 9, 2016,

3 In these porches was laid a great multitude of
disabled people—the blind, the lame, people with
withered appendages[313]—waiting for the moving of the
water.
*[4 For an angel went down at certain times[314] into the pool
and stirred up the water. Whoever then first stepped in, after
the stirring of the water, was made whole of whatever disease
he had.]* [315]
5 A certain man was there who had been sick thirty-
eight years.

---

http:// www.biblicalarchaeology.org/ daily/ biblical-sites-places/ jerusalem/ the-bethesda-pool-site-of-one-of-jesus%E2%80%99-miracles/

313 **5:3. *"People with withered appendages."*** These words are translated as "withered" in the KJV. A number of translations, including the NIV, end the sentence here with "people with withered appendages" or "withered," resuming the narrative with 5:5.

314 **5:4. *"Certain times."*** The word for "time," translated here as "certain times," is *kairos*.

315 **5:4. *"For an angel went down at certain times into the pool and stirred up the water. Whoever then first stepped in, after the stirring of the water, was made whole of whatever disease he had."*** The earliest and best available manuscripts omit this verse. These words may represent a superstition held by some in the first century but omitted by the Gospel writer out of a concern that tales about angels might distract from the more essential emphasis on the Son of God. At some point in the transmission of the text from one copy to another, a scribe might have added the traditionally held words of 5:4 as a plausible explanation for the "moving of the water" reference in 5:3. Michael S. Heiser, "Who Took Verse 4 out of My Bible?" *Christianity.com*, accessed October 10, 2012, http:// www.christianity.com/ 11627917/.

6 When Jesus saw him lying down and knew that he
had been in this condition a long time, he said to him,
"Do you want to be made whole?"[316]
7 The disabled man answered him, "Sir, when the
water is stirred, I have no one to put me into the pool,
but while I am coming, someone else steps down in
front of me."[317]
8 Jesus said to him, "Rise, take up your mat, and walk."
9 And immediately the man was made whole, took up
his mat, and walked.[318] The day this happened was the
Sabbath.

---

[316] **5:6.** ***"When Jesus saw him lying down and knew that he had been in this condition a long time, he said to him, 'Do you want to be made whole?'"*** Jesus sensed the discouraged state of this man. The text says that Jesus knew the man had been in this condition a long time—thirty-eight years. When people have been afflicted that long, their hope for a healing often fades. In some cases, they can even get so used to a lifestyle and identity of affliction that they no longer desire to be healed; they accept their afflicted state as normal. If this man were to receive a healing, he would have to make a lot of adjustments, including changing his daily routine and working a job. Jesus' question, "Do you want to be made whole?" awakened what might have been a dormant desire. Jesus wanted him to express that desire.

[317] **5:7.** ***"'Sir, when the water is stirred, I have no one to put me into the pool, but while I am coming, someone else steps down in front of me.'"*** The man did not answer Jesus' question. He did not express a desire to be healed; rather, he tried to explain the rationale behind why he had not yet been healed.

[318] **5:9.** ***"Immediately the man was made whole, took up his mat, and walked."*** A most unusual thing happened. The man did not say that he wanted to be healed. Neither is there any indication in this story that the man had faith in the Son of God. There is no evidence of him having faith for his own healing. Jesus simply commanded the man to rise, take up his bed, and walk! If the man did have faith, it

> 10 ¶ Then the Jews said to the man who had been cured, "It is the Sabbath day; it is not lawful for you to carry your mat."[319]
> 11 He answered them, "The man who made me whole—he is the one who said to me, 'Take up your mat, and walk.'"

---

might have been expressed through the fact that he had come to this pool repeatedly for so many years hoping for a healing. Or it might have been expressed in the one thing that he did next. He obeyed Jesus' simple command; he rose to his feet. He was healed! Then he took up his bed and walked.

There is a lesson to be learned here regarding the several ways that healing faith can be demonstrated: (1) through the person in need of healing (Matthew 9:27-29), (2) through others on behalf of the afflicted (Matthew 8:5-10), (3) through a person or persons functioning in a ministry of healing (1 Corinthians 12:9; James 5:14-16). In this case, the man was healed through Jesus' initiative as functioned in his own ministry of healing.

This story contains a helpful example for individuals functioning in the ministry of healing. When ministering healing to others, sometimes it is helpful to ask the person to test their healing by taking a faith action. People being healed of eyesight disorders may try to read something they could not read before. Those with speech problems may attempt to say words they could not previously pronounce. A person with a back problem might be asked to incrementally increase back movement until it can be verified that the back pain has decreased. As was the case with the passage at hand, a lame person may be asked to stand. Often it is at that moment of testing the healing that the actual healing takes place, for it is an exercise of faith to even attempt the test.

[319] **5:10.** ***"' It is the Sabbath day; it is not lawful for you to carry your mat.'"*** The man who had been healed was accused of breaking the law on the Sabbath by obeying Jesus' command to take up his bed and walk. The only law that had been broken was some man-made rabbinical rule. The man had not violated God's law.

12 Then they asked him, "What man said to you, 'Take
up your mat, and walk?'"
13 But the man who was healed did not know who it
was, for Jesus had already removed himself from the
crowd that was in that place.
14 Afterward Jesus found him in the temple[320] and said
to him, "Look at[321] what has happened; you have been
made whole. Stop sinning, so that something worse
does not happen to you."[322]
15 The man left and told the Jews that it was Jesus who
had made him whole.

---

[320] **5:14.** ***"Afterward Jesus found him in the temple."*** Due to his previous affliction, this is the first time in thirty-eight years that he had been allowed the opportunity to enter the house of the Lord. Over the years, a tradition had developed out of an incident recorded in 2 Samuel 5:8, forbidding the blind and the lame from entering the temple. Since the days of Moses, physical defects (e.g., blindness, crippled appendages, deformities, dwarfism, kyphosis, running sores, and damaged testicles) had disqualified individuals from approaching the curtain and the altar in the tabernacle (Leviticus 21:16-23) and the temple.

It is interesting to note that on another occasion, when Jesus overthrew the money changers, "the blind and the lame came to him in the temple, and he healed them" (Matthew 21:14). While still blind and lame, they entered the temple—the place where they had been previously forbidden, and while there with Jesus, they received their healing.

[321] **5:14.** ***"'Look at.'"*** The KJV translates, "behold."

[322] **5:14.** ***"'Stop sinning, so that something worse does not happen to you.'"*** It is not known what sin this man might have been committing. Jesus' words suggest that sin *can* open the door for affliction.

16 Because of this, the Jews persecuted Jesus and sought to kill him, because he had done these things on the Sabbath.[323]

The Third Discourse: Deity and Sonship of Christ (5:17-47)

17 ¶ But Jesus answered them, "My Father[324] is working right now, and just like him, I am also working."[325]
18 Because of this, the Jews sought even more to kill him, because not only had he broken the Sabbath, but he also said that God was his Father, making himself equal with God.[326]

---

[323] **5:16.** ***"The Jews persecuted Jesus and sought to kill him, because he had done these things on the Sabbath."*** In the eyes of the Jews, Jesus had violated rabbinical *traditions* related to the Sabbath. It is important to note that Jesus did not break *God's law* by healing on the Sabbath.

[324] **5:17.** ***"'My Father.'"*** Those who heard Jesus speak interpreted his "my Father" reference as equivalent to him saying, "I am the Son of God." Jesus was not trying to hide the fact that he was and is the Son of God. He had already identified himself as such in 2:16 and 3:16, and he continued to do so throughout this Gospel. See also 2:16; 5:43; 6:32, 65; 8:19, 28, 38, 49, 54; 10:17-18, 25, 29, 30, 32, 37; 12:26-27; 14:2, 7, 12, 20-21, 23, 28; 15:1, 8, 10, 15, 23-24; 16:10; 18:11; 20:17, and 21.

[325] **5:17.** ***"'My Father is working right now, and just like him, I am also working.'"*** Jesus was in effect saying, "My Father is working right now! He isn't waiting for tomorrow or some other day. He didn't decide to do this yesterday. He is working right now, so that means right now is the time for me to align my actions with his!"

[326] **5:18.** ***"Making himself equal with God."*** See note for "my Father" in 5:17.

19 Then Jesus answered and said to them, "I tell you the truth,[327] the Son can do nothing on his own.[328] He can only do what he sees the Father doing;[329] for whatever the Father is doing, that is also what the Son is doing.[330]

Pause and Reflect
1. Jesus only did what he saw the Father doing. What might God be invisibly and quietly doing in your situation or circumstances?
2. How might you sharpen your perception of God's voice and movements in your life?
3. How might increased spiritual perception improve your life and service unto Christ and other people?

---

[327] **5:19.** ***"'I tell you the truth.'"*** The KJV translates, "Verily, verily." The Greek words here are a transliteration of the Hebrew expression, "Amen, amen." It was a way of saying, "You can be certain of what I am about to tell you."

[328] **5:19.** ***"'The Son can do nothing on his own.'"*** See 5:30.

[329] **5:19.** ***"'The Son can do nothing on his own. He can only do what he sees the Father doing.'"*** The theme of spiritual vision and prophetic guidance is highlighted once again. Jesus can do nothing on his own; he can only do what he *sees* his Father doing. If Jesus had to rely on seeing and knowing what his Father was doing, how much more so should those who minister in his name. In any given situation, people who minister in Jesus' name should first discern what the Father *is* doing in the matter before they spring into action. Waiting for divine leading can make the difference between random ministry guesswork and ministry precision that aligns perfectly with the purposes of the Father. This passage is a key verse for those who desire to function in supernatural Christian ministry.

[330] **5:19.** ***"'Whatever the Father is doing, that is also what the Son is doing.'"*** Jesus' continual practice was to align his words and actions with the words and actions of his Father. See 8:26; 12:49-50.

> 20 For the Father loves the Son[331] and shows him all things that he is doing. And he will show him greater works[332] than these, so that you may marvel.[333]
> 21 For as the Father raises up the dead and gives them life, even so the Son gives life to whom he desires to give it.[334]
> 22 For the Father judges no man, but he has committed all judgment to the Son,[335]

---

[331] **5:20.** ***"'The Father loves the Son.'"*** This expression occurs earlier in 3:35. In both instances, the Father's love for the Son has ramifications for what the Father has entrusted to his Son.

[332] **5:20.** ***"'He will show him greater works.'"*** The word, *erga,* translated here as "works," is often used as a reference to "miracles" and is one of four words in the New Testament translated "miracles." The word is used in 5:20, 36; 14:11; as well as in other places. The other three words for miracles are *semeion,* meaning a "sign," as in 2:11, 18 23; *terata,* meaning "wonders"; and *dunameis,* meaning "mighty works."

[333] **5:20.** ***"'So that you may marvel.'"*** The supernatural dynamic taking place between the Father and the Son served the intentional purpose of causing people to marvel. Later in 5:36, Jesus stated it clearly: his miraculous works were evidences that the Father had sent him. As Easton notes, our Lord "appealed to miracles as a conclusive proof of his divine mission" (5:20, 36; 10:25, 38). "Miracle." Dictionary.com. *Easton's 1897 Bible Dictionary,* accessed September 16, 2012, http:// dictionary. reference.com/ browse/ miracle. The specific miraculous work in view in 5:20 is an occurrence of prophetic ministry. The text would suggest that the Father delights in people marveling at prophetically guided supernatural ministry; he seems to like the "wow!" effect.

[334] **5:21.** ***"'As the Father raises up the dead and gives them life, even so the Son gives life to whom he desires to give it.'"*** The Son gives life just as the Father gives life. Jesus claimed to have powers that belong to God alone.

[335] **5:22.** ***"'He has committed all judgment to the Son.'"*** This thought is taken further in 5:27 where Jesus is identified as the Son of man.

23 so that all may honor the Son, even as they honor
the Father. He who does not honor the Son does not
honor the Father who has sent him.[336]
24 I tell you the truth,[337] he who hears my word and
believes in him who sent me[338] has eternal life.[339] He

---

336 **5:23.** ***"'He who does not honor the Son does not honor the Father who has sent him.'"*** During Jesus' days of walking the earth, he was fully authorized as the Son to represent his Father. The hidden truth regarding honor is that it opens the way for an exchange with the one who is honored. Virtues and graces carried by the one who is honored become accessible. When one honors the Son, that person gains access to things that the Father has entrusted to the Son.

337 **5:24.** ***"'I tell you the truth.'"*** See the note for 5:19.

338 **5:24.** ***"'He who hears my word and believes in him who sent me.'"*** The present participles translated here as "hears" and "believes," might be better translated, "is hearing" and "believing," emphasizing continuous action. These are not one time occurrences. The expectation is that the hearing and the believing are present and ongoing activities.

Hearing alone is not enough. The mind and heart must be convinced that the message and the one who has authorized the message are worthy of trust. It is right and good to believe in the message, but here Jesus draws the focus to believing in the Father—the one who sent him. Ultimately the divine Person—God—is the focus of faith. Faith is not just about trusting what God says or what he can do; it is about trusting the Father—even trusting his heart. Such is the essence of belief.

339 **5:24.** ***"'Eternal life.'"*** Eternal life is not just a blessing that one receives after death; it is a gift received by faith and experienced even in one's terrestrial journey prior to physical death. It is the present-day life of heaven—a life that originates from the eternal realm. See also 3:15-16, 36; 4:14, 36; 5:39; 6:27, 40, 47, 54, 68; 10:28; 12:25, 50; and 17:2.

> shall not come into condemnation, but he has passed from death unto life.[340]
> 25 I tell you the truth,[341] the hour is coming, and the hour has already come,[342] when the dead will hear the voice of the Son of God, and they that hear will live.[343]
> 26 For as the Father has life in himself, so he has given to the Son to have life in himself,
> 27 and has also given him authority to execute judgment, because he is the Son of man.[344]

---

[340] **5:24.** ***"'Passed from death unto life.'"*** Passing "from death unto life" occurs at the moment a person places his or her faith in the Son of God.

[341] **5:25.** ***"'I tell you the truth.'"*** See the note for 5:19.

[342] **5:25.** ***"'The hour is coming, and the hour has already come.'"*** These words provide a glimpse into the "already, but not yet" aspect of God's kingdom. This expression also appears in 4:23. See the note for 4:23.

[343] **5:25.** ***"'The dead will hear the voice of the Son of God, and they that hear will live.'"*** For the dead to hear anything is normally impossible. The dead cannot hear, because they are dead. However, when it is the Son of God speaking, that which was impossible suddenly becomes reality. The dead do not hear the Son because *they decide* to hear him, for the dead can decide nothing. It is the voice of the Son that creates the ability to hear.

The dead experiencing life through hearing the voice of the Son is both a present and a future reality. It is part of the "already but not yet" nature of God's kingdom. (See the note for 4:23.) Eternal life is received at the moment a person hears the voice of the Son and places his or her faith in him, but there will also be a day—the resurrection day—when believers will hear his voice and physically rise from the dead. See 5:28-29.

[344] **5:27.** ***"'Son of man.'"*** The expression, "son of man," brings emphasis to the humanity of Jesus. Some also consider it a Messianic reference to Daniel 7:13-14: "In my vision at night I looked, and there before me was one like a son of man, coming

28 Do not marvel at this, for the hour is coming in
which all who are in the graves will hear his voice
29 and will come forth—they that have done good,[345]
unto the resurrection of life,[346] and they that have done
evil, unto the resurrection of damnation.[347]
30 I can of my own self do nothing.[348] As I hear, I judge;
and my judgment is just because I do not seek my own
will, but the will of the Father who has sent me.

---

with the clouds of heaven. He approached the Ancient of Days and was led into his presence. He was given authority, glory and sovereign power; all nations and peoples of every language worshiped him. His dominion is an everlasting dominion that will not pass away, and his kingdom is one that will never be destroyed." See 1:51; 3:13-14; 5:27; 6:27, 53, 62; 8:28; 12:23, 34 and 13:31.

[345] **5:29.** ***"'They that have done good.'"*** Judgment is on the basis of works, because works provide the proof or evidence of what is truly in the heart. According to 6:29, the "work" that God requires is faith or belief in the one he has sent. For other references to judgment on the basis of works, see Matthew 12:36-37; 16:27; Romans 2:6-10; 14:12; 1 Corinthians 3:13-15; 2 Corinthians 5:10; Ephesians 6:8; Colossians 3:25; Revelation 2:23; 20:12; 22:12. Believers are *not* saved by works (Ephesians 2:9), but they *are* "his workmanship, created in Christ Jesus unto good works" (Ephesians 2:10). Faith without works is "dead" (James 2:17). Saving faith is a faith that manifests itself through works. The works in view here are not the works of the law. These works are the result of faith and the product of grace.

[346] **5:29.** ***"'Unto the resurrection of life.'"*** Jesus spoke of "the resurrection of life"—the resurrection of the righteous. The righteous will be resurrected before the resurrection of the unrighteous (Matthew 27:52-53; 1 Corinthians 15:51-52; Revelation 20:4-6).

[347] **5:29.** ***"'Unto the resurrection of damnation.'"*** Jesus spoke of a "resurrection of damnation"—the resurrection of the unrighteous (Revelation 20:11-15).

[348] **5:30.** ***"'I can of my own self do nothing.'"*** Jesus indicated that he could do nothing by himself (5:19, 30). Although he walked this earth as God incarnate, he

31 If I bear witness of myself, my testimony[349] would
not be accepted as true.[350]

32 ¶ "There is another who bears witness of me, and I
know that the witness that he testifies of me is true.
33 You have sent people to John to inquire about me,[351]
and John has borne witness to the truth.[352]
34 It is not that I need to receive testimony[353] from man,
but I say these things that you might be saved.[354]
35 He was a burning and shining light, and you were
willing for a season to rejoice in his light.

36 ¶ "Yet I have greater testimony[355] than that of John,
for the works[356] that the Father has given me to finish,

---

chose not to exercise his divine prerogatives while he walked upon the earth. In all of his works, he relied upon the Father and the Spirit in a way that is similar to how all who minister in his name rely upon God.

[349] **5:31.** **"*'Testimony.'*"** See 3:11, 3:32-33; 5:34, 36; 8:13-14, 17; 12:18; 19:35 and 21:24.

[350] **5:31.** ***"'If I bear witness of myself, my testimony would not be accepted as true.'"*** According to Deuteronomy 17:6, a person could not testify on his own behalf. Two witnesses were required.

[351] **5:33.** ***"'You have sent people to John to inquire about me.'"*** The KJV translates, "Ye sent unto John."

[352] **5:33.** ***"'Truth.'"*** See note for "full of grace and truth" in 1:14.

[353] **5:34.** ***"'Testimony.'"*** See note for "testimony" in 5:31.

[354] **5:34.** ***"'I say these things that you might be saved."*** Jesus draws the attention of his hearers to the testimony of John the Baptist concerning him. If they would believe the testimony of John the Baptist, they would be saved.

[357]those same works that I do bear witness of me, that
the Father has sent me.[358]
37 The Father himself who has sent me has also
testified of me. You have never heard his voice nor
seen what he is like.
38 You do not have his word remaining in you, for you
do not believe the one whom he has sent.[359]

---

[355] **5:36.** ***"'Testimony.'"*** See 3:11, 3:32-33; 5:31, 34; 8:13-14, 17; 12:18; 19:35 and 21:24.

[356] **5:36.** ***"'The works.'"*** The word, *erga,* is translated twice as "works"; it is a word often used as a reference to "miracles." See also 5:20 (see footnote) and 14:11. *Erga* is one of four words in the New Testament translated "miracles." The other three words for miracles are *semeion,* meaning a "sign," as in 2:11, 18 23; *terata,* meaning "wonders"; and *dunameis,* meaning "mighty works."

[357] **5:36.** ***"'The works that the Father has given me to finish.'"*** Jesus came to finish specific works assigned to him by his Father. He came to complete a mission.

[358] **5:36.** ***"'The works that the Father has given me to finish, those same works that I do bear witness of me, that the Father has sent me.'"*** Jesus stated it clearly: his miraculous works are evidences that the Father has sent him. As Easton notes, our Lord "appealed to miracles as a conclusive proof of his divine mission" (5:20, 36; 10:25, 38). "Miracle." Dictionary.com. *Easton's 1897 Bible Dictionary,* accessed September 16, 2012, http:// dictionary. reference.com/ browse/ miracle.

[359] **5:37-38.** ***"'You have never heard his voice.... for you do not believe the one whom he has sent.'"*** The positive implication of these negative words is that by believing Jesus, people can become empowered to hear the Father's voice, see what he is like, and experience the transforming reality of his word taking residence in their lives.

39 ¶ "Search the scriptures, since you are supposing that you have eternal life[360] in them.[361] The scriptures are witnesses testifying about me,
40 yet you are not willing to come to me, that you might have life.
41 I am not looking for[362] glory[363] from men,
42 But I know you, that you do not have the love of God in you.
43 I have come in my Father's[364] name, and you do not receive me.[365] If another shall come in his own name, him you will receive.

---

[360] **5:39.** ***"'Eternal life.'"*** See also 3:15-16, 36; 4:14, 36; 5:24; 6:27, 40, 47, 54, 68; 10:28; 12:25, 50; and 17:2.

[361] **5:39.** ***"'Search the scriptures, since you are supposing that you have eternal life in them.'"*** At this point, these Jews had a higher regard for the scriptures than they had for Jesus. In essence, they were elevating the scriptures above God, for Jesus was and is God in the flesh. Only God could give eternal life, and he had purposed to give that life through Jesus, his Son. The scriptures had no power to impart this life, but the scriptures did testify of the one who does have that power. While the Bible is sacred, it is to never hold an idolatrous place in the human heart, replacing the presence of the very God of whom its words testify.

[362] **5:41.** ***"'Looking for.'"*** These words are more literally translated "receiving."

[363] **5:41.** ***"'Glory.'"*** Instead of "glory," the KJV translates, "honour."

[364] **5:43.** ***"'My Father.'"*** Jesus openly referenced God the Father as his Father, affirming his identity as the Son of God. See also 2:16; 5:17; 6:32, 65; 8:19, 28, 38, 49, 54; 10:17-18, 25, 29, 30, 32, 37; 12:26-27; 14:2, 7, 12, 20-21, 23, 28; 15:1, 8, 10, 15, 23-24; 16:10; 18:11; 20:17, and 21.

[365] **5:43.** ***"' I have come in my Father's name, and you do not receive me.'"*** By not receiving Jesus, these Jews had not received the Father.

44 How can you believe—you who receive glory from one another and do not seek the glory that comes from God alone?[366]
45 Do not think that I will accuse you to the Father;[367]
Moses—the one you have relied upon, he is the one who accuses you.[368]
46 For if you had believed Moses, you would have believed me, for he wrote about me.[369]

---

[366] **5:44. *"'How can you believe—you who receive glory from one another and do not seek the glory that comes from God alone?'"*** An important principle is presented: the seeking of approval (or "glory") from peers and others distracts from the pursuit of pleasing God alone.

[367] **5:45. *"'Do not think that I will accuse you to the Father.'"*** Jesus did not come into the world to bring condemnation. See also 3:17 and 12:47.

[368] **5:45. *"'Moses—the one you have relied upon, he is the one who accuses you.'"*** How is it that Moses accuses them? The Law came through Moses, illuminating the sinful state of the human heart and revealing man's dire need for a savior. Furthermore, as 5:46 indicates, Moses wrote about the Christ, thus leaving the Jews without excuse.

[369] **5:46. *"'Moses... wrote about me.'"*** Reference is made to Moses' testimony. His testimony is contained in the Pentateuch—the first five books of the Old Testament. What did Moses prophetically testify concerning Jesus? In the scriptures written by Moses, he spoke of Jesus in the follow terms:

1. He is the promised "seed of the woman" who was destined to bruise the serpent's head.
2. He is the promised "seed of Abraham," through whom all nations of the earth would be blessed.
3. He is "the Shiloh, to whom the gathering of the people should be."
4. He is "that prophet, who should be like unto himself, to whom the people of Israel should hearken."

47 But if you do not believe his writings, how will you believe my words?"

Harmony of the Gospels			
	Matthew	**Mark**	**Luke**
Plucking Grain on the Sabbath	12:1-8	2:23-28	6:1-5
Miracles	12:9-21	3:1-12	6:6-11
The Twelve	10:2-4	3:13-19	6:12-16
The Sermon on the Mount	5:1-7:29		6:17-49
Healing of the Centurion's Servant	8:5-13		7:1-10
Raising the Widow's Son at Nain			7:11-17
Messengers from John the Baptist	11:2-19		7:18-35
Denouncing of the Cities of Galilee	11:20-24		
Call to the Meek and Suffering	11:25-30		
Jesus' Feet Anointed			7:36-50
Second Ministry Tour in Galilee			8:1-3
Parable of the Sower	13:1-23	4:1-20	8:4-15
Parable of the Lamp		4:21-25	8:16-18
Parable of the Seed Growing Secretly		4:26-29	

---

5. He is represented throughout the Mosaic Law in types, shadows and symbols, as the New Testament epistle to the Hebrews is careful to explain.

John Gill, *Exposition of the Bible*; accessed October 10, 2012, http:// www.biblestudytools.com/ commentaries/ gills-exposition-of-the-bible/ john-5-46.html.

	Matthew	Mark	Luke
Parable of the Wheat and the Tares	13:24-30		
Parable of the Grain of Mustard Seed	13:31-32	4:30-32	13:18-19
Parable of the Leaven	13:33		13:20-21
Regarding Parables	13:34-35	4:33-34	
Parable of the Wheat and Tares Explained	13:36-43		
Parables of the Treasure, the Pearl and the Net	13:44-52		
Jesus' Mother and Brothers	12:46-50	3:31-35	8:19-21
Reception at Nazareth	13:53-58	6:1-6	
Third Ministry Tour in Galilee	9:35-38; 11:01	6:6	
Sending Forth the Twelve	10:5-42	6:7-13	9:1-6
Herod's Opinion of Jesus	14:1-2	6:14-16	9:7-9
Death of John the Baptist	14:3-12	6:17-29	

CHAPTER 6

Jesus Presents Himself to the Multitudes (6:1-71)

The Fourth Sign: Feeding of the Five Thousand (6:1-14)

After these things, Jesus went over the Sea of
Galilee, which is the Sea of Tiberias.[370]
2 And a great multitude[371] followed him
because they saw the miraculous signs that he
performed on those who were sick.
3 And Jesus went up into a mountain,[372] and there he
sat with his disciples.
4 The Passover,[373] a feast of the Jews, was near.

---

[370] **6:1. *"Sea of Tiberias."*** The Sea of Tiberias was also known as the Sea of Galilee and the Sea of Gennesaret.

[371] **6:2. *"A great multitude."*** In anticipation of Passover, a large number of people would have been passing through this region on their pilgrimage to Jerusalem. "John 6:4," *Meyer's New Testament Commentary, Bible Hub,* accessed January 9, 2016, http://biblehub.com/commentaries/john/6-4.htm.

[372] **6:3. *"Jesus went up into a mountain."*** According to Luke 9:10, the mountain referenced would have been near Bethsaida.

5 ¶ When Jesus then lifted up his eyes and saw a great
multitude coming toward him, he said to Philip, "From
where shall we buy bread that these may eat?"
6 He said this to test him, for he already knew what he
would do.
7 Philip answered, "Two hundred denarii[374] worth of
bread would not be enough, even if every person only
took a little."
8 One of his disciples, Andrew, Simon Peter's brother,
said to him,
9 "There is a boy here who has five loaves of bread and
two small fish, but what are they among so many?"[375]
10 Jesus said, "Have the people sit down."[376] There was
much grass there, so, the men sat down—about five
thousand in number.

---

[373] **6:4. *"Passover."*** John's repeated reference to the Passover highlights the significance that it held for the telling of the Gospel story. See 2:13, 23; 11:55; 12:1; 13:1; 18:28, 39; and 19:14. The celebration was in the month of Nisan (March-April).

[374] **6:7. *"'Two hundred denarii.'"*** A denarius was a Roman silver coin. In light of Matthew 20:2-13, it appears that a denarius was the typical wage for a full day of work. A person would have to work over six months to earn two hundred denarii.

[375] **6:8-9. *"One of his disciples, Andrew, Simon Peter's brother, said to him, 'There is a boy here who has five loaves of bread and two small fish, but what are they among so many?'"*** As he had done before, Andrew brought someone to Jesus. This time he brought a little boy whose seemingly insignificant gift would initiate a history-making miracle. In John's Gospel, every time Andrew appeared, he brought someone to Jesus:

1. In 1:41 he brought his brother, Simon.
2. In the text at hand he brought the boy with the loaves and fishes.
3. In 12:20-22 he brought the Greeks who wanted to see Jesus.

11 Then Jesus took the loaves, and when he had given thanks, he distributed them to the disciples, and the disciples to them who were sitting.[377] They did the same with the fish, giving the people as much as they wanted.[378]

---

[376] **6:10.** ***"'Have the people sit down.'"*** The word translated, "sit down," more literally translates, "lie down." See the note for 6:11.

[377] **6:11.** ***"Jesus took the loaves, and when he had given thanks, he distributed them to the disciples, and the disciples to them who were sitting."*** The loaves and fishes passed from the hands of the boy into the hands of Jesus. Then Jesus thanked God for the gift, he blessed the gift, and he handed to his disciples the five loaves and the two small fish. The disciples then distributed the bread to the people who were "sitting."

"Sitting." Instead of sitting, they were probably reclining, as the Greek word, *anakeimai,* would suggest. In that day, it was not uncommon for people to recline while they ate. See note for 6:10.

[378] **6:11.** ***"They did the same with the fish, giving the people as much as they wanted."*** Allow your imagination to capture what was going on here. With a few broken loaves and fishes in their hands, the disciples looked out over the vast multitude—a crowd of over five thousand people. As the disciples stepped forward to distribute that meager amount of blessed food, a great miracle manifested in their hands. There is no indication in this narrative that the miracle occurred in the hands of Jesus. It appears that the miracle took place as his disciples started distributing the food.

Furthermore, the people were not just given a snack to hold them over; they were given "as much as they wanted." Here is seen the generosity of God. Ministering from a culture of abundance rather than scarcity is the normative pattern for those who would serve in Jesus' name.

12 When they were filled, he said to his disciples,
"Gather up the fragments that remain so that nothing
is wasted."[379]
13 Then they gathered them and filled twelve baskets
with the fragments produced from the five loaves of
bread—the fragments that exceeded what was
needed[380] for those who were fed.
14 Seeing the miracle that Jesus did, the people said,
"This is truly the prophet who is to come into the
world." [381]

---

[379] **6:12.** ***"'Gather up the fragments that remain so that nothing is wasted.'"*** Even in times of great abundance, measures should be taken to prevent wastefulness. God expects good stewardship from his people over the resources that he entrusts into their hands.

[380] **6:13.** ***"The fragments that exceeded what was needed."*** The kingdom of heaven exposes and confronts a "barely enough to get by" mindset. The Father delights in manifesting provision that exceeds the need. The disciples had faithfully ministered to the multitude. Out of the surplus, the Lord now blessed them with more than enough provision for their own need.

[381] **6:14.** ***"'This is truly the prophet who is to come into the world.'"*** "The prophet" refers back to a prophecy in Deuteronomy 18:15-18 stating that one day a prophet similar to Moses would appear.

Pause and Reflect

With a handful of food, Jesus fed a multitude. Little can be much when Jesus is present.

1. What is the impossible need, task or situation in your life?
2. What has God already given you—whether great or small—that has the potential to become his miraculous provision for the situation you are facing?
3. Will you now use the small things God has given you and trust him for the increase?

Harmony of the Gospels

	Matthew	Mark	Luke
Feeding of the five thousand	14:13-21	6:30-44	9:10-17

15 ¶ Knowing that they were about to come and snatch him away to make him a king, Jesus retreated again into a mountain alone.[382]

The Fifth Sign:
Walking on the Water (6:16-21)

16 When evening came, his disciples went down to the sea.[383]

---

[382] **6:15.** ***"Jesus retreated again into a mountain alone."*** Although Jesus is forever King of kings, enthronement as an earthly king was not something that he desired. It would have been a major derailment of his mission, had the people had their way. For this reason, it was necessary for him to retreat.

[383] **6:16.** ***"Down to the sea."*** "Up" and "down" are references to elevation and not points on the compass. See 2:12, 13; 4:49; 5:1; 7:8, 10, 14; 11:55; and 12:20. This sea is the Sea of Galilee. It is also known as the Sea of Gennesaret or the Sea of Tiberias.

17 Stepping into the ship, they went over the sea
toward Capernaum. It was already dark, and Jesus had
not yet come to them.
18 And the sea arose because of a great wind that blew.
19 Then having rowed about twenty-five or thirty-
stadia,[384] they beheld Jesus walking on the sea and
coming near the ship. They were afraid.[385]
20 But he said to them, "It is I. Do not be afraid."
21 Then they willingly received him into the ship, [386]
and immediately the ship was at the land to which they
were going.[387]

---

[384] **6:19. *"Having rowed about twenty-five or thirty-stadia."*** A stadia is a distance of about 600 feet. They had rowed a distance of about three miles.

[385] **6:19. *"They were afraid."*** This account of the story says that the disciples were "afraid." Matthew 14:26 also speaks of them being terrified, but Matthew's account also adds that when the disciples saw Jesus walking on the water, they cried out, "It's a ghost!"

[386] **6:16-21a.** Matthew's account adds information about Peter walking on the water as well (Matthew 14:28-31). In response to Jesus' summons to "come," Peter did in fact walk on water, but then he began to doubt and started to sink. This was not Peter's finest hour. John may have omitted Peter's part in this story from his Gospel for two reasons:

1. Peter was already deceased at the time of John's writing, and he wanted to be careful to honor his departed friend, not dishonor him.
2. Drawing attention to Peter's miraculous attempt had the potential of distracting the reader from John's intentional emphasis on the personhood of Jesus. This was not supposed to be a Gospel about the miracles worked by Jesus' disciples.

[387] **6:21. *"Immediately the ship was at the land to which they were going."*** Some hold that the word "immediately" in this text suggests an instantaneous supernatural transport of the vessel directly to the party's destination.

Harmony of the Gospels			
	Matthew	**Mark**	**Luke**
Jesus Walking on the Water	14:22-33	6:45-52	
Miracles in Gennesaret	14:34-36	6:53-56	

The Fourth Discourse: The Bread of Life (6:22-71)

22 ¶ The following day, the crowd standing on the
other side of the sea knew that there had been only one
boat there—the one Jesus' disciples had entered—and
that Jesus had not left with his disciples in that boat.
His disciples had gone away alone.
23 Other boats came from Tiberias near to the place
where they had eaten bread after the Lord had given
thanks.
24 When the crowd saw that neither Jesus nor his
disciples were there, they got into those boats and went
to Capernaum looking for Jesus.
25 When they found him on the other side of the sea,
they said to him, "Rabbi, when did you arrive here?"
26 Jesus answered and said, "I tell you the truth,[388] you
do not seek me because you saw the miracles but
because you ate the loaves and were filled.[389]

---

[388] **6:26.** ***"I tell you the truth."*** The KJV translates, "Verily, verily." The Greek words here are a transliteration of the Hebrew expression, "Amen, amen." It was a way of saying, "You can be certain of what I am about to tell you."

[389] **6:26.** ***"You do not seek me because you saw the miracles but because you ate the loaves and were filled."*** The miracles were intended to bear witness that Jesus was and is in fact the Son of God. However, these people were not yet motivated by

> 27 Do not labor[390] for the perishable food[391] but for the lasting food that endures unto eternal life; [392] the Son of man[393] will give it to you,[394] for God the Father has placed his seal[395] upon him."[396]

---

that truth. They were motivated to follow Jesus out of a belief that he would meet their needs. At this point, they were not motivated out of a sense of personal devotion to him.

[390] **6:27.** ***"'Do not labor.'"*** This thought concerning "labor" prompted the question regarding working the "works of God" in 6:28.

[391] **6:27.** ***"'Do not labor for the perishable food.'"*** "Perishable food" is food that is useful for a time, but its ability to strengthen and sustain life is temporary. With the passing of time, it spoils or becomes useless. In the Old Testament, when the Hebrews hoarded manna, it spoiled. When they kept looking to God daily, it was always fresh.

[392] **6:27.** ***"'The lasting food that endures unto eternal life.'"*** "Lasting food" is food that does not spoil and continues to be beneficial for the sustaining of life, even with the passing of time. In fact, it "endures unto eternal life." Not only does this food remain useful forever, but those who are nourished by it will live forever. For additional references to eternal life in John's Gospel, see 3:15-16, 36; 4:14, 36; 5:24, 39; 6:40, 47, 54, 68; 10:28; 12:25, 50; and 17:2.

[393] **6:27.** ***"'Son of man.'"*** The expression, "son of man," brings emphasis to the humanity of Jesus. Some also consider it a Messianic reference to Daniel 7:13-14: "In my vision at night I looked, and there before me was one like a son of man, coming with the clouds of heaven. He approached the Ancient of Days and was led into his presence. He was given authority, glory and sovereign power; all nations and peoples of every language worshiped him. His dominion is an everlasting dominion that will not pass away, and his kingdom is one that will never be destroyed." See 1:51; 3:13-14; 5:27; 6:27, 53, 62; 8:28; 12:23, 34 and 13:31.

[394] **6:27.** ***"'The Son of man will give it to you.'"*** People may "labor" for this "lasting food," but actually this food is not provided as the result of human labor. The Son of Man *gives* this lasting food. This truth is illustrated with the miraculous

28 Then they said to him, "What shall we do that we
might work the works of God?"[397]
29 Jesus answered and said to them, "This is the work
of God: that you believe on him whom he has sent."[398]
30 Then they said to him, "What sign will you perform
then, that we may see and believe you? What
supernatural work do you have to show?[399]
31 Our fathers ate manna in the desert; as it is written,
'He gave them bread from heaven to eat.'"
32 Then Jesus said to them, "I tell you the truth, Moses
did not give you that bread from heaven, but my
Father[400] gives you the true bread from heaven.

---

feeding of the five thousand in 6:1-14. When Jesus fed that multitude, it was not the result of human labor. He generously *gave* to them all that they needed, plus some more. He gave them all that they *wanted* (6:11).

[395] **6:27.** ***"'His seal.'"*** This "seal" is a seal of approval and authenticity.

[396] **6:27.** ***"'God the Father has placed his seal upon him.'"*** The KJV translates, "for him hath God the Father sealed."

[397] **6:28.** ***"'What shall we do that we might work the works of God?'"*** This question was prompted by Jesus' reference to "labor" in 6:27.

[398] **6:29.** ***"'This is the work of God: that you believe on him whom he has sent.'"*** The "works of God" cannot be defined in terms of human labor or effort. Working the "works of God" is a matter of trust and devotion. It involves the inclination of the heart and the alignment of a person's life with the one whom the Father has sent.

[399] **6:30.** ***"'What supernatural work do you have to show?'"*** The KJV translates, "what dost thou work?" To the reader who already knows the full Gospel story, it seems incredible that these people did not already believe. It would appear that the works Jesus had already accomplished would have been sufficient.

33 For the bread of God is he[401] who comes down from
heaven and gives life to the world."
34 Then said they to him, "Lord, give us this bread all
the time!"
35 Jesus said to them, "I am the bread of life.[402] He who
comes to me will never hunger, and he who believes in
me will never thirst.[403]
36 But as I said to you, you have seen me, and still you
do not believe.[404]

---

[400] **6:32.** ***"'My Father.'"*** Jesus openly referenced God the Father as his Father, affirming his identity as the Son of God. See also 2:16; 5:17, 43; 6:65; 8:19, 28, 38, 49, 54; 10:17-18, 25, 29, 30, 32, 37; 12:26-27; 14:2, 7, 12, 20-21, 23, 28; 15:1, 8, 10, 15, 23-24; 16:10; 18:11; 20:17, and 21.

[401] **6:33.** ***"'The bread of God is he....'"*** This "bread" is a person. People may have many needs in life, but satisfaction is only temporarily found in having those needs met. Only Jesus can satisfy the longing of the human soul. See notes for 6:35.

[402] **6:35.** ***"'I am the bread of life.'"*** In 6:35 and 6:48, "I am the bread of life" is the first of seven "I am" statements in this Gospel. The other six statements are found in 8:12; 10:7; 10:14; 11:25; 14:6; and 15:1. At this moment when he said, "I am the bread of life," many in the crowd began to doubt (6:41).

[403] **6:35.** ***"'He who comes to me will never hunger, and he who believes in me will never thirst.'"*** Receiving the one who provides is a greater gift than receiving the provision. The provision can be depleted, but the one who provides remains with the believer forever, seeing to it that the flow of provision never ceases. The key is to rightly set one's faith upon the one who provides. When the believer hears Jesus say, "I am the bread of life," then his or her response should be, "You are all I want, and you are all that I will ever need."

[404] 6:36. ***"'Still you do not believe.'"*** Supernatural ministry affects the hearts and minds of people, causing them to believe upon Jesus. See 2:11, 23; 4:48, 53; 7:31; 10:37-38; 11:15, 45, 48; 12:11; 14:11; and 20:30-31. However, some see his miracles and still do not believe. See 7:5; and 12:37.

37 All that the Father gives me will come to me, and I
will never cast out any person who comes to me.
38 I came down from heaven,[405] not to do my own will,
but the will of him who sent me.[406]
39 This is the will of the Father who has sent me: that I
should lose none of those he has given me, [407] but that I
should raise them back to life at the last day.[408]
40 This is the will of him that sent me: that every
person who beholds the Son[409] and believes on him

---

[405] **6:38.** ***"'I came down from heaven.'"*** Jesus' claim to have come from a realm beyond the earth—heaven—was undoubtedly a jolt to many who were listening.

[406] **6:38.** ***"' I came down from heaven, not to do my own will, but the will of him who sent me.'"*** Jesus' devotion to the one who sent him provides an example for all who minister in his name. Serving self-interests is not the believer's purpose. Deviation from divine mandate is not an option. Obeying and pleasing God is the highest priority.

[407] **6:39.** ***"' This is the will of the Father who has sent me: that I should lose none of those he has given me.'"*** It was the Father's will that Jesus "lose none" of the disciples that he had been given. However, Jesus would still have to fulfill his mission, if he was to "lose none." It was necessary for him to suffer the cross-death and to be raised from the dead. If he were to somehow bypass death on the cross, then all would have been lost. Thankfully, he did not avoid or bypass the offering of himself. As a result, out of those who are given to Jesus, he will "lose none."

[408] **6:39.** ***"'That I should raise them back to life at the last day.'"*** The concept of "the last day" appears in a number of places in this Gospel. Jesus referred to "the last day" as a time when he will raise to life those who have believed on him (6:39, 40, 44 and 54). Martha confessed her faith that God would raise her brother, Lazarus, from the dead on "the last day" (11:24). Finally, Jesus spoke of "the last day" as a time when those who have rejected him will be judged by the very words that they have rejected (12:48).

may have eternal life;[410] and I will raise him up at the
last day."[411]
41 Then the Jews murmured at him, because he said, "I
am the bread that came down from heaven."
42 And they said, "Isn't this Jesus the son of Joseph[412]
whose father and mother we know? How is it then that
he said, 'I came down from heaven'?"
43 Jesus answered and said to them, "Do not murmur
among yourselves.
44 No one is able to come to me, unless the Father who
has sent me draws him;[413] and I will raise him up at the
last day.[414]

---

[409] **6:40.** ***"'Every person who beholds the Son.'"*** Beholding the Son involves the intentional fixation of a person's attention upon him.

[410] **6:40.** ***"'Eternal life.'"*** See also 3:15-16, 36; 4:14, 36; 5:24, 39; 6:27, 47, 54, 68; 10:28; 12:25, 50; and 17:2.

[411] **6:40.** ***"'I will raise him up at the last day.'"*** Regarding the concept of "the last day," see the note for 6:39.

[412] **6:42.** ***"'The son of Joseph.'"*** Joseph was not Jesus' biological father. Mary was his biological mother, but Jesus had no father other than God. According to Matthew 1:18, "She [Mary] was found to be with child through the Holy Spirit."

[413] **6:44.** ***"'No one is able to come to me, unless the Father who has sent me draws him.'"*** According to *Thayer's Lexicon,* the metaphorical use of the word translated "draw" conveys the idea of being drawn by an inward power. Also see 6:65, where Jesus described the ability to come to him as something that is *given* by the Father.

[414] **6:44.** ***"'I will raise him up at the last day.'"*** Regarding "the last day," see the note for 6:39.

45 It is written in the prophets, 'And they shall all be
taught by God.'[415] Therefore, every person who has
heard from the Father and has learned from him comes
to me.
46 No man has seen the Father,[416] except for the one
who is from God; he has seen the Father.
47 I tell you the truth,[417] he who believes in me has
eternal life.[418]
48 I am that bread of life.[419]
49 Your fathers ate manna in the wilderness and are
dead.
50 This is the bread that comes down from heaven, so
that any may eat of it and not die.
51 I am the living bread that came down from heaven:
if any man eats of this bread, he will live forever. And
the bread that I will give is my flesh, which I will give
for the life of the world."[420]

---

[415] **6:45.** ***"'And they shall all be taught by God.'"*** This line is a quote from Isaiah 54:13. Here Jesus rightly equates himself with God.

[416] **6:46.** ***"'No man has seen the Father.'"*** See 1:18.

[417] **6:47.** ***"'I tell you the truth.'"*** See note for 6:26.

[418] **6:47.** ***"'Eternal life.'"*** See also 3:15-16, 36; 4:14, 36; 5:24, 39; 6:27, 40, 54, 68; 10:28; 12:25, 50; and 17:2.

[419] **6:48.** ***"'I am that bread of life.'"*** See note for 6:35 pertaining to Jesus' statement, "I am the bread of life."

[420] **6:51.** ***"'The bread that I will give is my flesh, which I will give for the life of the world.'"*** Jesus' words are a foreshadowing of his approaching cross-death.

52 Then the Jews quarreled among themselves, saying,
"How can this man give us his flesh to eat?"
53 Then Jesus said to them, "I tell you the truth,[421]
unless you eat the flesh of the Son of man[422] and drink
his blood, you have no life in you.[423]
54 Whoever eats my flesh and drinks my blood has
eternal life,[424] and I will raise him up at the last day.[425]
55 For my flesh truly is food, and my blood truly is
drink.
56 He who eats my flesh[426] and drinks my blood dwells
in me and I in him.

---

[421] **6:53.** ***"'I tell you the truth.'"*** See the note for 6:26.

[422] **6:53.** ***"'Son of man.'"*** The expression, "son of man," brings emphasis to the humanity of Jesus. Some also consider it a Messianic reference to Daniel 7:13-14: "In my vision at night I looked, and there before me was one like a son of man, coming with the clouds of heaven. He approached the Ancient of Days and was led into his presence. He was given authority, glory and sovereign power; all nations and peoples of every language worshiped him. His dominion is an everlasting dominion that will not pass away, and his kingdom is one that will never be destroyed." See 1:51; 3:13-14; 5:27; 6:27, 53, 62; 8:28; 12:23, 34 and 13:31.

[423] **6:53.** ***"'Unless you eat the flesh of the Son of man and drink his blood, you have no life in you.'"*** Jesus' mysterious words were a foreshadowing of that which he would make clear during his last supper with his disciples. At that time, in reference to the bread, he would say, "Take, eat; this is my body." Then in reference to the wine, he would say, "Drink all of it, for this is my blood of the new testament, which is shed for many for the remission of sins" (Matthew 26:26-28).

[424] **6:54.** ***"'Eternal life.'"*** See also 3:15-16, 36; 4:14, 36; 5:24, 39; 6:27, 40, 47, 68; 10:28; 12:25, 50; and 17:2.

[425] **6:54.** ***"'I will raise him up at the last day.'"*** See the note for 6:39.

57 As the living Father has sent me and as I live
because of the Father, so he that eats me, that person
shall live because of me.
58 This is that bread that came down from heaven. This
is not like the bread that your fathers ate; they ate
manna and are now dead. He who eats this bread will
live into eternity."
59 These things he said in the synagogue as he taught
in Capernaum.
60 Then many of his disciples who heard this said,
"This is a difficult saying; who is able hear it?"
61 When Jesus knew in himself that his disciples
murmured at it, he said to them, "Does this offend
you?
62 What if you behold the Son of man[427] ascending up
to where he was before?[428]

---

[426] **6:56.** ***"'He who eats my flesh.'"*** The word, *trogo*, translated, "eats," can also be translated, "gnaw," "crunch" or "chew." It appears that Jesus may have been intentionally using language that would have required spiritual perception to be understood. In a sense, he was also offending the mind to reveal what was in the heart.

[427] **6:62.** ***"'Son of man.'"*** See 6:53 note.

[428] **6:62.** ***"'What if you behold the Son of man ascending up to where he was before?'"*** Jesus in effect was saying,

> You have seen my miracles, and you have not truly placed your faith in me. I have told you plainly who I am, and you are offended and do not believe. If I were to go flying up into the sky right now, is that any greater than what I have already done and said? Do you think that would cause you to believe? No! The same unbelief that has been ruling your heart until now would continue to do so, even if I were to visibly ascend into the heavens!

> 63 It is the spirit that gives life; the flesh profits nothing. The words that I speak to you—they are spirit, and they are life.[429]
> 64 But there are some of you who do not believe." For Jesus knew from the beginning who they were that did not believe and who would betray him.

---

[429] **6:63. *"'It is the spirit that gives life; the flesh profits nothing. The words that I speak to you—they are spirit, and they are life.'"*** In the previous verses, Jesus' hearers were offended for at least two reasons:

1. His words made it sound like he wanted them to physically digest his body and blood.
2. He claimed to be the bread that came down from heaven.

With that context in mind, the following expanded interpretive paraphrase represents one way to understand verse 63:

> Trying to comprehend my words from a *fleshly* or *natural* point of view will result in totally missing what I have come to reveal. It is the *spirit* that gives life, and it is *your spirit* that receives this life. When I spoke of you eating my flesh and drinking my blood, do you really think I was suggesting that you should become cannibals? Digesting my physical body would accomplish nothing! Likewise, trying to receive spiritual realities with your natural intellect will accomplish nothing! The words that I speak to you—they are to be received by your spirit. If you will do that, you will find my words to be life-giving words.

When Jesus spoke, those who truly believed on him could sense that there was something going on here that was beyond their natural ability to comprehend. It did not make sense to their mind, but they knew that somewhere within those mysterious words was a compelling truth that summoned them. The divine mystery drew them further into a pursuit of the heart of God's Son. In application, believers would do well to cultivate spiritual sensitivities to spiritual things, and not to expect their intellects to serve as capable receptors of spiritual realities. Intellectual understanding is important, but the mystical aspects of life in Jesus cannot be received by the natural man; they are spiritually received. See 1 Corinthians 2:14.

65 And he said, "This is why I said to you that no one is able to come to me, unless the ability to come is given to him from my Father."[430]

Harmony of the Gospels			
	Matthew	**Mark**	**Luke**
Washed Hands	15:1-20	7:1-23	
The Syrophoenician Woman	15:21-28	7:24-30	
Healings	15:29-31	7:31-37	
Feeding of the Four Thousand	15:32-39	8:1-9	
The Sign from Heaven	16:1-4	8:10-13	
The Leaven of the Pharisees	16:5-12	8:14-21	
Healing of a Blind Man		8:22-26	

66 ¶ As a result of this incident, many of Jesus' disciples went back to their former way of life and no longer walked with him.
67 Then Jesus said to the Twelve, "Will you also go away?"
68 Simon Peter answered him, "Lord, to whom shall we go? You have the words of eternal life.[431]

---

[430] **6:65.** ***"'This is why I said to you that no one is able to come to me, unless the ability to come is given to him from my Father.'"*** See 6:44, where the God-given ability to come to the Son is presented in terms of being drawn by an inward power.

"'My Father.'" Jesus openly referenced God the Father as his Father, affirming his identity as the Son of God. See also 2:16; 5:17, 43; 6:65; 8:19, 28, 38, 49, 54; 10:17-18, 25, 29, 30, 32, 37; 12:26-27; 14:2, 7, 12, 20-21, 23, 28; 15:1, 8, 10, 15, 23-24; 16:10; 18:11; 20:17, and 21.

69 And we believe and are sure that you are the Christ,
the Son of the living God."[432]
70 Jesus answered them, "Haven't I chosen you twelve,
and yet one of you is a devil?"[433]
71 He spoke of Judas Iscariot, the son of Simon, for he
was the one who would betray him, being one of the
Twelve.

Harmony of the Gospels			
	Matthew	**Mark**	**Luke**
Peter's Profession of Faith	16:13-19	8:27-29	9:18-20
Jesus' Death Foretold (#1)	16:20-28	8:30-38; 9:1	9:21-27
The Transfiguration	17:1-9	9:2-10	9:28-36
The Coming of Elijah	17:10-13	9:11-13	
Healing of a Lunatic	17:14-21	9:14-29	9:37-42
Jesus' Death Foretold (#2)	17:22-23	9:30-32	9:43-45
Money in the Mouth of a Fish	17:24-27		
The Little Child	18:1-5	9:33-37	9:46-48
A Person Casting Out Demons		9:38-41	9:49-50

---

[431] **6:68.** ***"'Eternal life.'"*** See also 3:15-16, 36; 4:14, 36; 5:24, 39; 6:27, 40, 47, 54; 10:28; 12:25, 50; and 17:2.

[432] **6:69.** ***"'We believe and are sure that you are the Christ, the Son of the living God.'"*** Also see Peter's confession concerning Christ in Matthew 16:16.

[433] **6:70.** ***"'Haven't I chosen you twelve, and yet one of you is a devil?'"*** "Devil" can also be translated "adversary." Even after Peter had made a confession (6:68-69) that could have potentially relieved the tension in the air, Jesus still pressed the point regarding true belief in him. He highlights the fact that even among the Twelve there was one who was not a true believer.

	Matthew	**Mark**	**Luke**
Offences	18:6-9	9:42-48	17:02
The Lost Sheep	18:10-14		15:4-7
Forgiveness	18:15-17		
Binding and Loosing	18:18-20		
Parable of the Unmerciful Servant	18:21-35		
Salt with Fire		9:49-50	

Chapter 7

Conflict over Moses (7:1 – 8:11)

After these things, Jesus walked in Galilee, for he would not walk in Judea, because the Jews sought to kill him.
2 The Jews' Feast of Tabernacles[434] was near.
3 Then his brothers[435] said to him, "Depart from here, and go into Judea so that your disciples may also see the works that you do.
4 For no one seeking to be known publicly does anything in secret. If you are doing these things, show yourself to the world."
5 His brothers said these things because neither did they believe in him.[436]

---

[434] **7:2.** ***"The Jews' Feast of Tabernacles was near."*** The origin of the feast is found in Leviticus 23:42-43. For the benefit of Gentile readers, the association of particular feasts with Jewish tradition is also made in 2:13 and 11:55.

[435] **7:3.** ***"His brothers."*** The brothers of Jesus were named James, Joseph (Joses), Judas (Jude or Judah) and Simon (Mark 6:3). His brothers were also mentioned in 2:12.

> 6 Then Jesus said to them, "My time[437] has not yet
> come, but any time is right for you.
> 7 The world[438] cannot hate you, but it hates me, because
> I testify of its true condition—that the works of the
> world are evil.
> 8 Go ahead and go up[439] to this feast; I am not going to
> go up right now, for my time[440] has not yet fully come."

---

[436] **7:3-5. *"His brothers said to him, 'Depart from here,.... show yourself to the world.' His brothers said these things because neither did they believe in him."*** With unbelief and a tone of sarcasm and mockery, Jesus' brothers in essence said,

> Get on with your mission! What's the use with you hanging around here? Get on your way into Judea so that your disciples there can see how amazing you are! You can't become famous by remaining here in hiding. That is what you want, right? You want to be famous, don't you? If you are so amazing, get out there; show yourself to the world!

[437] **7:6. *"'My time.'"*** The word here is *kairos*, meaning, "a fixed and definite time," an "opportune or seasonable time," or "the right time." *"kairos," Thayer's Greek Lexicon, Blue Letter Bible,* accessed January 10, 2016, https:// www.blueletterbible.org/ lang/ lexicon/ lexicon.cfm?t=kjv&strongs=g2540. In this Gospel, when referring to the approaching hour or time for Jesus to face the crucifixion, John seems to use *hora* (2:4; 7:30; 8:20; 12:23, 27; 13:1; and 17:1) and *kairos* (7:6-8) interchangeably with little intended differentiation of meaning.

[438] **7:7. *"'The world.'"*** In some contexts, such as 7:7, "the world" means, as Thayer suggests, "the ungodly multitude; the whole mass of men alienated from God, and therefore hostile to the cause of Christ." *"kosmos," Thayer's Greek Lexicon, Blue Letter Bible,* accessed January 10, 2016, https:// www.blueletterbible.org/ lang/ lexicon/ lexicon.cfm?t= kjv&strongs= g2889.

[439] **7:8. *"'Go up.'"*** "Up" and "down" are references to elevation and not points on the compass. See 2:12, 13; 4:49; 5:1; 6:16; 7:10, 14; 11:55; and 12:20.

[440] **7:8. *"'My time.'"*** See note for "my time" in 7:6.

9 Having said these words to them, he remained in Galilee.

10 ¶ But after his brothers had gone up, he also went up[441] to the feast—not openly, but in secret.

Harmony of the Gospels			
	Matthew	**Mark**	**Luke**
Journey to Jerusalem			9:51
Fire from Heaven			9:52-56
Answers to Disciples	8:19-22		9:57-62

11 Then the Jews looked for him at the feast and said, "Where is he?"
12 And there was much whispering among the people concerning him, for some said, "He is a good man." Others said, "No, he deceives the people."
13 But no one spoke openly of him for fear of the Jews.[442]

---

[441] **7:10.** ***"Gone up… went up."*** See note regarding "go up" in 7:8.

[442] **7:13.** ***"No one spoke openly of him for fear of the Jews."*** In at least five places in this Gospel, behavior was motivated out of fear of the Jews:

1. The first occurrence is here in 7:13 where people were afraid to speak openly of Jesus because of their fear of the Jews.
2. The second is in 9:22 where the parents of a man healed from blindness were afraid to testify concerning their son's healing.
3. The third is in 12:42 where many of the chief Jewish rulers who believed in Jesus did not openly confess him "because of the Pharisees;" they feared that they might be put out of the synagogue.

> 14 ¶ About the middle of the feast, Jesus went up[443] into the temple and taught.
> 15 And the Jews marveled, saying, "How is this man so acquainted with the sacred writings, having never learned?"
> 16 Jesus answered them and said, "My doctrine is not mine, but it is his that sent me.
> 17 If any man is willing to do his will, he will know concerning the doctrine, whether it is of God or whether I am speaking from myself.[444]
> 18 He that speaks from himself seeks his own glory, but he that seeks the glory of the one who sent him, that man is true, and no unrighteousness is in him.
> 19 Didn't Moses give you the law,[445] and yet none of you keeps the law? Why are you seeking to kill me?"[446]

---

4. The fourth is in 19:38 where Joseph of Arimathaea was secretive regarding his allegiance to Jesus because of his fear of the Jews.
5. The fifth is in 20:19 following Jesus' resurrection; at that time, the disciples assembled secretly behind closed doors because they feared the Jews.

[443] **7:14.** ***"Went up."*** See note regarding "go up" in 7:8.

[444] **7:17.** ***"'If any man is willing to do his will, he will know concerning the doctrine, whether it is of God or whether I am speaking from myself.'"*** When a person's will or desire is set upon pleasing God, that person's perception of truth increases. Furthermore, perception of truth increases as one walks in truth already received.

[445] **7:19.** ***"'Didn't Moses give you the law.'"*** In subtle ways, the writer confronts the heresy of Cerinthus and others like him who taught that salvation could only come through obedience to Jewish law. The author is careful to honor Moses' rightful place in the history of redemption, while elevating the fullness of salvation as manifested in and through Jesus. See 1:17; 1:45; 7:23 and 8:5.

20 The crowd answered and said, "You have a
demon.[447] Who is seeking to kill you?"[448]
21 Jesus answered and said to them, "I have done one
work,[449] and you all marvel.
22 Moses gave circumcision to you—not because it is of
Moses, but of the patriarchs—and you circumcise a
man on the Sabbath day.
23 If a man on the Sabbath day receives circumcision
that the Law of Moses should not be broken, are you
angry at me because I have made a man's whole body
well on the Sabbath day?[450]
24 Do not judge according to the appearance, but judge
righteous judgment."

---

[446] **7:19.** ***"'Why are you seeking to kill me?'"*** Beginning in 5:16, the Jews were trying to find a way to kill Jesus.

[447] **7:20.** ***"'You have a demon.'"*** On at least two other occasions, Jesus was accused of being demonized (8:48, 52 and 10:20).

[448] **7:20.** ***"'You have a demon. Who is seeking to kill you?'"*** The people in the crowd made it seem as though no one was trying to kill Jesus. However, according to 7:25, it was known in Jerusalem that the Jews were trying to kill him.

[449] **7:21.** ***"'I have done one work.'"*** The one notable work or miracle on the mind of these Jews was the healing of the lame man on the Sabbath during Jesus' previous visit to Jerusalem (5:1-16).

[450] **7:23.** ***"'If a man on the Sabbath day receives circumcision that the Law of Moses should not be broken, are you angry at me because I have made a man's whole body well on the Sabbath day?'"*** Jesus contrasts the receiving of an "affliction"—the painful cutting of the flesh associated with circumcising a male—against the healing of an affliction. In essence he is pointing out how strange it is that these Jews condone afflicting on the Sabbath, but they condemn healing an affliction on the Sabbath.

25 Then some of the people of Jerusalem said, "Isn't
this the man they are seeking to kill?[451]
26 Look at this! He speaks boldly, and they say nothing
to him! Could it be that the rulers have become
convinced that this is truly the Christ?
27 But we know where this man comes from. When
Christ comes, no man will know where he is from."[452]
28 Then Jesus cried out in the temple as he taught,
saying, "You both know me, and you know from
where I have come! I have not come of myself, but he
that sent me is true, whom you do not know.
29 But I know him, for I am from him, and he has sent
me."
30 Then they sought to take him, but no man laid
hands on him because his hour[453] had not yet come.[454]

---

[451] **7:25. "*'Isn't this the man they are seeking to kill?'*"** In 7:20, the people in the crowd made it seem as though no one was trying to kill Jesus; however, 7:25 indicates that it was known in Jerusalem that the Jews were trying to kill him.

[452] **7:27. "'No man will know where he is from.'"** The idea that the origin of the Messiah would be unknowable is without definitive support in Hebrew Scripture. In fact, the scriptures *do* give clues to the Messiah's origin: for instance, he was to rise from the tribe of Judah (Genesis 49:10), Bethlehem Ephratah (Micah 5:2) and Galilee (Isaiah 9:1-2). The Galilee and Bethlehem origins appear contradictory, until the complete narrative of Jesus' birth and childhood are taken into consideration.

The expressed opinion, "No man will know where he is from," was probably the popular thought of the day. On the other hand, it *is* true that prophecies related to the coming of Messiah are a bit mysterious. In light of the veiled nature of the Messianic expectation, it is understandable that these Jews could have formed the belief stated in 7:27.

31 Yet many of the people believed on him and said, "When Christ comes, will he do more miracles than these which this man has done?"[455]

32 ¶ The Pharisees[456] heard that the people murmured such things concerning Jesus, and the Pharisees and the chief priests sent officers to take him.[457]

---

[453] **7:30. *"Hour."*** The word translated "hour" is *hora,* meaning "any definite time, point of time, moment." "*hora,*" *Thayer's Greek Lexicon, Blue Letter Bible,* accessed January 10, 2016, https:// www.blueletterbible.org/ lang/ lexicon/ lexicon.cfm?t= kjv&strongs= g5610. In this Gospel, when referring to the approaching hour or time for Jesus to face the crucifixion, John seems to use *hora* (2:4; 7:30; 8:20; 12:23, 27; 13:1; and 17:1) and *kairos* (7:6-8) interchangeably with little intended differentiation of meaning.

[454] **7:30. *"His hour had not yet come."*** "His hour" is a reference to Jesus' divinely appointed time to die.

[455] **7:31. *"'When Christ comes, will he do more miracles than these which this man has done?'"*** In other words, "What more proof could anyone want? Look at all that this man has done! Certainly he is the Christ."

Supernatural ministry affects the hearts and minds of people, causing them to believe upon Jesus. See 2:11, 23; 4:48, 53; 10:37-38; 11:15, 45, 48; 12:11; 14:11; and 20:30-31. However, some see his miracles and still do not believe. See 6:36; 7:5; and 12:37.

[456] **7:32. *"Pharisees."*** The Pharisees were a sect noted for their strict observance of Jewish practices, adherence to oral laws and traditions, belief in an afterlife and the coming of Messiah. They are mentioned in 1:24; 3:1; 4:1; 7:32, 45-48; 8:3, 13; 9:13, 15, 16, 40; 11:46, 47, 57; 12:19, 42; 18:3.

[457] **7:32. *"The Pharisees and the chief priests sent officers to take him."*** The officers do not succeed in arresting Jesus. When the officers later return to the Pharisees and the chief priests, their report suggests that *they* were the ones who were arrested—captivated by the words of Jesus (7:45-49).

33 Then Jesus said to them, "I am with you a little
while longer, and then I go to him who sent me.
34 You will look for me and will not find me, and
where I am, you cannot come."[458]
35 Then said the Jews among themselves, "Where will
he go that we will not find him? Will he go to the
dispersed Jews among the Gentiles and teach the
Gentiles as well?[459]
36 What is this saying he has said: 'You will look for
me and will not find me,' and, 'Where I am, you cannot
come?'"[460]

The Fifth Discourse: The Life-Giving Spirit (7:37-44)

37 In the last day, that great day of the feast,[461] Jesus
stood and cried,[462] saying, "If any man is thirsty, let him
come unto me and drink!

---

[458] **7:34.** ***"'Where I am, you cannot come.'"*** More literally this line would read, "Where I am, to that place you cannot come." See 7:36.

[459] **7:35.** ***"'Will he go to the dispersed Jews among the Gentiles and teach the Gentiles as well?'"*** The Pharisees reasoned that Jesus might have been implying that he was going to embed himself among the Gentiles. They realized that Jesus knew that religious Jews would never venture into Gentile cities to look for him. The Pharisees thought that Jesus might have come up with a clever plan for disappearing from their sight.

[460] **7:36.** ***"'Where I am, you cannot come.'"*** More literally this line would read, "Where I am, to that place you cannot come." See 7:34.

[461] **7:37.** ***"In the last day, that great day of the feast."*** The reference here is to the last day of the Feast of Tabernacles.

38 He who believes on me, as the scripture has said,
out of his belly will flow rivers of living water!"[463]
39 (This he spoke of the Spirit which they who believed
on him would receive, for the Holy Spirit had not yet
been given[464] because Jesus had not yet been glorified.)

40 ¶ When the people heard this saying, many of them
said, "Truly, this is the Prophet."
41 Others said, "This is the Christ."
But some said, "Shall Christ come out of Galilee?[465]

---

[462] **7:37. *"Jesus stood and cried."*** In the midst of a multitude, Jesus stood and cried out in a loud voice with the intent of being heard by all.

[463] **7:37-38. *"'If any man is thirsty, let him come unto me and drink! He who believes on me, as the scripture has said, out of his belly will flow rivers of living water.'"*** For an earlier and similar instance of Jesus using this water metaphor, see 4:14.

Traditionally on the last day of the Feast of Tabernacles, The priests would fill golden vessels with water from a stream flowing beneath the temple mount. They would then pour the water on the altar and sing Isaiah 12:3: "With joy shall you draw water out of the wells of Salvation." This ceremony was performed with the sounding of trumpets and ecstatic celebration. The joy was so great that some have said, "Whoever had not witnessed it had never seen rejoicing at all." Robert Jamieson, A. R. Fausset and David Brown, *Commentary Critical and Explanatory on the Whole Bible* (1871), accessed July 31, 2014, http:// www.biblestudytools.com/ commentaries/ jamieson-fausset-brown/ john/ john-7.html.

[464] **7:39. *"The Holy Spirit had not yet been given."*** After Jesus' resurrection, he imparted the Holy Spirit to his disciples with this declaration: "Receive the Holy Spirit!" (See 20:22.) John's words in 7:39 may have been in anticipation of the later impartation account, or his words may have been in anticipation of the outpouring that would come following Jesus' ascension on the Day of Pentecost (Acts 2:1-41).

42 Haven't the Scriptures said that Christ comes from the seed of David and out of the town of Bethlehem where David was from?"
43 So there was a division among the people because of him.
44 Some of them would have taken him, but no man laid hands on him.

45 ¶ Then the officers came to the chief priests and Pharisees,[466] and the chief priests and Pharisees said to them, "Why haven't you brought him?"[467]
46 The officers answered, "Never has a man spoken like this man."
47 Then the Pharisees answered them, "Are you also deceived?
48 Have any of the rulers or any of the Pharisees believed on him?[468]

---

[465] **7:41.** ***"'Shall Christ come out of Galilee?'"*** This question is reminiscent of the words spoken by Nathanael in 1:46: "Can anything good come out of Nazareth?'" Nazareth was a tiny frontier community in the Galilee region not known for anything important. As suggested in the text at hand, members of the Judean elite were unimpressed with Jesus' humble Galilean origins. (See also 7:52.) Craig S. Keener, "Can Anything Good Come out of Nazareth?" *Bible Odyssey*, accessed January 5, 2016, http:// www.bibleodyssey.org/ places/ related-articles/ can-anything-good-come-out-of-nazareth.aspx.

[466] **7:45.** ***"Pharisees."*** See note on 7:32. The Pharisees are mentioned in 1:24; 3:1; 4:1; 7:32, 45-48; 8:3, 13; 9:13, 15, 16, 40; 11:46, 47, 57; 12:19, 42; 18:3.

[467] **7:45.** ***"'Why haven't you brought him?'"*** In 7:32, the chief priests and Pharisees sent these officers to arrest Jesus.

49 This throng—these people who do not know the
law, they are cursed."
50 Nicodemus[469] said to them, (the man who came to
Jesus by night, being one of them),
51 "Does our law judge any man before it hears him
and knows what he has done?"
52 They answered and said to him, "Are you also of
Galilee? Search the Scriptures and see; no prophet
arises out of Galilee." [470]
[53 And every man went to his own house.[471]

[468] **7:48.** ***"'Have any of the rulers or any of the Pharisees believed on him?'"*** The chief priests and Pharisees were saying, "We are the chief priests and Pharisees! *We* are the enlightened ones! If we who have superior discernment on such matters have not believed in him, neither should you!"

[469] **7:50.** ***"Nicodemus."*** Nicodemus appears the second time. He appears a total of three times in John's Gospel: 3:1-21; 7:45-51; and 19:39-42.

[470] **7:52.** ***"'No prophet arises out of Galilee.'"*** The chief priests and Pharisees failed to remember that Isaiah 9:1-2 speaks of the Messiah rising out of Galilee.

Craig S. Keener notes that members of the Judean elite were especially unimpressed with Jesus' rural Galilean origins. (See also 7:41-42.) Craig S. Keener, "Can Anything Good Come out of Nazareth?" *Bible Odyssey*, accessed January 5, 2016, http:// www.bibleodyssey.org/ places/ related-articles/ can-anything-good-come-out-of-nazareth.aspx.

[471] **7:53-8:11.** See note on 8:11.

CHAPTER 8

Jesus went to the mount of Olives.

2 Then early in the morning he came again into the
temple, and all the people came to him; and he sat down
and taught them.

3 The scribes and Pharisees[472] *brought to him a woman taken*
in adultery. When they had set her in the midst of them,

4 they said to him, "Teacher,[473] *this woman was caught in*
the very act of committing adultery.

5 Moses in the law commanded us that such should be
stoned[474]*, but what do you say?"*

6 They said this, tempting him, so that they might have
grounds to accuse him.[475] *But Jesus stooped down, and with*

---

[472] **8:3. *"Pharisees."*** The Pharisees were a sect noted for their strict observance of Jewish practices, adherence to oral laws and traditions, belief in an afterlife and the coming of Messiah. They are mentioned in 1:24; 3:1; 4:1; 7:32, 45-48; 8:3, 13; 9:13, 15, 16, 40; 11:46, 47, 57; 12:19, 42; 18:3.

[473] **8:4. *"'Teacher.'"*** The word translated "Teacher" is *didaskale,* derived from *didaskalos*. It is sometimes translated, "Master." In many places in other translations, the word *rabbi* is also translated, "Master."

[474] **8:5. *"'Moses in the law commanded us that such should be stoned.'"*** The scribes and Pharisees reference the law of Moses as it relates to capital punishment in cases of adultery. See Leviticus 20:10-21 and Deuteronomy 22:22.

his finger he wrote on the ground as though he did not hear them.
7 As they continued asking him, he lifted himself up and said to them, "He who is without sin among you, let him be the first to cast a stone at her."[476]
8 Again he stooped down and wrote on the ground.
9 And they who heard what he said, being convicted by their own conscience, departed one by one beginning from the oldest to the youngest. Jesus and the woman who was standing there were left alone.
10 When Jesus had lifted himself up and saw no one but the woman, he said to her, "Woman, where are your accusers? Has no man condemned you?"
11 She said, "No man, Lord."
And Jesus said to her, "Neither do I condemn you. Go, and stop sinning."[477]*]* [478]

---

[475] **8:6. *"They said this, tempting him, so that they might have grounds to accuse him."*** If Jesus could be caught contradicting the law of Moses, Jewish leaders would then have grounds for arresting him.

[476] **8:7. *"'He who is without sin among you, let him be the first to cast a stone at her.'"*** Jesus referred to "he who is without sin among you." It is noteworthy that the only one who was without sin among them—Jesus (Hebrews 4:15)—was not willing to condemn her, much less stone her. Justice was required, yet it was mercy that was demonstrated.

[477] **8:11. *"'Neither do I condemn you. Go, and stop sinning.'"*** Jesus did not condone the sin; rather, he was merciful toward the woman, offering her a way out of her sinful lifestyle.

[478] **7:53-8:11.** The earliest and best manuscripts do not include these words. Although Johannine authorship of 7:53-8:11 is doubtful, the ancient church regarded the account as authentic and inspired. A few manuscripts include it after John 7:36,

Conflict Over Abraham (8:12-59)

The Sixth Discourse:
The Light of the World (8:12-30)

12 ¶ Then Jesus spoke again to them, saying, "I am the
light of the world.[479] He who follows me will not walk
in darkness but will have the light of life."[480]
13 Then the Pharisees[481] said to him, "You testify on
your own behalf; your testimony[482] is invalid.[483]"

John 21:25, Luke 21:38 or Luke 24:53. Because the writing style is more like Luke's than John's, some believe that 7:53-8:11 was originally authored by Luke but excluded from the final draft of his Gospel for unknown reasons. It may have been among Luke's loose leaf research notes but not included due to a concern that he might run out of space on the scroll. At some point in the course of history, a scribe who appreciated the value of this account, found an opportunity to include it while he was making a copy of the Gospel According to John.

[479] **8:12.** ***"I am the light of the world."*** Here is the second of seven "I am" statements in this Gospel. The other six statements are found in 6:35, 48; 10:7; 10:14; 11:25; 14:6; and 15:1. Regarding Jesus being the "true light," see 1:9.

[480] **8:12.** ***"' He who follows me will not walk in darkness but will have the light of life.'"*** Regarding those who live and walk in the light, see 3:19-21 and 1 John 1:6-7. Those who follow Jesus will live a life liberated from spiritual darkness. Following this discourse, the next miracle that Jesus would perform would be that of healing a blind man—delivering a man from physical darkness so that he may walk in the light (9:1-12). There is a prophetic connection between 8:12 and 9:1-12.

[481] **8:13.** ***"Pharisees."*** See note on 8:3. The Pharisees are mentioned in 1:24; 3:1; 4:1; 7:32, 45-48; 8:3, 13; 9:13-16, 40; 11:46, 47, 57; 12:19, 42; 18:3.

[482] **8:13.** ***"'Testimony.'"*** See 3:11, 3:32-33; 5:31, 34, 36; 8:13-14, 17; 12:18; 19:35 and 21:24.

14 Jesus answered and said to them, "Although I testify
on my own behalf, my testimony[484] is still true, for I
know where I came from and where I am going. But
you do not know where I came from and where I am
going.[485]
15 You judge after the flesh;[486] I judge no one.[487]
16 Yet if I judge, my judgment is true, for I am not
alone. I judge with the Father who sent me.
17 It is also written in your law that the testimony[488] of
two men is true.[489]

---

[483] **8:13.** ***"'Your testimony is invalid.'"*** The words translated "invalid" can also be translated "not true." According to Deuteronomy 17:6, a person could not testify on his own behalf. Two witnesses were required.

[484] **8:14.** ***"'Testimony.'"*** See 8:13 note.

[485] **8:14.** ***"'I know where I came from and where I am going. But you do not know where I came from and where I am going.'"*** Where did Jesus come from, and where was he going? He came from "above" (8:23)--his place with the Father in the eternal realm, and he was returning to that glory. Although his hearers did not perceive this truth, in effect Jesus was saying, "My testimony is true, because I am God, the Son."

[486] **8:15.** ***"'You judge after the flesh.'"*** The Pharisees judged according to natural or physical perception, not according to spiritual perception.

[487] **8:15.** ***"'I judge no one.'"*** Jesus' mission was to bring salvation, not judgment. His approach to sinful humanity is always with a view toward "how can I save them," rather than, "how can I judge and condemn them." See 3:17.

[488] **8:17.** ***"'Testimony.'"*** See 3:11, 3:32-33; 5:31, 34, 36; 8:13-14; 12:18; 19:35 and 21:24.

[489] **8:17.** ***"'The testimony of two men is true.'"*** See the note for 8:13.

18 I am one who testifies on my own behalf, and the
Father who sent me testifies on my behalf."
19 Then they said to him, "Where is your father?"
Jesus answered, "You neither know me nor my
Father.[490] If you had known me, you would have
known my Father also."[491]
20 Jesus spoke these words in the treasury as he taught
in the temple, and no one laid hands on him, for his
hour[492] had not yet come.
21 Jesus said again to them, "I am going my way, and
you will seek me and will die in your sins. You cannot
come to the place where I go."
22 Then the Jews said, "Will he kill himself?" because
he said, "You cannot come to the place where I go."
23 He said to them, "You are from below; I am from
above.[493] You are of this world; I am not of this world.

---

[490] **8:19. *"'My Father.'"*** Jesus openly referenced God the Father as his Father, affirming his identity as the Son of God. See also 2:16; 5:17, 43; 6:32, 65; 8:28, 38, 49, 54; 10:17-18, 25, 29, 30, 32, 37; 12:26-27; 14:2, 7, 12, 20-21, 23, 28; 15:1, 8, 10, 15, 23-24; 16:10; 18:11; 20:17, and 21.

[491] **8:19. *"'If you had known me, you would have known my Father also.'"*** Jesus is the only way to the Father (14:6).

[492] **8:20. *"His hour."*** This term is a reoccurring reference to Jesus' divinely appointed time to die. The word translated "hour" is *hora,* meaning "any definite time, point of time, moment." "*hora,*" *Thayer's Greek Lexicon, Blue Letter Bible,* accessed January 10, 2016, https:// www.blueletterbible.org/ lang/ lexicon/ lexicon.cfm?t= kjv&strongs= g5610. In this Gospel, when referring to the approaching hour or time for Jesus to face the crucifixion, John seems to use *hora* (2:4; 7:30; 8:20; 12:23, 27; 13:1; and 17:1) and *kairos* (7:6-8) interchangeably with little intended differentiation of meaning.

24 For this reason, I said to you that you will die in
your sins, for if you do not believe that I am who I am,
you will die in your sins."[494]
25 Then they said to him, "Who are you?"
And Jesus said to them, "I am the same person that I
said from the beginning.
26 I have many things to say and to judge of you, but
he who sent me is true, and I speak to the world the
things that I have heard from him."[495]
27 They did not understand that he spoke to them of
the Father.
28 Then Jesus said to them, "When you have lifted up[496]
the Son of man,[497] then you will know that I am who I

---

[493] **8:23.** ***"'You are from below; I am from above.'"*** These words answer the mystery in 8:14 regarding Jesus' place of origin; he came from "above."

[494] **8:23-24.** ***"'You are of this world; I am not of this world. For this reason, I said to you that you will die in your sins, for if you do not believe that I am who I am, you will die in your sins.'"*** Sin and death belong to this realm known as "this world." Freedom and life belong to the "not of this world" realm.

[495] **8:26.** ***"'I speak to the world the things that I have heard from him.'"*** Jesus' continual practice was to align his words and actions with the words and actions of his Father. See 5:19; 12:49-50.

[496] **8:28.** ***"'When you have lifted up.'"*** The words "lifted up" signify exaltation as well as the manner of death by which Jesus would die—crucifixion. Also see 3:14 and 12:32-34.

[497] **8:28.** ***"'Son of man.'"*** The expression, "son of man," brings emphasis to the humanity of Jesus. Some also consider it a Messianic reference to Daniel 7:13-14:

> In my vision at night I looked, and there before me was one like a son of man, coming with the clouds of heaven. He approached the Ancient of Days and was led into his presence. He was given authority, glory and sovereign power; all

am[498] and that I do nothing of myself; but as my
Father[499] has taught me, I speak these things.[500]
29 He who sent me is with me; the Father has not left
me alone, for I always do those things that please him."
30 As he spoke these words, many believed in him.
31 Then Jesus said to those Jews who believed in him,
"If you continue in my word, then you are truly my
disciples;
32 And you will know the truth,[501] and the truth will set
you free."[502]

---

nations and peoples of every language worshiped him. His dominion is an everlasting dominion that will not pass away, and his kingdom is one that will never be destroyed.

See 1:51; 3:13-14; 5:27; 6:27, 53, 62; 12:23, 34 and 13:31.

[498] **8:28. *"'You will know that I am who I am.'"*** A more literal translation of "I am who I am" would simply be the two words, "I am." He is in effect saying, "When you have lifted me up, you will know that I am God."

[499] **8:28. *"'My Father.'"*** See note for 8:19.

[500] **8:28. *"'As my Father has taught me, I speak these things.'"*** See note for 8:26.

[501] **8:32. *"'You will know the truth.'"*** Following the Hebraic way of knowing, Jesus' words may be stated another way: "You will encounter and become intimately acquainted with the truth." In a sense, truth is synonymous with reality, yet truth is not just a set of facts. It is life and creation as seen through the lens of God's design and purpose. It is reality as seen and revealed from the Father's point of view. Seeing that Jesus is the ultimate personification of truth, one might even conclude that truth is a person more than it is a concept.

"'Truth.'" See the note for "full of grace and truth" in 1:14.

[502] **8:32. *"You will know the truth, and the truth will set you free."*** Steve Backlund, Francis Frangipane and others have emphasized that any area of a person's life that is not "glistening" with hope is an area where a stronghold exists.

Pause and Reflect

1. Are you feeling hopeless about a situation? What is that situation, and what is really going on there?
2. Knowing that hopelessness is caused by being under the influence of Satan's lies, what lie are you believing concerning this matter?
3. What is God's heart toward you in the midst of these circumstances? What do you think he is feeling, thinking or saying? In other words, what is truth in this matter? What does the Bible say? Once you discern what God is saying, make his words your declaration over your life. His words are always truth, and truth will set you free.
4. Jesus *is* the truth. Invite and expect him to show up in the midst of your trouble. Seek his presence, and steward his presence in your life. The presence of Jesus and hopelessness cannot coexist. Your partnership with the presence of Jesus—who is the truth—will drive out hopelessness and bring freedom every time.

33 ¶ They answered him, "We are Abraham's seed and
were never in bondage to any man.[503] How can you say,
"You will be made free?"

The absence of hope is evidence that the person believes a lie in that area. The underlying lie needs to be identified and countered with truth—what God thinks, feels and speaks about the matter. Furthermore, because truth is embodied in the person of Jesus, an increased awareness of his presence will make it very difficult for such lies to survive. When people become intimately acquainted with the truth, the truth will set them free.

[503] **8:33.** *"'We are Abraham's seed and were never in bondage to any man.'"* These descendants of Abraham who claimed to have never been "in bondage to any man" were with these very words believing a lie and denying the truth. The Jews

34 Jesus answered them, "I tell you the truth,[504]
whoever commits sin is the servant of sin.[505]
35 But the servant does not stay in the house forever;
the Son remains forever.
36 If the Son, therefore, shall make you free, you shall
truly be free.[506]
37 I know that you are Abraham's seed, but you seek to
kill me, because my word has no place in you.
38 I speak that which I have seen with my Father,[507]
and you do that which you have seen with your
father."[508]

---

had been in bondage to man at many points throughout their history. They were even currently oppressed under Roman dominion.

[504] **8:34.** ***"'I tell you the truth.'"*** The KJV translates, "Verily, verily." The Greek words here are a transliteration of the Hebrew expression, "Amen, amen." It was a way of saying, "You can be certain of what I am about to tell you."

[505] **8:34.** ***"'Whoever commits sin is the servant of sin.'"*** When a person sins, that person makes that sin their master. The only hope for freedom from this slavery is found in the Deliverer—Jesus, the Son of God.

[506] **8:36.** ***"'You shall truly be free.'"*** The KJV translates, "you shall be free indeed." The idea being conveyed here is that the promised freedom is not something that is figurative or a mere concept; it is a true freedom experienced in real life.

[507] **8:38.** ***"'I speak that which I have seen with my Father.'"*** See note for 8:26.

"'That which I have seen with my Father.'" Even prior to his incarnation, Jesus enjoyed face-to-face relationship with his Father. See note for "the Word was with God" in 1:1.

"'My Father.'" See note for 8:19.

[508] **8:38.** ***"'I speak that which I have seen with my Father, and you do that which you have seen with your father.'"*** There are two contrasting families in the earth: the

39 They answered and said to him, "Abraham is our
father."
Jesus said to them, "If you were Abraham's children,
you would do the same works that Abraham did.[509]
40 But now you seek to kill me, a man who has told
you the truth[510] that I have heard from God. Abraham
did not direct you to do this.
41 You do the deeds of your father."
Then said they to him, "We are not born of fornication;
we have one Father, even God."
42 Jesus said to them, "If God were your Father, you
would love me, for I proceeded forth and came from
God; neither did I come of myself, but he sent me.
43 Why do you not understand my speech? It is
because you cannot hear my word. [511]

---

children of God and the children of the devil. Who was the father of these people to whom Jesus was speaking? In 8:44 Jesus will tell them that their father is the devil.

[509] **8:39.** ***"'If you were Abraham's children, you would do the same works that Abraham did.'"*** Galatians 3:6-9 speaks of those who are the true children of Abraham.

[510] **8:40.** ***"Truth."*** See the note for "full of grace and truth" in 1:14.

[511] **8:43.** ***"'Why do you not understand my speech? It is because you cannot hear my word.'"*** The problem here is not simply about people being unwilling to hear or receive what Jesus was saying. The statement, "you cannot hear my word," conveys the idea that they did not have the capacity or the ability to hear. This problem is also noted in 3:10 and 6:63, and it is implied throughout John's Gospel. 1 Corinthians 2:14 (NIV) says, "The man without the Spirit does not accept the things that come from the Spirit of God, for they are foolishness to him, and he cannot understand them, because they are spiritually discerned."

44 You are of your father the devil, and you will do the
desires of your father. He was a murderer from the
beginning, and he did not abide in the truth[512] because
there is no truth in him.[513] When he speaks a lie, he
speaks out of his own nature,[514] for he is a liar and the
father of lies.[515]
45 And because I tell you the truth, you do not believe
me.
46 Which of you can prove that I am guilty of sin? If I
speak the truth,[516] why don't you believe me?
47 He that is of God hears God's words. Therefore, you
do not hear his words, because you are not of God."[517]

---

[512] **8:44.** ***"'Truth.'"*** See the note for "full of grace and truth" in 1:14.

[513] **8:44.** ***"'He [the devil] was a murderer from the beginning, and he did not abide in the truth because there is no truth in him.'"*** The association of "he was a murderer from the beginning" with "he did not abide in the truth" is an interesting connection. Why did Jesus say that the devil was a murderer from the beginning? He was a murderer in that he intentionally lured Adam and Eve into the realm of death by conceiving within them a lie—a lie that caused them to question God's goodness.

[514] **8:44.** ***"'When he [the devil] speaks a lie, he speaks out of his own nature.'"*** As someone has said, "When the devil lies, he is speaking in his native tongue."

[515] **8:44.** ***"'He is a liar and the father of lies.'"*** Not only does the devil lie, but he also conceives lies within human minds. In this sense, he is the father of lies. He plants seeds of lying thoughts—thoughts that at first seem reasonable. Often we think that these thoughts are *our* thoughts, and we fail to recognize them as fiery darts from the evil one (Ephesians 6:16). Before you know it, we have nurtured that thought and have ended up making it our own.

[516] **8:46.** ***"Truth."*** See the note for "full of grace and truth" in 1:14.

48 Then the Jews answered and said to him, "Aren't we
right when we say that you are a Samaritan[518] and have
a demon?"[519]
49 Jesus answered, "I do not have a demon, but I honor
my Father,[520] and you dishonor me.[521]
50 I do not seek my own glory. There is one who seeks
and judges.
51 I tell you the truth,[522] if a man keeps my word,[523] he
shall never behold death."[524]
52 Then the Jews said to him, "Now we know that you
have a demon.[525] Abraham and the prophets are dead,

---

[517] **8:47. *"'You do not hear his words, because you are not of God.'"*** Those who were listening on this day did not receive the truth, because Jesus' words were like a foreign language to them. Had these people been "of God," they would have received and understood.

[518] **8:48. *"'You are a Samaritan.'"*** The word "Samaritan" was frequently used as a term of derision.

[519] **8:48. *"'You... have a demon?'"*** This accusation was repeated on this occasion in 8:52. On at least two other occasions, Jesus was accused of being demonized (7:20 and 10:20).

[520] **8:49. *"'My Father.'"*** See note for 8:19.

[521] **8:49. *"'But I honor my Father, and you dishonor me.'"*** By dishonoring Jesus, the Jews were dishonoring the Father.

[522] **8:51. *"'I tell you the truth.'"*** See the note for 8:34.

[523] **8:51. *"'If a man keeps my word.'"*** Keeping Jesus' word is a matter of carefully attending to all that He says.

[524] **8:51. *"'He shall never behold death.'"*** When believers pass from this life, they do not enter the realm of death. Rather, they transition directly into the realm of eternal life. In this sense, believers never die. See 11:26.

and you say, 'If a man keeps my word, he shall never
taste of death.'[526]
53 Are you greater than our father Abraham who is
dead? And the prophets are dead. Who are you
making yourself out to be?"
54 Jesus answered, "If I honor myself, my honor is
nothing. It is my Father[527] who honors me—my Father,
whom you say is your God.
55 Yet you have not known him, but I know him. If I
should say, 'I do not know him.' I would be a liar like
you. But I do know him, and I attend carefully to his
word.
56 Your father Abraham rejoiced to see my day, and he
saw it and was glad."[528]

---

[525] **8:52. *"'Now we know that you have a demon.'"*** Here the Jews repeated the accusation first stated in 8:48. On at least two other occasions, Jesus was accused of being demonized (7:20 and 10:20).

[526] **8:52. *"'He shall never taste of death.'"*** These are the words of the Jews as they were misquoting Jesus, who actually said, "He shall never *behold* [emphasis mine] death" (8:51). In 8:52, the word translated "taste" comes from *geuomai,* which can be translated "experience" but is most commonly translated "taste." The Jews were not attempting to convey anything substantially different from what Jesus actually said. The difference was a difference in emphasis. In the heat of the moment they were exaggerating Jesus' statement. "Taste of death" was stronger language than "behold death," and the Jews were using the stronger expression to emphasize what they perceived to be the *impossibility* of Jesus' promise. "8:52," *Ellicott's Commentary for English Readers, Bible Hub,* accessed January 11, 2016, http://biblehub.com/commentaries/john/8-52.htm.

[527] **8:54. *"'My Father.'"*** See note for 8:19.

57 Then the Jews said to him, "You are not yet fifty
years old, and have you seen Abraham?"
58 Jesus said to them, "I tell you the truth,[529] before
Abraham was, I am."[530]
59 Then they took up stones to cast at him,[531] but Jesus
hid himself and left the temple. He passed through the
midst of them and disappeared.[532]

---

[528] **8:56. *"'Your father Abraham rejoiced to see my day, and he saw it and was glad.'"*** In what ways did Abraham anticipate the coming of the Son of God, and how did he see that day, as Jesus suggests? Abraham experienced an encounter with the preincarnate Son of God in Genesis 18:2ff. Furthermore, in Genesis 22:18, God promised him that through his seed, all nations of the earth would be blessed. According to Galatians 3:16, Jesus was that promised seed.

[529] **8:58. *"' I tell you the truth.'"*** See the note for 8:34.

[530] **8:58. *"'I am.'"*** Jesus unmistakably refers to himself as the "I AM." The actions of the Jews that follow demonstrate that they understood Jesus as claiming to be God.

[531] **8:59. *"They took up stones to cast at him."*** Another attempt would be made to stone Jesus later in 10:31. Later in 11:8, Jesus' disciples would try to prevent him from returning to Judea due to the threats made on his life in 8:59 and 10:31.

[532] **8:59. *"He passed through the midst of them and disappeared."*** The word, *paregen* (from *parago*), translated "passed by" in the KJV, is in some contexts a way of saying that something or someone has disappeared. See also 10:39.

Chapter 9

Conflict Over Who Messiah Is (9:1 – 10:42)

The Sixth Sign: Healing of the Blind Man (9:1-12)

And as Jesus passed by, he saw a man who had
been blind from the time of his birth.
2 His disciples asked him, "Rabbi, who
sinned, this man or his parents, causing him to be born
blind?"
3 Jesus answered, "Neither this man nor his parents
have sinned. What is important here is that the works
of God should be manifested in him.[533]

---

[533] **9:3. *"'What is important here is that the works of God should be manifested in him.'"*** The KJV translates, "but that the works of God should be made manifest in him." Many assume that what is intended here is that God intentionally allowed this man to be in this condition all of these years so that on this day Jesus might work a miracle. Such an understanding is technically possible; however, there are actually a number of alternative ways to understand Jesus' response. First, no matter what injustice afflicts a person, God's purpose is always to manifest his works. Second, neither this man nor his parents had sinned; but even if they had, sin would not be able to stop what Jesus was about to do. Sin cannot stop the God of mercy and grace from manifesting his works. Third, Jesus is redirecting the focus

4 I must work the works of him that sent me while it is
day. The night is coming when no man will be able to
work.
5 As long as I am in the world, I am the light of the
world."[534]
6 When he had spoken these words, he spat on the
ground, made clay out of the spittle and anointed the
eyes of the blind man with the clay.[535]
7 And said to him, "Go, wash in the pool of Siloam"[536]
(which by translation means, "Sent"). Then he went his
way, washed and came seeing.

8 ¶ Then the neighbors and those who saw him before
when he was blind said, "Isn't this the man who sat
and begged?"
9 Some said, "He is that man."

---

away from trying to assess the cause of the affliction. What is important here is not trying to affix blame or trying to determine cause. What is important is that God's works should be manifested in the situation. The paraphrase offered in the body of the text is based on this latter understanding.

[534] **9:5.** ***"'I am the light of the world.'"*** The miracle that Jesus was about to perform was a prophetic act demonstrating that he was in fact the Light of the world (8:12).

[535] **9:6.** ***"He spat on the ground, made clay out of the spittle and anointed the eyes of the blind man with the clay."*** No explanation is given of why Jesus chose this unprecedented method of healing. Healing ministry cannot be reduced to prescribed formulas and methods.

[536] **9:7.** ***"'The pool of Siloam.'"*** The pool of Siloam was probably used in Jewish rituals for cleansing.

Others said, "He resembles him."
But he said, "I am the man."
10 Then they said to him, "How were your eyes opened?"
11 He answered and said, "A man called Jesus made clay, anointed my eyes and said to me, 'Go to the pool of Siloam and wash.' I went, and while I was washing, I received sight."
12 Then they said to him, "Where is he?"
He said, "I do not know."

13 ¶ They led the man who had been blind to the Pharisees.[537]
14 It was the Sabbath[538] when Jesus made the clay and opened his eyes.
15 Then the Pharisees also asked him how he had received his sight. He said to them, "He put clay on my eyes, I washed, and now I see."
16 Then some of the Pharisees said, "This man is not of God, because he does not keep the Sabbath."
Others said, "How can a man who is a sinner do such miracles?" There was a division among them.

---

[537] **9:13. *"Pharisees."*** The Pharisees were a sect noted for their strict observance of Jewish practices, adherence to oral laws and traditions, belief in an afterlife and the coming of Messiah. They are mentioned in 1:24; 3:1; 4:1; 7:32, 45-48; 8:3, 13; 9:13-16, 40; 11:46, 47, 57; 12:19, 42; 18:3.

[538] **9:14. *"It was the Sabbath."*** This reference to the Sabbath anticipates the fact that the Pharisees would find reason to condemn this healing that took place on the Sabbath.

17 They said to the blind man again, "What do you say
about him, seeing that he has opened your eyes?"
He said, "He is a prophet."
18 But the Jews did not believe that the man who had
been blind had actually received his sight, until they
called his parents.
19 They asked them, "Is this your son who you say was
born blind? How then does he now see?"
20 His parents answered them and said, "We know
that this is our son and that he was born blind,
21 but by what means he now sees, we do not know.
Neither do we know who has opened his eyes. He is of
age; ask him. He will speak for himself."
22 His parents spoke these words because they feared
the Jews,[539] for the Jews had already agreed that if any

---

[539] **9:22.** ***"His parents spoke these words because they feared the Jews."*** Here is a noteworthy contrast between the man and his parents. The man's parents were fearful in the presence of the Jews, but their son was bold. Both the man and his parents were witnesses to the same miracle, but it affected them differently. What made the difference? It was the man, not the parents, who had the personal encounter with Jesus; and not only had Jesus opened his physical eyes, but he was opening his spiritual eyes as well. The parents had not had a transformational personal encounter. The parents were seeing with the eyes of flesh; their son was seeing with the eyes of his spirit.

In at least five places in this Gospel, behavior was motivated out of fear of the Jews:

1. The first occurrence is in 7:13 where people were afraid to speak openly of Jesus because of their fear of the Jews.
2. The second is here in 9:22 where the parents of a man healed from blindness were afraid to testify concerning their son's healing.

man did confess that Jesus was Christ, he should be
put out of the synagogue.[540]
23 Therefore, his parents said, "He is of age; ask him."
24 Again they called the man that was blind and said to
him, "Give God the praise; we know that this man is a
sinner."
25 He answered and said, "Whether he is a sinner or
not, I do not know. But one thing I do know: I was
blind, and now I see."[541]
26 They said to him again, "What did he do to you?
How did he open your eyes?"
27 He answered, "I have told you already, and you did
not hear. Why do you want to hear it again? Do you
also want to become his disciples?"
28 Then they reviled him and said, "You are his
disciple, but we are Moses' disciples.

---

3. The third is in 12:42 where many of the chief Jewish rulers who believed in Jesus did not openly confess him "because of the Pharisees;" they feared that they might be put out of the synagogue.
4. The fourth is in 19:38 where Joseph of Arimathaea was secretive regarding his allegiance to Jesus because of his fear of the Jews.
5. The fifth is in 20:19 following Jesus' resurrection; at that time, the disciples assembled secretly behind closed doors because they feared the Jews.

[540] **9:22. *"He should be put out of the synagogue."*** The man who had been healed of blindness would be put out of the synagogue in 9:34.

[541] **9:25. *"'I was blind, and now I see.'"*** The man's words provide a model testimony—simple, yet powerful: "This is what *was*; but then I met Jesus, and now this is what *is*."

29 We know that God spoke to Moses, but as for this
man, we do not know where he came from."[542]
30 The man answered and said to them, "This is an
extraordinary[543] thing: that you do not know where he
is from, and yet he has opened my eyes.[544]
31 We know that God does not hear sinners,[545] but if
any man is a worshipper of God and does his will, God
hears that man.[546]
32 Since the world began it has not been heard that any
man has opened the eyes of a person who was born
blind.
33 If this man were not of God, he could do nothing."
34 They answered and said to him, "You were born
steeped in sin,[547] and you dare to teach us?" And they
threw him out.[548]

---

[542] **9:29.** ***"'As for this man, we do not know where he came from.'"*** For these Pharisees, their inability to determine Jesus' origin became an excuse for not accepting his authority.

[543] **9:30.** ***"'Extraordinary.'"*** The KJV translates, "marvelous."

[544] **9:30.** ***"'This is an extraordinary thing: that you do not know where he is from, and yet he has opened my eyes.'"*** The man is implying, "Isn't it obvious where he is from? How could you miss it? He has opened my eyes! Don't you get it?"

[545] **9:31.** ***"'God does not hear sinners.'"*** The reference is to those who willfully continue in sin. Psalm 66:18 says, "If I had cherished sin in my heart, the Lord would not have listened." See also Isaiah 1:15. These words do not refer to repentant sinners praying for salvation.

[546] **9:31.** ***"If any man is a worshipper of God and does his will, God hears that man."*** See Psalm 34:15.

35 Jesus heard that they had thrown the man out, and
when he had found him,[549] he said to him, "Do you
believe in the Son of God?"
36 He answered and said, "Who is he, Lord, so that I
might believe in him?"
37 Jesus said to him, "You have seen him, and it is he
that is talking with you."
38 And he said, "Lord, I believe." And he worshipped
him.[550]

39 ¶ And Jesus said, "For judgment[551] I have come into
this world, that those who do not see might see,[552] and
that those who do see might become blind."[553]

---

[547] **9:34.** ***"You were born steeped in sin."*** In contrast to 9:3 where Jesus said that the man had not sinned, here the Pharisees accused him of being "steeped in sin."

[548] **9:34.** ***"They threw him out."*** In 9:22, John notes that the Jews had already decided to put out of the synagogue anyone confessing that Jesus was the Christ.

[549] **9:35.** ***"Jesus heard that they had thrown the man out, and when he had found him…."*** The wording here suggests that when Jesus heard that the man had been thrown out, he went looking for him.

[550] **9:38.** ***"He worshipped him."*** The man recognized that Jesus was the Son of God, and he worshipped him. Jesus permitted this man's expression and did not forbid it. Scripture teaches that only God is worthy of worship (Exodus 34:14). By permitting this reverential act, Jesus confirmed that he *is* God and that he *is* worthy of worship. He came into this world as the Word—the Word who *is* God (1:1). Jesus was self-aware of his divinity.

[551] **9:39.** ***"For judgment."*** By "judgment," Jesus did not mean "condemnation," for he did not come into the world to condemn the world (3:17; 12:47; 5:45). By "judgment,' he meant that he came to issue a judicial decision and declaration regarding the condition of the human heart. As seen in the words that follow, his

> 40 Some of the Pharisees[554] who were with him heard
> these words and said to him, "Are we also blind?"
> 41 Jesus said to them, "If you were blind, you would
> have no sin.[555] But now you say, 'We see;' therefore,
> your sin remains."[556]

---

coming brought spiritual sight to the spiritually blind, and his coming revealed the spiritual blindness of those who thought themselves to be the enlightened ones.

[552] **9:39.** ***"'That those who do not see might see.'"*** Having given sight to a blind man, Jesus spoke metaphorically of granting spiritual vision to the spiritually blind. Jesus came to open the eyes of those who acknowledge that they cannot see.

[553] **9:39.** ***"'That those who do see might become blind.'"*** Jesus continued to speak metaphorically. Those who think they are spiritually enlightened apart from Jesus are actually blind. Jesus came to make such people aware of their blindness so that they too might acknowledge their need for the salvation that only Jesus can bring.

[554] **9:40.** ***"Pharisees."*** The Pharisees were a sect noted for their strict observance of Jewish practices, adherence to oral laws and traditions, belief in an afterlife and the coming of Messiah. They are mentioned in 1:24; 3:1; 4:1; 7:32, 45-48; 8:3, 13; 9:13-16, 40; 11:46-47, 57; 12:19, 42; 18:3.

[555] **9:41.** ***"'If you were blind, you would have no sin.'"*** If these Jews had no knowledge of the truth and were willing to acknowledge their ignorance, then they would not be guilty of resisting the truth. However, they could not claim ignorance. They were among the most highly trained people in the world, as far as training in Scripture was concerned, yet they would not believe upon Jesus.

[556] **9:41.** ***"'But now you say, 'We see;' therefore, your sin remains.'"*** On one hand, the Pharisees claimed to have no need for the Light—Jesus. They said, "We see," thinking they could see fine without him. In reality, they could not see at all. They were deceiving themselves, for apart from Jesus, all are blind. On the other hand, their claim, "We see," was accurate. They were highly trained in Scripture. They had been given an abundance of revelation. They could in fact "see," and yet refused to believe. Their sin was much darker than the sin of those who had never known Scripture.

CHAPTER 10

The Seventh Discourse:
The Good Shepherd (10:1-21)

I tell you the truth,[557] he who does not enter by the gate into the sheepfold but climbs up some other way, that person is a thief and a robber.[558]
2 But he who enters in by the gate is the shepherd of the sheep.[559]

---

[557] **10:1.** ***"'I tell you the truth.'"*** In Greek, these words read, "Amen, amen." It was a way of saying, "You can be certain of what I am about to tell you."

[558] **10:1.** ***"'He who does not enter by the gate into the sheepfold but climbs up some other way, that person is a thief and a robber.'"*** In light of 10:8, "he who does not enter by the gate" is possibly a reference to false Messiahs who had attempted to lead the flock of God before Jesus arrived on the scene. However, the immediate religious context suggests that Jesus was speaking of the Jewish leaders of his day. In application, these words speak of influences other than Jesus that try to infiltrate and take captive the people of God. These words are also a warning to any who attempt to influence or lead the flock secretly, away from the view of those to whom oversight of the flock has been given. In Jesus' words, such are thieves and robbers.

[559] **10:2.** ***"'He who enters in by the gate is the shepherd of the sheep.'"*** Jesus is both the "gate" and the "shepherd" (10:7, 9, 11). Applying the imagery to church leadership, unlike "he who does not enter by the gate" (10:1), the one who aligns with the shepherd-heart of Jesus will not attempt to influence the flock secretly, out of view of God's appointed leadership.

> 3 To him the gatekeeper opens, and the sheep hear his voice.[560] He calls his own sheep by name[561] and leads them out.[562]
> 4 And when he leads his own sheep out, he goes before them,[563] and the sheep follow him, for they know his voice.[564]

---

[560] **10:3.** ***"'The sheep hear his voice.'"*** A characteristic of Jesus' followers is that they will listen for his voice. Those who are truly Jesus' sheep will hear and recognize his voice. See also 10:4.

[561] **10:3.** ***"'He calls his own sheep by name.'"*** Jesus knows each of his followers by name, and he wants each one to personally hear his call. He knows them individually, and he desires a close personal relationship with all of them.

[562] **10:3.** ***"'He... leads them out.'"*** The imagery here is of a flock being led out of a confined area where they had been secure and comfortable. The shepherd leads them away from the familiar and into places that are often unfamiliar. But the sheep are safe because the shepherd is there. Outside of the familiar environment of the sheepfold there are green pastures, paths to be taken, new adventures, challenges and possibly even dangers. However, with Jesus at the lead, the sheep remain secure.

The illusion can be that it is the sheepfold that keeps the sheep safe. It is not the sheepfold that keeps the sheep safe, for even thieves and robbers can make their way into the sheepfold. The basis of security is always found in the presence of the shepherd. When the shepherd is present, the sheep are safer in the midst of dangers than they would be within the familiar sheepfold without him present.

[563] **10:4.** ***"'He goes before them.'"*** Jesus does not drive the sheep like cattle. He goes before them as their protector and with perfect knowledge of where to take the flock.

[564] **10:4.** ***"'The sheep follow him, for they know his voice.'"*** The sound of the voice of Jesus is a sound that is worthy to be followed. One of the greatest things that can be impressed upon believers is to cultivate the hearing and knowing of his voice.

5 They will not follow a stranger, but they will flee
from him, for they do not know the voice of
strangers."[565]
6 Jesus spoke this parable to them, but they did not
understand what he was telling them.
7 Then Jesus said to them again, "I tell you the truth,[566]
I am the gate of the sheep.[567]
8 All that ever came before me are thieves and robbers,
but the sheep did not hear them.
9 I am the gate; if any man enters through me, he will
be saved, go in and out, and find pasture.
10 The only reason that the thief comes is to steal, to
kill and to destroy.[568] I have come that they might have
life, and that they might have it more abundantly.[569]

---

[565] **10:5.** ***"'They do not know the voice of strangers.'"*** True disciples of Jesus do not need to be trained to recognize an enemy's voice. They only need to become deeply acquainted with the voice of Jesus. When a person knows the voice of Jesus, the voice of a false shepherd will be recognized as false.

[566] **10:7.** ***"'I tell you the truth.'"*** See the note for 10:1.

[567] **10:7.** ***"'I am the gate of the sheep.'"*** The words "I am the gate of the sheep" present the third of seven "I am" statements in this Gospel. The other six statements are found in 6:35, 48; 8:12; 10:14; 11:25; 14:6; and 15:1.

[568] **10:10.** ***"'The only reason that the thief comes is to steal, to kill and to destroy.'"*** Those who attempt to influence the flock secretly are thieves and robbers (10:1). Their workings will only result in something being robbed, something or someone being killed, or something or someone being destroyed.

[569] **10:10.** ***"'I have come that they might have life, and that they might have it more abundantly.'"*** Jesus wants his disciples to enjoy the fullness of what God intended life to be from the very beginning. That is why he came—to make sure that such an abundant life would be made available.

> 11 I am the good shepherd: the good shepherd gives
> his life for the sheep.[570]
> 12 But a hired hand is not the shepherd, and he does
> not own the sheep. When he sees the wolf coming, he
> leaves the sheep and flees;[571] and the wolf catches them
> and scatters the sheep.[572]
> 13 The hired hand flees, because he is a hired hand,
> and he does not care for the sheep.
> 14 I am the good shepherd,[573] and I know my sheep,
> and I am known by my sheep—
> 15 as the Father knows me and as I know the Father.[574]
> And I lay down my life for the sheep.[575]

---

[570] **10:11.** ***"'The good shepherd gives his life for the sheep.'"*** In these words is found the secret in God's plan for making the abundant life (10:10) a possibility: the good shepherd was going to give his life for the sheep. See also 10:15.

[571] **10:12.** ***"'When he [a hired hand] sees the wolf coming, he leaves the sheep and flees.'"*** If a leader is not devoted to the sheep, or if a leader is influencing the sheep for personal gratification or gain, when trouble arises, that person is not likely to be willing to suffer personal harm for the sake of the flock.

[572] **10:12.** ***"'When he sees the wolf coming, he [a hired hand] leaves the sheep and flees; and the wolf catches them and scatters the sheep."*** Without the presence of a true shepherd, wolves will take advantage of the opportunity to "catch" and "scatter."

[573] **10:14.** ***"'I am the good shepherd.'"*** These words present the fourth of seven "I am" statements in this Gospel. The other six statements are found in 6:35, 48; 8:12; 10:7; 11:25; 14:6; and 15:1.

[574] **10:15.** ***"'I know my sheep, and I am known by my sheep—as the Father knows me and as I know the Father.'"*** Just as Jesus and his Father enjoyed a deep intimate relationship with one another, in a similar way, Jesus' followers would enjoy a deep intimate relationship with him.

16 I have other sheep who are not of this fold;[576] I must
also bring them. They will hear my voice, and there
will be one fold[577] and one shepherd.
17 Because of this my Father[578] loves me: I lay down my
life that I might take it again.[579]
18 No man takes it from me, but I lay it down
voluntarily. I have power to lay it down, and I have
power to take it again. This command I have received
from my Father."

---

[575] **10:15. *"'I lay down my life for the sheep.'"*** See also 10:11.

[576] **10:16. *"Other sheep who are not of this fold."*** These words are a reference to those who had not yet become Jesus' followers, including the Gentiles. The church should be reminded that there are many other people of every conceivable description that Jesus so desires to bring into his flock.

[577] **10:16. *"'They will hear my voice, and there will be one fold.'"*** Both Jewish and Gentile believers would come together as one fold. Galatians 3:26-29 says, "For you are all the children of God by faith in Christ Jesus. For as many of you as have been baptized into Christ have put on Christ. There is neither Jew nor Greek, there is neither bond nor free, there is neither male nor female; for you are all one in Christ Jesus. And if you are Christ's, then you are Abraham's seed and heirs according to the promise."

[578] **10:17. *"'My Father.'"*** Jesus openly referenced God the Father as his Father, affirming his identity as the Son of God. See also 2:16; 5:17, 43; 6:32, 65; 8:19, 28, 38, 49, 54; 10:17-18, 25, 29, 30, 32, 37; 12:26-27; 14:2, 7, 12, 20-21, 23, 28; 15:1, 8, 10, 15, 23-24; 16:10; 18:11; 20:17, and 21.

[579] **10:17. *"'Because of this my Father loves me: I lay down my life that I might take it again.'"*** An alternative rendering might be as follows: "Through this my Father expresses his love: I lay down my life that I might take it again."

19 ¶ Then there was a division again among the Jews
for these sayings,
20 and many of them said, "He has a demon[580] and is
not in his right mind; why do you listen to him?"
21 Others said, "These are not the words of a man who
has a demon. Can a demon open the eyes of the blind?"

22 ¶ Then came the Feast of Dedication[581] at Jerusalem,
and it was winter.
23 And Jesus walked in the temple in Solomon's porch.
24 Then the Jews came around him and said to him,
"How long will you keep us in suspense?[582] If you are
the Christ, tell us plainly."
25 Jesus answered them, "I told you, and you did not
believe;[583] the works that I do in my Father's[584] name,
they bear witness of me.[585]

---

[580] **10:20.** ***"'He has a demon.'"*** On at least two other occasions, Jesus was accused of being demonized (7:20 and 8:48, 52).

[581] **10:22.** ***"The Feast of Dedication."*** This feast is also known as "Hanukkah" or the "Feast of the Maccabees." It was an eight day observance in commemoration of the reconsecrating of the Temple after it had been desecrated under Antiochus Epiphanes (168 BC).

[582] **10:24.** ***"'How long will you keep us in suspense?'"*** "How long will you keep lifting our soul?" approximates a literal translation.

[583] **10:25.** ***"'I told you, and you did not believe.'"*** Jesus had already said more than enough to enlighten those who would believe. Nothing more needed to be said.

[584] **10:25.** ***"'My Father's.'"*** See note for "My Father" in 10:17.

26 But you do not believe, because you are not of my
sheep, as I said to you.
27 My sheep hear my voice,[586] and I know them,[587] and
they follow me.

---

[585] **10:25.** ***"'The works that I do in my Father's name, they bear witness of me.'"*** Jesus once again indicated that his miraculous works were evidences that the Father had sent him. As Easton notes, our Lord "appealed to miracles as a conclusive proof of his divine mission (5:20, 36; 10:25, 38). "Miracle," *Dictionary.com,* accessed September 16, 2012, *Easton's 1897 Bible Dictionary.* http:// dictionary. reference.com/ browse/ miracle.

[586] **10:27.** ***"'My sheep hear my voice.'"*** God has a history of communicating with his people. Throughout history he has spoken through creation (Psalm 19:1-4; Romans 1:20), Scripture (2 Timothy 3:16), prophetic guidance (1 Corinthians 12-14), wise counsel (James 3:17), personal desires (Philippians 2:13), and even circumstantial confirmations.

The ability to hear and discern the voice of Jesus can be developed. An earnest desire to hear Him is a good place to start. Consider the story of the woman named Mary who was captivated by Jesus and sat at His feet with a yearning to hear everything He had to say (Luke 10:38-42). Jesus wants such a relationship of love and friendship with His followers. He is hoping that we will all be like Mary, who loved Him so much that she could not get enough of listening to his voice.

Our very life depends on hearing and heeding God's voice. When Jesus was tempted by the devil to turn stones into bread, Jesus said, "It is written, 'Man does not live on bread alone, but on every word that comes from the mouth of God'" (Matthew 4:4). A spiritual life cannot be sustained by natural means. A spiritual life can only be sustained by the sound of God's voice. Cultivate a hunger for this kind of bread—"every word that comes from the mouth of God." Stir up a hunger for the sound of His voice. Have an attitude that says, "I can't wait to hear the next thing that He has to say. I can't wait to take the next thing that He says, devour it, embrace it, integrate it into my life, and act upon it."

Pause and Reflect
1. How do you plan to develop your ability to hear God's voice?

Expect to hear the Lord's voice. In addition to 10:27, consider these passages that elevate the expectation that God is ready to speak to us: Isaiah 30:21, Isaiah 50:4 and John 16:13.

In Mark 4:24, Jesus taught, "Consider carefully what you hear.... With the measure you use, it will be measured to you—and even more." God will measure to us "even more" revelation, if we will come to Him with the intent to "consider carefully" whatever He has to say to us. He also wants us to consider the size of the measure we are using to receive His words. How much are we expecting to receive? If we expect a thimble-full of revelation, that is how much we will receive, plus a little more. If we expect to fill a tanker truck with revelation, that is how much we will receive, plus a good deal more.

Our ability to hear God's voice will increase when we do the following:

1. Place a high value on the sound of His voice—His Word. Refuse to live your life without that sound.
2. Listen with the intent of carefully considering whatever He says. Before you even hear His voice, make the decision: "I am going to believe whatever He says. I am going to take it to heart. I am going to obey His instructions. I am going to live by what He says." When we are faithful with a little, He will trust us with more.
3. Listen with great expectation. Approach Him with a huge measure. The Lord will meet you to the level of your expectation, and then He will do something beyond that expectation simply because He loves you and wants to.

This commentary on 10:27 is based on a chapter entitled, "Your Calling," in the author's book, *Gateway to the Christian College Experience* (Canal Winchester, Ohio: Declaration Press, 2015), 48-54.

[587] **10:27. *"'I know them.'"*** In keeping with the Hebraic concept of knowledge, these words suggest that Jesus is intimately acquainted with his followers.

2. Describe what you believe God is saying to you in this season of your life? If you do not know for sure, describe what you might hope for him to be saying.
3. The voice of God anticipates your response. Write a prayer to your heavenly Father in response to what you think he is or might be saying.

28 And I give to them eternal life,[588] and they shall
never perish. Neither shall any man pluck them out of
my hand.
29 My Father,[589] who gave them to me, is greater than
all, and no man is able to pluck them out of my Father's
hand.
30 I and my Father are one."[590]
31 Then the Jews took up stones again to stone him.[591]

---

[588] **10:28.** ***"'Eternal life.'"*** See also 3:15-16, 36; 4:14, 36; 5:24, 39; 6:27, 40, 47, 54, 68; 12:25, 50; and 17:2.

[589] **10:29.** ***"'My Father.'"*** See note for 10:17.

[590] **10:30.** ***"'I and my Father are one.'"*** Jesus claimed to be one with the Father. These words speak of his unity with the Father, but they also speak of his equality with God. In light of the violent reaction of the Jews in the next verse, it is clear that they understood Jesus as saying that he was God.

Jesus wanted the unity between believers to resemble the unity that God the Father and God the Son enjoy together. See 10:30; 11:52; 17:11, 21-23.

[591] **10:31. "The Jews took up stones again to stone him."** The Jews had previously attempted to stone Jesus in 8:59. Later in 11:8, Jesus' disciples would try to prevent him from returning to Judea due to the threats made on his life in 8:59 and 10:31.

> 32 Jesus answered them, "Many good works I have shown you from my Father; for which of those works do you stone me?"
> 33 The Jews answered him, saying, "We do not stone you for a good work, but for blasphemy; and because you, being a man, make yourself out to be God."
> 34 Jesus answered them, "Isn't it written in your law, 'I said, you are gods?'[592]
> 35 If he called them gods, unto whom the word of God came, and the scripture cannot be broken,

---

[592] **10:34.** ***"Isn't it written in your law, 'I said, you are gods?'"*** What was Jesus saying? He was referring to Psalm 82:6 where the psalmist was rebuking or confronting the judges and magistrates of the day who had not been judging justly. In that context they were referred to as "gods"—not with the intent that they be regarded as deities; rather, the word *elohim* was used in the psalm as a reference to people holding positions of very high authority. The word, *elohim,* was sometimes used of rulers who received their authority directly from God. A good example would be when God spoke to Moses in Exodus 7:1 and told him that he had been made like God to Pharaoh. In the context of Psalm 82:6, the judges were being called upon to act with impartiality because even they were accountable to the Judge of all judges.

Now consider this terminology in the context of John 10. Jesus had just claimed to be the Son of God, in 10:25-30. The Jews responded by accusing him of blasphemy. Jesus then quoted Psalm 82:6, reminding them that the Scriptures refer to some people of authority as "gods." In effect, Jesus is saying,

> You charge me with blasphemy for using the title, 'Son of God,' yet your own Scriptures apply the title, 'gods,' to mere human rulers. If human rulers can be called 'gods,' how much more appropriate it should be to call the true Son of God as the Son of God—or even God.

36 do you say of him whom the Father has sanctified
and sent into the world, 'You blaspheme,' because I
said, 'I am the Son of God'?
37 If I do not do the works of my Father,[593] do not
believe me.
38 But if I do, even though you do not believe me,
believe the works,[594] so that you may know and believe
that the Father is in me, and I in him."[595]
39 Then they sought again to take him, but he
escaped[596] out of their hand
40 and went away again beyond Jordan into the place
where John baptized at the beginning of his ministry;[597]
and there he stayed.
41 Many resorted unto him and said, "John performed
no miracles, but all things that John spoke of this man
were true."
42 And many believed on him there.

---

[593] **10:37.** ***"'My Father.'"*** See note for 10:17.

[594] **10:38.** ***"'Believe the works.'"*** The word "works" is a reference to miracles. Supernatural ministry affects the hearts and minds of people, causing them to believe upon Jesus. See 2:11, 23; 4:48, 53; 7:31; 11:15, 45, 48; 12:11; 14:11; and 20:30-31. However, some see his miracles and still do not believe. See 6:36; 7:5; and 12:37.

[595] **10:38**. ***"'Believe the works, so that you may know and believe that the Father is in me, and I in him.'"*** See the footnote on 10:25.

[596] **10:39.** ***"He escaped."*** See also 8:59.

[597] **10:40.** ***"The place where John baptized at the beginning of his ministry."*** The place was probably Bethabara (1:28). Bethabara means "house of the ford," signifying that it was commonly a place where people crossed the river.

Harmony of the Gospels			
	Matthew	**Mark**	**Luke**
Mission of the Seventy in Galilee			10:1-16
The Return of the Seventy			10:17-24
The Good Samaritan			10:25-37
Mary and Martha			10:38-42
The Model Prayer	6:9-13		11:1-4
Effectual Prayer	7:7-11		11:5-13
Blasphemous Pharisees Reproved	12:22-37	3:20-30	11:14-23
The Unclean Spirit Returning	12:43-45		11:24-28
The Sign of Jonah	12:38-42		11:29-32
The Light of the Body	5:15; 6:22-23		11:33-36
The Pharisees	23:1-39		11:37-54
What to Fear	10:26-33		12:1-12
Covetousness	6:25; 6:33		12:13-31
Watchfulness			11:32-54
Galileans that Perished			13:1-9
Woman Healed on the Sabbath			13:10-17
The Grain of Mustard Seed	13:31-32	4:30-32	13:18-19
The Leaven	13:33		13:20-21
Journey toward Jerusalem			13:22
The Narrow Gate			13:23-30
Warning against Herod			13:31-33
Prophecy against Jerusalem	23:37-39		13:34-35

	Matthew	Mark	Luke
Healing of Dropsy on the Sabbath			14:1-6
Humility and Self-Exaltation			14:7-14
Parable of the Great Supper	22:1-14		14:15-24
The Cost of Discipleship	10:37-38		14:25-35
Parables of the Lost Sheep, Lost Coin and Lost Son			15:1-32
Parable of the Shrewd Manager			16:1-15
Additional Teachings			16:16-18
The Rich Man and Lazarus			16:19-31
Offences	18:6-15		17:1-4
Faith and Merit	17:20		17:5-10
The Ten Lepers			17:11-19
The Present and Coming Kingdom			17:20-37
Parable of the Unjust Judge			18:1-8
Parable of the Pharisee and the Publican			18:9-14
Divorce	19:1-12	10:1-12	
Infants Brought to Jesus	19:13-15	10:13-16	18:15-17
The Inquiring Rich Man	19:16-26	10:17-27	18:18-27
Promises to the Disciples	19:27-30	10:28-31	18:28-30
Laborers in the Vineyard	20:1-16		
Death of Christ foretold	20:17-19	10:32-34	18:31-34
Request of James and John	20:20-28	10:35-45	

	Matthew	**Mark**	**Luke**
Blind Men at Jericho	20:29-34	10:46-52	18:35-43
Zaccheus			19:1-10
Parable of the Ten Talents	25:14-30		19:11-28

CHAPTER 11

Conflict Over His Miraculous Power (11:1 – 12:36)

The Seventh Sign: Raising of Lazarus (11:1-46)

Now a certain man was sick, named Lazarus,
of Bethany—the town of Mary and her sister
Martha.
2 (It was that Mary, who anointed the Lord with
ointment and wiped his feet with her hair,[598] whose
brother Lazarus was sick.)
3 Then his sisters sent unto him, saying, "Lord, behold,
your friend[599] is sick."
4 When Jesus heard that, he said, "This sickness is not
ending in death, but it is making way for[600] the glory of

---

[598] **11:2.** ***"It was that Mary, who anointed the Lord with ointment and wiped his feet with her hair."*** This story is told in 12:3.

[599] **11:3.** ***"Your friend."*** This expression is translated in the KJV as, "he whom thou lovest." The word here for "lovest" or "love" is *phileo*, a word that carries the idea of friendship or brotherly love.

[600] **11:4.** ***"'Making way for.'"*** These words are a paraphrase of *huper*, literally translated "for the sake of." The use of the paraphrase brings out the intended

God,[601] that the Son of God might be glorified[602]
through it."
5 Jesus loved Martha, and her sister, and Lazarus.
6 When he had heard that Lazarus was sick, Jesus
remained where he was for two days.[603]
7 After that he said to his disciples, "Let's go into Judea
again."
8 His disciples said to him, "Rabbi, recently the Jews
have sought to stone you,[604] and you are going there
again?"
9 Jesus answered, "Aren't there twelve hours in the
day?[605] If any man walks in the day, he does not
stumble, for he sees the light of this world.[606]

---

meaning that the sickness was not leading to death; rather, with Jesus present, the potential for the situation would change. That which might have previously led to death would be transformed into an opportunity for God to be glorified. It is not the sickness itself that would bring glory to God; rather, the miracle that was about to occur would bring glory to him.

601 **11:4.** ***"Glory of God."*** Here in 11:4, in 11:40 and in 2:11, the manifestation of Jesus' "glory" is associated with him working miracles.

602 **11:4.** ***"'Might be glorified.'"*** Derivatives of the word "glory" often convey the idea of esteem, honor and praise.

603 **11:6.** ***"Jesus remained where he was for two days."*** This delay would result in feelings of disappointment among others who knew and loved Lazarus. See 11:21, 32 and 37. This delay also initiated a cause and effect sequence that would take Jesus to the cross. Because of the delay, Lazarus died. Because Lazarus died, Jesus raised him back to life. Because Jesus raised him back to life, the Sanhedrin convened. As a result of the Sanhedrin convening, both Jewish and Roman authorities crucified the Son of God.

604 **11:8.** ***"'Recently the Jews have sought to stone you.'"*** See 8:59 and 10:31.

10 But if a man walks in the night, he stumbles,
because there is no light in him."[607]
11 These things he said, and after that he said to them,
"Our friend Lazarus sleeps, but I go that I may awaken
him out of sleep."
12 Then his disciples said, "Lord, if he is sleeping, he
will get well."
13 But Jesus had spoken concerning his death, yet they
thought that he was talking about resting in sleep.
14 Then Jesus said to them plainly, "Lazarus is dead.
15 And I am glad for your sakes that I was not there, so
that you may believe.[608] Let's go to him."

---

[605] **11:9. *"'Aren't there twelve hours in the day?'"*** The disciples were concerned that Jesus might be arrested and killed, if he were to return to Judea. Jesus' response suggested that such darkness could not come until its appointed time. Just as the darkness of night cannot come until the hours of daylight have been completed, so his death could not come until the completion of his appointed work.

[606] **11:9. *"'The light of this world.'"*** The reference here is to natural sunlight. Jesus uses the imagery of a man walking in natural sunlight as a metaphor to set up his contrasting reference in 11:10 to a man who walks in spiritual darkness without any light within him.

[607] **11:10. *"'If a man walks in the night, he stumbles, because there is no light in him.'"*** Without the internal illumination that Jesus brings, a person remains in spiritual darkness. If a person attempts to conduct his or her life in spiritual darkness, that person will stumble.

[608] **11:15. *"'So that you may believe.'"*** Supernatural ministry affects the hearts and minds of people, causing them to believe upon Jesus. See 2:11, 23; 4:48, 53; 7:31; 10:37-38; 11:45, 48; 12:11; 14:11; and 20:30-31. However, some see his miracles and still do not believe. See 6:36; 7:5; and 12:37.

16 Then Thomas (the one called Didymus)[609] said to his fellow disciples, "Let us also go, that we may die with him."

17 When Jesus came, he found that Lazarus had already been in the grave four days.[610]

18 Bethany was near Jerusalem, about fifteen stadia[611] away.

19 Many of the Jews came to Martha and Mary to comfort them concerning their brother.

20 As soon as Martha heard that Jesus was coming, she went and met him, but Mary sat still in the house.

21 Then Martha said to Jesus, "Lord, if you had been here, my brother would not have died.[612]

22 But I know that even now, whatever you will ask of God, he will give it to you."

---

[609] **11:16. *"Thomas (the one called Didymus)."*** Both the name Thomas (Hebrew) and the name Didymus (Greek) mean "twin." The fact that Thomas is singled out by the Greek form of his name implies that he may have been known among the Gentile recipients of this Gospel. Reference to his Greek name is also made in 20:24 and 21:2.

[610] **11:17. *"In the grave four days."*** For some Jews, it was customary for relatives to visit the grave during the first three days to see if the dead had come to life again. In this case, three days had already passed. Kaufmann Kohler, "Burial," *Jewish Encyclopedia,* accessed January 22, 2016, http:// www.jewishencyclopedia.com/ articles/ 3842-burial. At this point, there was no hope for Lazarus being revived.

[611] **11:18. *"About fifteen stadia."*** A stadia is a distance of about 600 feet. Bethany was not quite two miles from Jerusalem.

[612] **11:21. *"'Lord, if you had been here, my brother would not have died.'"*** Martha was convinced of Jesus' ability to heal. Mary would speak the same words in 11:32.

23 Jesus said to her, "Your brother will rise again."
24 Martha said to him, "I know that he will rise again
in the resurrection at the last day."[613]
25 Jesus said to her, "I am the resurrection and the
life.[614] He who believes in me, even if he dies, he will
live.[615]
26 And every person who lives and believes in me will
never die.[616] Do you believe this?"

---

[613] **11:24.** ***"'The last day.'"*** The concept of "the last day" appears in a number of places in this Gospel. Jesus referred to "the last day" as a time when he will raise to life those who have believed on him (6:39, 40, 44 and 54). Martha confessed her faith that God would raise her brother, Lazarus, from the dead on "the last day" (11:24). Finally, Jesus spoke of "the last day" as a time when those who have rejected him will be judged by the very words that they have rejected (12:48).

[614] **11:25.** ***"'I am the resurrection and the life.'"*** This line is the fifth of seven "I am" statements in this Gospel. The other six statements are found in 6:35, 48; 8:12; 10:7; 10:14; 14:6; and 15:1.

Jesus did not say, "I will be resurrected, and I will live." He did not say, "I will resurrect believers, and I will give them life," as though resurrecting and the giving of life were *services* he would provide. He said, "*I am* the resurrection and the life." Jesus is the "*I AM*" (Exodus 3:14). Jesus is God, and as God, he *is* the resurrection and the life. "Resurrection" and "life" are inseparable from the person of Jesus Christ.

[615] **11:25.** ***"'He who believes in me, even if he dies, he will live.'"*** Eternal life begins at the moment a person comes to faith in Christ. For the believer, existence is not about the fulfilling of one's appointed days upon the earth only to face an inevitable end called "death." Followers of Jesus enjoy an existence characterized by *life*. For them, the final word is never "death." For them, the final word is always "life." Believers do not live their lives in anticipation of death. Believers live their lives in anticipation of life, and if death does occur, they continue to live as they transition into a realm of more life.

27 She said to him, "Yes, Lord, I have believed that you are the Christ, the Son of God—the one who was to come into the world."
28 When she had said these things, she went away and summoned Mary her sister privately, saying, "The Teacher has come, and he calls for you."[617]
29 As soon as she heard that, she arose quickly and came unto him.
30 Jesus had not yet come into the town, but he was in that place where Martha had met him.
31 The Jews were in the house with Mary comforting her. When they saw that she rose up hastily and went out, they followed her, saying, "She is going to the grave to mourn there."
32 Then when Mary came to where Jesus was and saw him, she fell down at his feet, saying to him, "Lord, if you had been here, my brother would not have died."[618]

---

[616] **11:26.** ***"'Will never die.'"*** "Will not die in eternity" would be a more literal translation of *me apothane eis ton aiona*. Often "not... in eternity" is rendered as "never."

[617] **11:28.** ***"'He calls for you.'"*** Although the words of Jesus' call for Mary are not recorded, apparently Jesus had asked Martha to go and get Mary.

[618] **11:32.** ***"'Lord, if you had been here, my brother would not have died.'"*** Martha spoke the same words in 11:21. Mary and Martha had no doubt that Jesus was able and willing to heal. There was a settled confidence in these sisters regarding the power of Jesus' presence.

33 When Jesus saw her weeping and the Jews who
came with her also weeping, he groaned in the spirit
and was troubled.[619]
34 And he said, "Where have you placed him?" They
said to him, "Lord, come and see."
35 Jesus wept.[620]
36 Then the Jews said, "Behold how he loved him!"
37 Some of them said, "Couldn't this man who opened
the eyes of the blind have also done something to
prevent this man from dying?"
38 Then Jesus, groaning again in himself, came to the
tomb. It was a cave, and a stone was laid upon it.
39 Jesus said, "Take the stone away."[621]
Martha, the sister of him who was dead, said to him,
"Lord, by this time his body is already giving out an
odor, for he has been dead four days."[622]

---

[619] **11:33.** ***"He groaned in the spirit and was troubled."*** Verses 33, 35 and 38 provide a glimpse into the depth of Jesus' grief over the death of Lazarus. Although Jesus knew that he was about to raise Lazarus from the dead, he still felt the pain of the separation, and he was empathetic toward the broken hearts of the people around him.

[620] **11:35.** ***"Jesus wept."*** This verse is the shortest verse in the Bible.

[621] **11:39.** ***"'Take the stone away.'"*** This moment must have been unsettling to everyone who saw what was happening. Here faith took action. Jesus refused to accept the status quo. Although Jesus was empathetic toward the sorrow of his friends, and although he too felt the pain of Lazarus' death, he refused to partner with the sorrow and pain. He did not come to strike a truce with death and suffering. He came to wage war against this darkness and to triumph.

[622] **11:39.** ***"'He has been dead four days.'"*** See note for 11:17.

40 Jesus said to her, "Didn't I say to you,[623] that if you would believe, you would see the glory of God?"[624]

41 Then they took the stone away from the place where the one who had died was lying. And Jesus lifted up his eyes, and said, "Father, I thank you that you have heard me.

42 I have known that you always hear me, but because of the crowd of people standing around me, I give thanks to you,[625] that they may believe that you have sent me."

43 When he had said these things, he cried out with a loud voice, "Lazarus, come out!"[626]

44 And he who had died came out, having his feet and hands bound in burial cloths, and his face was bound about with a burial napkin. Jesus said to them, "Loose him, and let him go."

---

[623] **11:40.** ***"'Didn't I say to you.'"*** On one hand, these words and the words that follow appear to reference an undocumented previous occasion when Jesus had spoken to Martha. On the other hand, the words that follow may be a rewording of the emphasis Jesus made in 11:23-25.

[624] **11:40.** ***"'Didn't I say to you, that if you would believe, you would see the glory of God.'"*** Here in 11:40, in 11:4 and in 2:11, the manifestation of Jesus' "glory" is associated with him working miracles.

[625] **11:42.** ***"'I give thanks to you.'"*** These words are a paraphrase of "I said it"—a reference to Jesus publicly thanking the Father for having heard him in 11:41.

[626] **11:43.** ***"He cried out with a loud voice, 'Lazarus, come out!'"*** In one moment, Jesus was engaged in an intimate prayer to his Father. In the next moment, his voice thundered. He suddenly shifted from praying to shouting an authoritative command to the dead man.

45 Then many of the Jews who came to Mary and had
seen the things that Jesus did, believed in him.[627]
46 Yet some went out from them to the Pharisees[628] and
told them the things that Jesus had done.[629]

47 ¶ Then the chief priests and the Pharisees[630] gathered
the Sanhedrin, and they said, "What are we to do,
seeing that this man is performing many miraculous
signs?
48 If we allow him to continue like this, everyone will
believe in him,[631] and the Romans will come and take
away both our place and our nation."[632]

---

[627] **11:45. *"Believed in him."*** Supernatural ministry affects the hearts and minds of people, causing them to believe upon Jesus. See 2:11, 23; 4:48, 53; 7:31; 10:37-38; 11:15, 48; 12:11; 14:11; and 20:30-31. However, some see his miracles and still do not believe. See 6:36; 7:5; and 12:37.

[628] **11:46. *"Pharisees."*** The Pharisees were a sect noted for their strict observance of Jewish practices, adherence to oral laws and traditions, belief in an afterlife and the coming of Messiah. They are mentioned in 1:24; 3:1; 4:1; 7:32, 45-48; 8:3, 13; 9:13-16, 40; 11:46, 47, 57; 12:19, 42; 18:3.

[629] **11:45-46. *"Then many of the Jews... believed in him. Yet some went out from them to the Pharisees and told them the things that Jesus had done."*** The polarization of reactions to this astounding miracle is amazing. The same miracle that caused many to believe caused others to run to the authorities with accusation.

[630] **11:47. *"Pharisees."*** See note on 11:46.

[631] **11:48. *"'Everyone will believe in him.'"*** For the association between supernatural ministry and faith, see 2:11, 23; 4:48, 53; 7:31; 10:37-38; 11:15, 45; 12:11; 14:11; and 20:30-31. However, some see his miracles and still do not believe. See 6:36; 7:5; and 12:37.

49 One of them named Caiaphas, being the high priest
that same year,[633] said to them, "You know nothing at
all.
50 Neither do you consider that it is expedient for us
that one man should die for the people, so that the
whole nation does not perish."[634]
51 He did not speak this by himself, but being high
priest that year, he prophesied that Jesus should die for
that nation.[635]

---

[632] **11:48.** ***"'The Romans will come and take away both our place and our nation.'"*** As long as the people of Judea paid tribute to Rome and as long as there were no disturbances, the Jews were allowed to continue in their own way of governing and in their own traditions of worship. In the text at hand, the Sanhedrin was concerned that Jesus' rise as a leader might lead to disturbances that would give the Romans cause to intervene in unfavorable ways.

[633] **11:49.** ***"Being the high priest that same year."*** See the note for 18:13.

[634] **11:50.** ***"'It is expedient for us that one man should die for the people, so that the whole nation does not perish.'"*** See 18:14. The words that Caiaphas spoke had significance beyond his intent. He thought of this "one man" as a nuisance threatening the wellbeing of the nation. The Spirit thought of this "one man" as the Savior whose death would redeem the nation.

[635] **11:51.** ***"Being high priest that year, he prophesied that Jesus should die for that nation."*** Under the new covenant, the Spirit of God would be poured out upon all flesh. Under the old covenant, the Spirit of God came upon people holding particular offices (e.g., prophets, priests and kings) at particular times. Caiaphas was functioning as high priest under the old covenant, and because he held that office at this time, the Spirit of God was upon him, whether he recognized it or not. There is an interesting application that one might make here for those who are under the new covenant. All Spirit-filled followers of Jesus would do well to recognize that the Spirit of God is in them. Because of that fact, they should be

52 And not for the sake of that nation only, but that he
should also gather the scattered children of God[636]
together into one.[637]
53 From that day forward, they took counsel together
to put him to death.[638]
54 Then Jesus no longer walked openly among the
Jews, but he went from that place into a rural area near
the wilderness, into a city called Ephraim.[639] He stayed
there with his disciples.

55 ¶ The time for the Jews' Passover[640] was near, and
many went out from the countryside up to Jerusalem
[641]before the Passover to purify themselves.

---

especially aware of how powerful and significant their words can be, both for good and for evil.

[636] **11:52. *"The scattered children of God."*** These words would have captured the attention of John's Gentile readers. In this context, the writer views the entire human family as "the scattered children of God." Jesus came to save both Jew and Gentile.

[637] **11:52. *"Together into one."*** Jesus wanted the unity between believers to resemble the unity that God the Father and God the Son enjoy together. See 10:30; 11:52; 17:11, 21-23.

[638] **11:53. *"They took counsel together to put him to death."*** The raising of Lazarus from the dead triggered the convening of this council, and the convening of this council set into motion the sequence of events that took Jesus to the cross.

[639] **11:54. *"Ephraim."*** Ephraim was located about fifteen miles northwest of Jerusalem. By foot, it would have taken about five hours to walk from Jerusalem to Ephraim.

[640] **11:55. *"The Jews' Passover."*** John's repeated reference to the Passover highlights the significance that it held for the telling of the Gospel story. See 2:13, 23;

56 Then they looked for Jesus and said among themselves as they stood in the temple, "What do you think? Will he come to the feast or not?"
57 Both the chief priests and the Pharisees[642] had given a command, that if any man knew where he was, he should let it be known so that they might take him.

6:4; 12:1; 13:1; 18:28, 39; and 19:14. For the benefit of Gentile readers, the association of particular feasts with Jewish tradition is also made in 2:13 and 7:2.

[641] **11:55.** ***"Up to Jerusalem."*** "Up" and "down" are references to elevation and not points on the compass. See 2:12, 13; 4:49; 5:1; 6:16; 7:8, 10, 14; and 12:20.

[642] **11:57.** ***"Pharisees."*** The Pharisees were a sect noted for their strict observance of Jewish practices, adherence to oral laws and traditions, belief in an afterlife and the coming of Messiah. They are mentioned in 1:24; 3:1; 4:1; 7:32, 45-48; 8:3, 13; 9:13-16, 40; 11:46-47, 57; 12:19, 42; 18:3.

CHAPTER 12

Six days before the Passover,[643] Jesus came to Bethany,[644] the home of Lazarus—the man who had been dead and who Jesus had raised from the dead.

2 There they made him a supper,[645] and Martha served. Lazarus was one of them that sat at the table with Jesus.

3 Then Mary took a pound of pure nard ointment (very rare and costly[646]) and anointed the feet of Jesus. Then

---

[643] **12:1.** ***"Passover."*** John's repeated reference to the Passover highlights the significance that it held for the telling of the Gospel story. See 2:13, 23; 6:4; 11:55; 13:1; 18:28, 39; and 19:14.

[644] **12:1.** ***"Jesus came to Bethany."*** In light of the fact that "Jesus no longer walked openly among the Jews" (11:54), he and his disciples must have been careful to not draw attention as they walked for over five hours from Ephraim (11:54) to Bethany.

[645] **12:2.** ***"There they made him a supper."*** See the parallel account of this supper in Luke 10:38-42.

[646] **12:3.** ***"Very rare and costly."*** The value of this ointment is noted in 12:5.

she wiped off his feet with her hair, and the house was filled with the aroma of the ointment.
4 One of his disciples (Judas Iscariot, Simon's son, who would betray him) said,
5 "Why wasn't this ointment sold for three hundred denarii[647] and given to the poor?"
6 He said this, not because he cared for the poor, but because he was a thief. He had possession of the money chest, and he would take for himself what was put in it.
7 Jesus said, "Leave her alone![648] She has kept this ointment for the day of my burial.
8 You always have the poor with you, but you will not always have me with you."[649]

---

[647] **12:5. *"'Three hundred denarii.'"*** A denarius was a Roman silver coin. In light of Matthew 20:2-13, a denarius was the typical wage for a full day of work. The value of this ointment was close to one year's wages.

[648] **12:7. *"'Leave her alone!'"*** Jesus was saying, "Back off!" When this account is viewed alongside the parallel account in Luke 10:38-42, it is interesting to note that Mary was attacked twice for her devotion during Jesus' visit. First, her sister Martha accused her of being lazy—wasting time at Jesus' feet while she should have been helping to prepare and serve the meal. Second, as is seen here in chapter 12, Judas accused her of being wasteful with resources. People who become passionate and extravagant in their devotion to Jesus are often misunderstood and suffer resistance.

[649] **12:8. *"'You always have the poor with you, but you will not always have me with you.'"*** On this occasion, Mary had a narrow window of time in which she could express her love to Jesus. The time would come to minister to the poor, but this was not such a time. On one hand, we minister to Jesus by ministering to the poor (Matthew 25:31-46). On the other hand, ministering to the poor must never replace ministering to Jesus, and extravagant expressions of the heart toward him must never be condemned.

9 A vast multitude of the Jews knew that he was there.
They did not come for Jesus' sake only, but that they
might see Lazarus also, whom he had raised from the
dead.[650]

10 ¶ But the chief priests consulted that they might put
Lazarus to death also,[651]
11 because many of the Jews went away and believed
on Jesus because of him.[652]

Harmony of the Gospels			
	Matthew	**Mark**	**Luke**
The Anointing by Mary	26:6-13	14:3-9	7:36-50

[650] **12:9. *"They did not come for Jesus' sake only, but that they might see Lazarus also, whom he had raised from the dead."*** Those whose lives have been impacted by supernatural signs and wonders have the potential of becoming a living sign and wonder, drawing others to the glory of God's Son.

[651] **12:10. *"The chief priests consulted that they might put Lazarus to death also."*** The chief priests would not succeed in killing Lazarus. History reveals that Lazarus fled to Cyprus where he was eventually ordained by Paul and Barnabas as the first Bishop of Kition. He died his second death in 63 A.D. while serving in Kition, Cyprus. On his sarcophagus this inscription was made in Hebrew: "Lazarus of the four days and the friend of Christ." John Sanidopoulos, "What Happened to Lazarus After He Rose From the Dead," *Mystagogy*, April 27, 2013, accessed January 23, 2016, http:// www.johnsanidopoulos.com/ 2013/ 04/ what-happened-to-lazarus-after-he-rose.html.

[652] **12:11. *"Many of the Jews... believed on Jesus because of him."*** Supernatural ministry affects the hearts and minds of people, causing them to believe upon Jesus. See 2:11, 23; 4:48, 53; 7:31; 10:37-38; 11:15, 45, 48; 14:11; and 20:30-31. However, some see his miracles and still do not believe. See 6:36; 7:5; and 12:37.

12 ¶ On the next day,[653] many people were coming to
the feast. When they heard that Jesus was coming to
Jerusalem,
13 they took branches of palm trees,[654] went forth to
meet him, and cried, "Hosanna![655] Blessed is the King of
Israel who comes in the name of the Lord!"[656]
14 And Jesus, when he had found a young donkey, sat
on it, fulfilling the scripture that says,
15 "Do not fear, daughter of Zion. Behold, your King is
coming, sitting on a donkey's colt."[657]

---

[653] **12:12.** ***"On the next day."*** The day referenced was the Sunday before Jesus' crucifixion.

[654] **12:13.** ***"Branches of palm trees."*** In ancient times, kings and heroes of war were welcomed with the waving of palm branches. Palm branches were also placed on the road in front of them as they entered the city. The practice was like the modern day custom of rolling out the red carpet. Some believe that the palm branches were an intentional connection with the Old Testament reference to their use for the Feast of Tabernacles (Leviticus 23:40).

[655] **12:13.** ***"'Hosanna!'"*** The shout, "Hosanna!" was an Aramaic expression of joy and praise. It was originally a cry meaning "save us" (Psalm 118:25), but over time, it became a declaration of praise for anticipated deliverance or for deliverance already granted. John H. Stek, "Hosanna," *Baker's Evangelical Dictionary of Biblical Theology* (Grand Rapids, Michigan: Baker Books, 1996), accessed January 23, 2016, http:// www.biblestudytools.com/ dictionaries/ bakers- evangelical- dictionary/ hosanna.html.

[656] **12:13.** ***"'Hosanna! Blessed is the King of Israel who comes in the name of the Lord!'"*** The crowd that praised Jesus on this day fully expected that he was entering the city as their Messiah and that he had come to deliver them. This occasion was not the first time that the people wanted to make Jesus their king (6:15). The incident of Jesus raising Lazarus from the dead combined with this exaltation of Jesus as Messiah greatly accelerated his movement toward the cross.

16 At first his disciples did not understand these
things, but when Jesus was glorified, then they
remembered that these things were written about him
and that they had done these things to him.
17 Then the crowd that was with him when he called
Lazarus out of the grave and awakened him from the
dead testified[658] to what they had witnessed.
18 Because of their testimony,[659] the crowd that heard
he had done this miracle came to meet him.
19 Then the Pharisees[660] said among themselves, "Do
you see? We are accomplishing nothing! Look, the
world is following him as their leader!"[661]

---

[657] **12:15.** ***"'Do not fear, daughter of Zion. Behold, your King is coming, sitting on a donkey's colt.'"*** See Zechariah 9:9.

[658] **12:17.** ***"Testified."*** The KJV translates, "bare record." The Greek word is a form of *martyreo*, meaning "to be a witness."

[659] **12:18.** ***"Testimony."*** See 3:11, 3:32-33; 5:31, 34, 36; 8:13-14, 17; 19:35 and 21:24.

[660] **12:19.** ***"Pharisees."*** The Pharisees were a sect noted for their strict observance of Jewish practices, adherence to oral laws and traditions, belief in an afterlife and the coming of Messiah. They are mentioned in 1:24; 3:1; 4:1; 7:32, 45-48; 8:3, 13; 9:13-16, 40; 11:46-47, 57; 12:19, 42; 18:3.

[661] **12:19.** ***"'Look, the world is following him as their leader!'"*** The KJV translates, "Behold, the world is gone after him." See 3:26.

Harmony of the Gospels			
	Matthew	**Mark**	**Luke**
Jesus Enters Jerusalem	21:1-11	11:1-10	19:29-44
Jesus' Second Cleansing of the Temple	21:12-16	11:15-18	19:45-48
The Barren Fig Tree	21:17-22	11:11-14; 19-23	
Prayer and Forgiveness	6:14-15	11:24-26	
Questioning the Chief Priests	21:23-27	11:27-33	20:1-8
Parable of the Two Sons	21:28-32		
Parable of the Wicked Vineyard Tenants	21:33-46	12:1-12	20:9-18
Parable of the Wedding Garment	22:1-14		14:16-24
Taxes to Caesar	22:15-22	12:13-17	20:20-26
The Resurrection and Marriage	22:23-33	12:18-27	20:27-40
The Great Commandment	22:34-40	12:28-34	
David's Son and Lord	22:41-46	12:35-37	20:41-44
The Hypocrisy and Ambition of the Pharisees	23:1-39	12:38-40	20:45-47
The Widow's Mite		12:41-44	21:1-4
Jerusalem's Destruction and Jesus' Return Foretold	24:1-51	13:1-37	21:5-36
Parable of the Ten Virgins	25:1-13		
Parable of the Talents	25:14-30		19:11-27
The Last Judgment	25:31-46		

20 ¶ There were some Greeks among them that came
up[662] to worship at the feast.
21 They came to Philip, who was of Bethsaida of
Galilee, and asked him, saying, "Sir, we want to see
Jesus."
22 Philip came and told Andrew, and again, Andrew[663]
and Philip told Jesus.

23 ¶ Jesus answered them, saying, "The hour[664] has
come that the Son of man[665] should be glorified.[666]

---

[662] **12:20.** ***"Came up."*** "Up" and "down" are references to elevation and not points on the compass. See 2:12, 13; 4:49; 5:1; 6:16; 7:8, 10, 14; and 11:55.

[663] **12:22.** ***"Andrew."*** Andrew frequently brought people to Jesus:

1. In 1:41 he brought his brother, Simon.
2. In 6:8 he brought the boy with the loaves and fishes.
3. In the text at hand, he brought the Greeks who wanted to see Jesus.

[664] **12:23.** ***"'Hour.'"*** In this Gospel, when referring to the approaching hour or time for Jesus to face the crucifixion, John uses *hora* (2:4; 7:30; 8:20; 12:23, 27; 13:1; and 17:1) and *kairos* (7:6-8) interchangeably.

[665] **12:23.** ***"'Son of man.'"*** The expression, "son of man," brings emphasis to the humanity of Jesus. Some also consider it a Messianic reference to Daniel 7:13-14:

> In my vision at night I looked, and there before me was one like a son of man, coming with the clouds of heaven. He approached the Ancient of Days and was led into his presence. He was given authority, glory and sovereign power; all nations and peoples of every language worshiped him. His dominion is an everlasting dominion that will not pass away, and his kingdom is one that will never be destroyed.

See 1:51; 3:13-14; 5:27; 6:27, 53, 62; 8:28; 12:34 and 13:31.

[666] **12:23.** ***"'The hour has come that the Son of man should be glorified.'"*** Jesus was speaking of his death. He already knew that he was approaching death, but

24 I tell you the truth,[667] if the kernel of the grain does not fall into the ground and die, it remains alone. But if it dies, it brings forth much fruit.
25 He who loves his life will lose it, and he who hates his life in this world, will keep it for eternal life.[668]
26 If any man serves me, let him follow me. Where I am, there my servant will be also. If any man serves me, my Father[669] will honor him.
27 Now my soul is troubled, and what shall I say? Father, save me from this hour?[670] But it was for this purpose that I came to this hour.
28 Father, glorify your name!"
Then a voice came from heaven, saying, "I have both glorified it, and I will glorify it again."

---

with the approaching of these Gentiles, it was one more confirmation that the time had come for him to lay down his life. His death would be necessary, not only for the salvation of the Jews but also for the salvation of the whole world, including the Gentiles. The scene recorded in 12:20-23 is an indicator that Jesus' mission to the entire human race—Jew and Gentile—was about to become obvious.

[667] **12:24.** ***"I tell you the truth."*** The KJV translates, "Verily, verily." The Greek words here are a transliteration of the Hebrew expression, "Amen, amen." It was a way of saying, "You can be certain of what I am about to tell you."

[668] **12:25.** ***"Eternal life."*** See also 3:15-16, 36; 4:14, 36; 5:24, 39; 6:27, 40, 47, 54, 68; 10:28; 12:50; and 17:2.

[669] **12:26.** ***"My Father."*** Jesus openly referenced God the Father as his Father, affirming his identity as the Son of God. See also 2:16; 5:17, 43; 6:32, 65; 8:19, 28, 38, 49, 54; 10:17-18, 25, 29, 30, 32, 37; 12:26-27; 14:2, 7, 12, 20-21, 23, 28; 15:1, 8, 10, 15, 23-24; 16:10; 18:11; 20:17, and 21.

[670] **12:27.** ***"Hour."*** See the note for "hour" in 12:23.

29 Then the crowd of people standing there and
hearing the sound of the voice said that it thundered.
Others said, "An angel spoke to him."[671]
30 Jesus answered and said, "This voice did not come
because of me, but because of you.
31 Now is the judgment of this world. Now the prince
of this world will be cast out.[672]
32 And if I be lifted up[673] from the earth, I will draw all
men unto me."
33 He said this signifying what kind of death he was
about to die.

---

[671] **12:29. *"The crowd of people standing there and hearing the sound of the voice said that it thundered. Others said, 'An angel spoke to him.'"*** The text provides an example of how people perceive the supernatural in different ways. Some will continue to conclude that the experience can be explained naturally, and others will know that what they have experienced was indeed supernatural.

[672] **12:31. *"'Now is the judgment of this world. Now the prince of this world will be cast out.'"*** The events that were about to transpire constituted the "judgment of this world" and the casting out of "the prince of this world." "The prince of this world" was Satan. These are not just figurative expressions. Something was accomplished in the cross-death and resurrection of Jesus that was decisive and final. Through the events at hand, the "prince" was being displaced from his seat of authority. There is a mystery here that may not be completely understood, yet it should be completely embraced by faith. In fulfillment of the ancient prophecy, the serpent was about to strike the heel of the Seed of the woman, but in the process, the serpent's head would be crushed (Genesis 3:15). The Son of God was manifested for this purpose: to destroy the works of the devil (1 John 3:8).

[673] **12:32. *"'If I be lifted up.'"*** Regarding Jesus being "lifted up," also see 3:14 and 8:28. The words that follow in 12:34 suggest that the crowd understood Jesus' reference to being "lifted up" as a description of his approaching death.

34 The crowd answered him, "We have heard out of
the law that Christ remains forever. How can you say,
'The Son of man[674] must be lifted up'? Who is this Son
of man?"
35 Then Jesus said to them, "For a little while, the light
is still with you. Walk while you have the light, so that
darkness does not come upon you, for he who walks in
darkness does not know where he is going.
36 While you have light, believe in the light, so that
you may be the children of light." Jesus spoke these
things, departed and hid himself from them.

They Would Not Believe on Him (12:37-50)

37 ¶ Although he had performed so many miracles
before them, they still did not believe in him,[675]
38 that the saying of Isaiah the prophet might be
fulfilled, which he spoke, "Lord, who has believed our
report? And to whom has the arm of the Lord been
revealed?"

---

[674] **12:34.** *"'Son of man.'"* See 12:23 note.

[675] **12:37.** ***"They still did not believe in him."*** Supernatural ministry affects the hearts and minds of people, causing them to believe upon Jesus. See 2:11, 23; 4:48, 53; 7:31; 10:37-38; 11:15, 45, 48; 12:11; 14:11; and 20:30-31. However, some see his miracles and still do not believe. See 6:36; and 7:5.

39 They could not believe,[676] because again Isaiah said,
40 "He has blinded their eyes and hardened their heart,
that they might not see with their eyes nor understand
with their heart and be converted, and I should heal
them."[677]
41 These things Isaiah said when he saw his glory and
spoke of him.

---

[676] **12:39. *"They could not believe."*** The text does not say that "they *would not* believe." It says that "they *could not* believe." Why did they lack the ability to believe? The next verse provides the answer.

[677] **12:40. *"'He has blinded their eyes and hardened their heart, that they might not see with their eyes nor understand with their heart and be converted, and I should heal them.'"*** Here John quotes Isaiah 6:9-10. Without consideration of the context, it would appear that God arbitrarily decides and predetermines who will or will not believe. Not so. We must understand that these words were spoken of a people who had already been given more than enough opportunity to believe and repent. Applying Isaiah's words to the Jews who were rejecting Jesus, they were already in a hypocritical state where their hearts were not truly toward God. In fact in one place, Jesus indicated that they did not even believe Moses (5:45-47). When light and grace have been repeatedly rejected and ignored, there ultimately comes a point when God blinds the eyes and hardens the heart.

Some who are steeped in unbelief erroneously think that if they could first see or understand spiritual realities, then they would believe. Not so. Seeing is not believing; rather, believing is seeing. Believing always precedes the ability to see and understand spiritual realities. Yes, it was God who blinded their eyes and hardened their hearts, yet this same God gladly opens the eyes and softens the hearts of any who will respond to the revelation of his goodness. He will transform their lives and heal them completely, if they will only respond. He does not want anyone to perish. His desire is for everyone to come to repentance (2 Peter 3:9).

42 ¶ Nevertheless, many among the chief rulers also believed in him,[678] but because of the Pharisees[679] they did not confess him, so that they might not be put out of the synagogue,
43 for they loved the praise of men more than the praise of God.[680]

---

[678] **12:42.** ***"Nevertheless, many among the chief rulers also believed in him."*** Any who may yet think God to be something less than good because he blinds the eyes and hardens the heart of some should take a close look at these first few words of verse 42: "Nevertheless, many among the chief rulers also believed in him." Even within this group of religious leaders that had blinded eyes and hardened hearts, there were some who yet came to faith in Jesus! God is merciful.

[679] **12:42.** ***"Because of the Pharisees."*** In at least five places in this Gospel, behavior was motivated out of fear of the Jews:

1. The first occurrence is in 7:13 where people were afraid to speak openly of Jesus because of their fear of the Jews.
2. The second is in 9:22 where the parents of a man healed from blindness were afraid to testify concerning their son's healing.
3. The third is here in 12:42 where many of the chief Jewish rulers who believed in Jesus did not openly confess him "because of the Pharisees;" they feared that they might be put out of the synagogue.
4. The fourth is in 19:38 where Joseph of Arimathaea was secretive regarding his allegiance to Jesus because of his fear of the Jews.
5. The fifth is in 20:19 following Jesus' resurrection; at that time, the disciples assembled secretly behind closed doors because they feared the Jews.

The Pharisees were a sect noted for their strict observance of Jewish practices, adherence to oral laws and traditions, belief in an afterlife and the coming of Messiah. They are mentioned in 1:24; 3:1; 4:1; 7:32, 45-48; 8:3, 13; 9:13-16, 40; 11:46-47, 57; 12:19, 42; 18:3.

[680] **12:43.** ***"They loved the praise of men more than the praise of God."*** Devotion to Jesus can result in loss of social acceptance. "What will they think of me?" a

44 ¶ Jesus cried and said, "He who believes in me does
not believe in me, but in him who sent me.
45 And he who sees me sees him that sent me.
46 I have come as a light into the world so that every
person who believes in me should not remain in the
darkness.
47 If anyone ever hears my words and does not believe,
I do not judge him; for I did not come to judge the
world,[681] but I came to save the world.
48 He who rejects me and does not receive my words
has one who judges him. The word that I have spoken,
that same word will judge him in the last day.[682]
49 For I have not spoken of myself, but the Father who
sent me, he gives me direction,[683] what I should say and
what I should speak.[684]

---

person may ask. Love for "the praise of men" is in reality a fear of man, and it should never reign in the heart. Love for "the praise of men" takes on different forms. It can manifest as selfish ambition, and on the other extreme it can manifest as insecurity. The question is this: to whom does a person look to gain their sense of validation and significance? The answer to that question will reveal who is controlling that person's life. Only Jesus deserves that place in the life of a believer.

[681] **12:47.** ***"'I did not come to judge the world.'"*** See also 3:17 and 5:45.

[682] **12:48.** ***"'The last day.'"*** The concept of "the last day" appears in a number of places in this Gospel. Jesus referred to "the last day" as a time when he will raise to life those who have believed on him (6:39, 40, 44 and 54). Martha confessed her faith that God would raise her brother, Lazarus, from the dead on "the last day" (11:24). Finally, Jesus spoke of "the last day" as a time when those who have rejected him will be judged by the very words that they have rejected (12:48).

[683] **12:49.** ***"'He gives me direction.'"*** "Direction" can be translated, "commandment."

50 And I know that his direction[685] is life—eternal life.[686]
Therefore, whatever the Father says to me, that is what
I speak."[687]

Harmony of the Gospels			
	Matthew	**Mark**	**Luke**
Passover and Conspiracy	26:1-5	14:1-2	22:1-2
Judas Iscariot	26:14-16	14:10-11	22:3-6

---

[684] **12:49.** ***"'What I should say and what I should speak.'"*** In this verse, there is a slight shade of difference in meaning between "say" and "speak." A person may *say* something orally, graphically, symbolically or in writing. When a person *speaks*, he or she is specifically using vocal faculties.

[685] **12:50.** ***"'His direction.'"*** See 12:49.

[686] **12:50.** ***"'Life—eternal life.'"*** These words are an expanded translation of "life eternal." This expansion has been made to bring emphasis to the life-giving impact of the command of God as fulfilled through the works and word of Jesus, and to bring emphasis to the eternal quality of this life. For additional references to eternal life in John's Gospel, see 3:15-16, 36; 4:14, 36; 5:24, 39; 6:27, 40, 47, 54, 68; 10:28; 12:25; and 17:2.

[687] **12:50.** ***"'Whatever the Father says to me, that is what I speak.'"*** Jesus' continual practice was to align his words and actions with the words and actions of his Father. See 5:19; 8:26; 12:49-50.

Chapter 13

The Faith of the Disciples (13:1 – 17:26)

Now before the feast of the Passover,[688] when Jesus knew that his hour[689] was approaching when he would depart out of this world unto the Father, having loved his own who were in the world, he loved them unto the end.
2 Supper had ended, and the devil had now put it into
the heart of Judas Iscariot, Simon's son, to betray him.[690]

---

688 **13:1. *"Passover."*** John's repeated reference to the Passover highlights the significance that it held for the telling of the Gospel story. See 2:13, 23; 6:4; 11:55; 12:1; 18:28, 39; and 19:14.

689 **13:1. *"His hour."*** This expression is a reoccurring reference to Jesus' divinely appointed time to die. The word translated "hour" is *hora,* meaning "any definite time, point of time, moment." "*hora,*" *Thayer's Greek Lexicon, Blue Letter Bible,* accessed January 10, 2016, https:// www.blueletterbible.org/ lang/ lexicon/ lexicon.cfm?t= kjv&strongs= g5610. In this Gospel, when referring to the approaching hour or time for Jesus to face the crucifixion, John seems to use *hora* (2:4; 7:30; 8:20; 12:23, 27; 13:1; and 17:1) and *kairos* (7:6-8) interchangeably with little intended differentiation of meaning.

690 **13:2.** A literal translation would make 13:2-4 a long and awkward run-on sentence. To simplify the flow for the reader, here verse 2 has been translated as a complete sentence, yet it still qualifies that which takes place in verse 4.

3 Jesus knew that the Father had given all things into his hands, and that he had come from God and was going to God.[691]
4 Knowing these things,[692] He rose from supper, laid aside his garments, took a towel and girded himself.[693]
5 After that he poured water into a basin and began to wash the disciples' feet[694] and to wipe them with the towel that was wrapped around his waist.

---

691 **13:3.** ***"Jesus knew that the Father had given all things into his hands, and that he had come from God and was going to God."*** Jesus was fully aware of his identity and of the authority he had been given. As with 13:2, in the Greek this verse is part of a larger sentence that begins with verse 2 and ends with verse 4. To simplify the flow for the reader, verse 3 has been translated as a complete sentence, yet it still serves to qualify verse 4.

692 **13:4.** ***"Knowing these things."*** These words are not in the Greek for this verse; however, they have been inserted in this translation to support the connection of verses 2 and 3 with verse 4. This connection is clear in the Greek for verses 2 through 4.

By connecting verses 2 through 4, we see the heart of Jesus. He knew that Judas was going to betray him, yet as the following lines will show, Jesus knelt as a servant before his betrayer and washed his feet. Jesus was also fully aware of his own identity and of the authority he had been given, yet he voluntarily took on the role of a servant.

Knowing that the time had come for him to be "going to God" (13:3), he wanted to make the most of every moment. He wanted to make sure that his disciples were given the essentials that they would need before he departed. The lesson that he was teaching them by washing their feet would be essential for their life and ministry.

693 **13:4.** ***"He rose from supper, laid aside his garments, took a towel and girded himself."*** In the sight of his disciples, Jesus took the form of a servant. See Philippians 2:1-11.

6 Then he came to Simon Peter, and Peter said to him,
"Lord, you are washing my feet?"
7 Jesus answered and said to him, "You do not know
what I am doing right now, but you will know later."
8 Peter said to him, "You should never wash my
feet."[695]
Jesus answered him, "If I do not wash you, you have
no part with me."
9 Simon Peter said to him, "Lord, not only my feet, but
my hands and my head as well!"
10 Jesus said to him, "He who has already taken a bath
only needs to wash his feet; he is totally clean.[696] And
you are clean, but not all."

---

[694] **13:5.** ***"Wash the disciples' feet."*** Jesus and his disciples lived in a world where people walked everywhere they went. The roads were dusty and often dirty; consequently, the feet of pedestrians became dusty and dirty. Whatever was on the road ended up sticking to their feet. Upon entering a home, it was a welcomed blessing whenever a servant would offer to wash the feet of a visitor.

[695] **13:8.** ***"'You should never wash my feet.'"*** The washing of a guest's feet was a task for a servant. For Peter it seemed inappropriate for a man of Jesus' stature to take on the role of a servant. Jesus was not only a rabbi, but he was also the Messiah and the Lord.

[696] **13:10.** ***"'He who has already taken a bath only needs to wash his feet; he is totally clean.'"*** A person who has already taken a bath may leave his home and walk dusty roads getting his feet dirty, but that does not mean that he needs to take a bath again when he steps into the house. He only needs to have his feet washed, for it is only his feet that have been dirtied.

Likewise, the person who has been cleansed of his sins may yet walk through this fallen world and pick up some of its defilement along the way. Whether that person actually commits a sin or not, at times he may become soiled, even by the

> 11 He said this because he knew who would betray
> him; therefore, he said, "You are not all clean."
> 12 After he had washed their feet, he took his garments
> and sat down again. Then he said to them, "Do you
> know what I have done to you?
> 13 You call me Teacher and Lord, and you are right, for
> that is what I am.
> 14 If I then, your Lord and Teacher, have washed your
> feet, you also ought to wash one another's feet.
> 15 For I have given you an example, that you should
> do as I have done to you.[697]

---

sins of others. That person does not need to "get saved" all over again, but that person may need to receive the merciful cleansing of the Lord for the defiling dust of sin picked up while walking through life.

[697] **13:14-15.** ***"If I then, your Lord and Teacher, have washed your feet, you also ought to wash one another's feet. For I have given you an example, that you should do as I have done to you."*** If Jesus, their Lord, knelt before these disciples as their servant, then they should become servants one to another. This is a powerful picture of what it looks like to be a servant; however, this passage is about something more than just serving one another in a general sense. Jesus was teaching his disciples that they were to serve one another in a very specific way. With servant-hearts they were to refuse to have judgmental attitudes regarding defilements that their fellow-disciples might have picked up along the way. There was to be no place in their hearts for an attitude that would say, "Oh, look at those dirty feet! You should not have let your feet get dirty! You should have known better!" Rather, they were to look upon one another in such times with hearts of humility and mercy, and they were to minister to one another cleansing, grace, forgiveness and release.

There are times when I have washed the feet of my brothers in the Lord. On those occasions while kneeling before them and pouring water over their feet, I have spoken words something like these:

16 I tell you the truth,[698] the servant is not greater than his lord; neither is he that is sent greater than he that sent him.
17 If you know these things, you are happy, if you do them.[699]

18 ¶ "I am not talking about all of you; I know whom I have chosen. But that the Scriptures might be fulfilled, he who eats bread with me has lifted up his heel against me.[700]

My brother, I know how walking through this world can cause defiling things to stick to us—things that we do not want in our lives. I know, because it has happened to me. As I wash your feet, may you now be cleansed of such things, in Jesus' name. May all of the dust of the past be washed from your feet, so that you may walk from this day forward with none of that sticking to you.

[698] **13:16.** ***"'I tell you the truth.'"*** The KJV translates, "Verily, verily." The Greek words here are a transliteration of the Hebrew expression, "Amen, amen." It was a way of saying, "You can be certain of what I am about to tell you."

[699] **13:17.** ***"'If you know these things, you are happy, if you do them.'"*** There is happiness in obeying Jesus; there is happiness in serving others out of honor for Jesus; and there is happiness in being one of God's agents for ministering cleansing to one another in Jesus' name.

[700] **13:18.** ***"'He who eats bread with me has lifted up his heel against me.'"*** See Psalm 41:9. The idea of someone lifting a heel against Jesus may come from the imagery of a horse lifting its heel and giving a vicious kick to his master who has trusted him and fed him. E. Cobham Brewer, *Dictionary of Phrase and Fable* (n.p.: publisher, 1898), accessed March 4, 2013, http:// www.bartleby.com/ 81/ 10249.html. Albert Barnes offers another possibility, suggesting that the figure is of a runner in a race attempting to trip another. Albert Barnes, *Barnes' Notes on the New Testament* (Grand Rapids, Michigan: Kregel Publications, 1962), 330.

> 19 I am telling you this before it comes, so that when it
> happens, you may believe that I am who I am.
> 20 I tell you the truth,[701] he who receives whoever I
> send receives me, and he who receives me receives him
> that sent me."
> 21 When Jesus had said this, he was troubled in spirit,
> and testified and said, "I tell you the truth,[702] that one
> of you will betray me."
> 22 Then the disciples looked at one another, wondering
> who it was that he was talking about.
> 23 One of Jesus' disciples—the disciple whom he
> loved—was reclining in his bosom.[703]
> 24 Then Simon Peter nodded to that disciple, signaling
> that he should ask who it was that Jesus was talking
> about.

---

[701] **13:20.** ***"'I tell you the truth.'"*** See the note for 13:16.

[702] **13:21.** Ibid.

[703] **13:23.** ***"One of Jesus' disciples—the disciple whom he loved—was reclining in his bosom."*** The men were reclining at the table, leaning on their left arms with their heads toward the table. "The disciple whom he loved"—John—was reclining at the position to the right of Jesus. John's back was to Jesus, and he was leaning against Jesus' chest.

In John's Gospel, there are five direct references to a disciple whom Jesus loved (13:23; 19:26; 20:2; 21:7; and 21:20). Many scholars believe that this disciple is the Apostle John, the author of this Gospel. It is unlikely that John was elevating himself above his peers or implying that Jesus had a lesser love for the other disciples. He repeatedly referenced the love of Jesus because he had been so profoundly impacted by Jesus' love. In fact, John is now known as the Apostle of love, due to his emphasis on love found in the body of biblical literature attributed to him.

25 He then leaned back against Jesus' chest and said to
him, "Lord, who is it?"
26 Jesus answered, "It is the one to whom I will give a
morsel of bread when I have dipped it." And when he
had dipped the morsel of bread, he gave it to Judas
Iscariot, the son of Simon.[704]
27 After Judas had taken the morsel, Satan entered into
him.[705] Then Jesus said to him, "That which you do, do
quickly."
28 Yet no one at the table[706] knew why he said this to
him.
29 Because Judas had possession of the money chest,
some of them thought Jesus had said to him, "Buy the
things that we need for the feast," or that he should
give something to the poor.
30 Then, having received the morsel, he went out
immediately. It was night.

---

[704] **13:26.** ***"When he had dipped the morsel of bread, he gave it to Judas Iscariot, the son of Simon."*** The ease with which Jesus handed Judas the morsel of bread suggests that Judas was reclining in the position to the left of Jesus. Judas was reclining at the place considered to be a seat of honor.

[705] **13:27.** ***"Satan entered into him."*** Satan was able to enter into Judas only because the disciple had already opened his heart to darkness. Evidences of Judas' hypocrisy had already manifested prior to this moment (6:70-71; 12:4-6; and 13:2).

[706] **13:28.** ***"At the table."*** A more precise translation for *anakeimenon* would be "reclining at the table." In this historical and cultural context, reclining was the normal posture at the table.

31 ¶ When he had gone out, Jesus said, "Now the Son
of man[707] is glorified, and God is glorified in him.
32 If God be glorified in him, God shall also glorify him
in himself and shall immediately glorify him.
33 Little children, I will not be with you much longer.
You will look for me, and as I said to the Jews, 'You
cannot come to the place where I go.'[708] So, now I am
saying the same thing to you.
34 A new commandment I give unto you: that you love
one another. Just as I have loved you, so you are to love
one another.[709]

---

[707] **13:31.** ***"'Son of man.'"*** The expression, "son of man," brings emphasis to the humanity of Jesus. Some also consider it a Messianic reference to Daniel 7:13-14: "In my vision at night I looked, and there before me was one like a son of man, coming with the clouds of heaven. He approached the Ancient of Days and was led into his presence. He was given authority, glory and sovereign power; all nations and peoples of every language worshiped him. His dominion is an everlasting dominion that will not pass away, and his kingdom is one that will never be destroyed." See 1:51; 3:13-14; 5:27; 6:27, 53, 62; 8:28; 12:23 and 34.

[708] **13:33.** ***"'You cannot come to the place where I go.'"*** These are the words that Jesus spoke to the Jews in 7:34-36 and 8:21-22.

[709] **13:34.** ***"'A new commandment I give unto you: that you love one another. Just as I have loved you, so you are to love one another.'"*** There is a command aspect to this passage, but first notice that Jesus said, "Just as I have loved you, so you are to love one another." First, let Jesus love you! Yes, love is a command to be obeyed, but first love is an experience to be experienced. Jesus wants us to have an encounter with his love. It is not until we have personally encountered the transforming love of Jesus that we are then empowered to love one another.

There is an old commandment to love found in Leviticus 19:18, that says, "love your neighbor as yourself." That command focused on each Hebrew loving his fellow Hebrew. (It was unthinkable to consider a non-Jewish person his neighbor.)

35 In this all will know that you are my disciples, if you
have love for one another."[710]

Under this command to love, love for oneself becomes the standard by which he measures love for his fellow Hebrew. The Hebrew would desire to do unto others as he would desire others to do unto him.

Jesus shows us something new and different: a new commandment. According to the new commandment here in 13:34, we are to love one another as Jesus has loved us. Obeying this command requires us to first experience his love for us. It requires us to be observant of *the way* he loves. It requires us to sense his heart. It requires us to ask the question, "Jesus, what is your heart toward this person? What are your thoughts regarding him or her? Whatever your heart is toward this person, that is the heart that I choose to have. I choose to agree and align my heart with *your* affections." This is far greater than merely loving another person the way that we would love ourselves. This is very Jesus-centered. It actually causes us to love others more than "as yourself." So, we continually ask, "What would Jesus do? What would Jesus say? How would Jesus love?"

[710] **13:35.** ***"'In this all will know that you are my disciples, if you have love for one another.'"*** Proof of one's standing as a disciple is the subject. How will people know that we are Jesus' disciples? Will they know it through us manifesting all of the gifts of the Spirit? Will they know it through us displaying a knowledge of the scriptures that makes people think we are awesome? Will they know it through us praying so much that the toes of our shoes and the knees on our pants have holes in them? Will they know it because we pay our tithes and don't miss a single church service? Will they know it because we are vocal on all of the moral, social and political issues facing our day? Not likely. According to 13:35, "By this all men will know that you are my disciples, if you love one another." In effect, Jesus is saying,

> When you obey this command to love one another, the world will know that you are my disciples because they will recognize the pattern. When they see the way that you relate to one another, they will see me! They will look at you and say, 'Look at how that person loves! That person loves just like Jesus! That person must be one of Jesus' disciples!'

Harmony of the Gospels			
	Matthew	**Mark**	**Luke**
Seder	26:17-30	14:12-26	22:7-23
Contention			22:24-30

36 ¶ Simon Peter said to him, "Lord, where are you
going?"
Jesus answered, "Where I am going, you cannot follow me to that place now, but you will follow me afterwards."
37 Peter said to him, "Lord, why can't I follow you now? I will lay down my life for your sake."[711]
38 Jesus answered him, "Will you lay down your life for my sake? I tell you the truth, before the rooster crows, you will have renounced me three times."[712]

Harmony of the Gospels			
	Matthew	**Mark**	**Luke**
Jesus Foretells Peter's Fall	26:31-35	14:27-31	22:31-39

---

[711] **13:37. *"'I will lay down my life for your sake.'"*** Later in 21:18-19, Jesus prophesies the kind of death Peter would die. Peter would indeed be given the opportunity to follow Jesus even unto death.

[712] **13:38. *"'Before the rooster crows, you will have renounced me three times.'"*** See the fulfillment of Jesus' prophecy in 18:27.

CHAPTER 14

Do not let your heart be troubled.[713] You believe in God; believe also in me.
2 In my Father's[714] house are many rooms. If it were not so, I would have told you. I go to prepare a place for you.
3 And if I go and prepare a place for you, I will come again and receive you unto myself, that where I am, there you may be also.[715]

---

713 **14:1. *"'Do not let your heart be troubled.'"*** Without a doubt, Jesus' words in 13:38 must have troubled Peter and anyone else listening. It is fitting that in Jesus' next breath he would say, "Do not let your heart be troubled."

714 **14:2. *"'My Father's.'"*** Jesus openly referenced God the Father as his Father, affirming his identity as the Son of God. See also 2:16; 5:17, 43; 6:32, 65; 8:19, 28, 38, 49, 54; 10:17-18, 25, 29, 30, 32, 37; 12:26-27; 14:2, 7, 12, 20-21, 23, 28; 15:1, 8, 10, 15, 23-24; 16:10; 18:11; 20:17, and 21.

715 **14:2-3. *"'In my Father's house are many rooms.... I go to prepare a place for you. And if I go and prepare a place for you, I will come again and receive you unto myself, that where I am, there you may be also.'"*** These two verses begin a new stream of thought. Here Jesus speaks in terms resembling what a bridegroom would say to his bride-to-be at the time of betrothal. It was customary for the bridegroom to announce that he was going to return to his father's house to prepare a room that he and his bride would occupy after their marriage. Once the room was ready, he would come again for the bride and receive her unto himself, so that where he lived, the bride would live also.

4 And you know where I am going, and you know the
way."[716]
5 Thomas said to him, "Lord, we do not know where
you are going. How can we know the way?"
6 Jesus said to him, "I am the way, the truth[717] and the
life.[718] No man comes to the Father, if he does not come
through me.[719]
7 If you had known me, you would have also known
my Father.[720] From this point forward, you know him.
You have even seen him."
8 Philip said to him, "Lord, show us the Father, and it
will be sufficient for us."
9 Jesus said to him, "Have I been with you all this time,
and still you have not known me, Philip? He who has

---

716 **14:4. *"'You know the way.'"*** In light of 14:6, it is clear that Jesus was referring to himself as "the way."

717 **14:6. *"'Truth.'"*** See the note for "full of grace and truth" in 1:14.

718 **14:6. *"'I am the way, the truth and the life.'"*** Jesus answers the question that Thomas asked in 14:5. "I am the way, the truth and the life" is the sixth of seven "I am" statements in this Gospel. The other six statements are found in 6:35, 48; 8:12; 10:7; 10:14; 11:25; and 15:1.

719 **14:6. *"'No man comes to the Father, if he does not come through me.'"*** These words are a sober reminder that Jesus is the only way to the Father. Acts 4:12 (NIV) says, "Salvation is found in no one else, for there is no other name under heaven given to men by which we must be saved."

720 **14:7. *"'My Father.'"*** See note for "'My Father's'" in 14:2.

seen me has seen the Father.[721] How can you say then,
'Show us the Father?'
10 Do you not believe that I am in the Father and that
the Father is in me? The words that I speak to you, I do
not speak of myself, but the Father who dwells in me,
he does the works.
11 Believe me when I say that I am in the Father and
that the Father is in me; or at least believe me because
of the miracles.[722]

---

[721] **14:9.** ***"'He who has seen me has seen the Father.'"*** Jesus is not saying that he is the Father. He is the revelation of the Father.

[722] **14:11.** ***"'Believe me when I say.... Believe me because of the miracles.'"*** Jesus referenced two factors that cause people to believe in him: his words and miracles (*erga,* literally meaning, "works," but often used as a reference to miracles). *Erga,* translated "miracles," "miraculous works," or "works," is one of four words in the New Testament translated, "miracles." The word is used in 5:20, 36; 14:11; and in other places. The other three words for miracles are *semeion,* meaning a "sign," as in 2:11, 18 23; *terata,* meaning "wonders"; and *dunameis,* meaning "mighty works."

Supernatural ministry affects the hearts and minds of people, causing them to believe upon Jesus. See 2:11, 23; 4:48, 53; 7:31; 10:37-38; 11:15, 45, 48; 12:11; and 20:30-31. However, some see his miracles and still do not believe. See 6:36; 7:5; and 12:37.

12 I tell you the truth, anyone who has faith in me,[723] the works[724] that I do, he will also do.[725] And he will do even greater works than these,[726] because I go to my Father.[727]

---

723 **14:12. *"'Faith in me.'"*** Faith focuses on the person of Jesus more than it focuses on his works. His works flow out of who he *is*. Focusing on *him* is essential to stability in faith. His works from situation to situation may change; who he *is* remains constant, never changing.

724 **14:12. *"'Works.'"*** *Erga,* translated here as "works," is the same word translated as "miracles" in 14:11.

725 **14:12. *"'The works that I do, he will also do.'"*** Jesus has not only set the example as to how ministry should be conducted; he has also invited us to participate with him in his works. Doing the miraculous works that Jesus did and participating with him in what he is still doing is normative for those who have faith in him.

726 **14:12. *"'He will do even greater works than these.'"*** Did Jesus mean greater in quality or greater in quantity? A case could be made in support of both interpretations. Either way, the thought of such a thing is mind-boggling. Jesus wanted his disciples to go further than he had gone with his mission and works. As leaders in ministry paving the way for others to minister supernaturally, our desire should be for those who follow us to take whatever we have done and go much further with it. As some would say it, "May my ceiling become your floor." For a similar emphasis on "greater things," see 1:50 and its corresponding footnote.

727 **14:12. *"'Because I go to my Father.'"*** How does Jesus going to the Father cause greater works to be affected in the life of the believer? First, when Jesus returned to the Father, he sent back to the earth the promised Holy Spirit (John 16:7 and Acts 2:33). Second, because of our mystical union with Jesus, when Jesus went to the Father, we went to the Father. In fact, Ephesians 2:6 (NIV) says, "God raised us up with Christ and seated us with him in the heavenly realms in Christ Jesus."

Pause and Reflect

1. Carefully review 14:12, and consider the magnitude of the works that Jesus performed. Do you have faith in him? If so, then he promised that you would perform the same miraculous works that he did. In what ways does that thought stretch you?
2. Jesus continued, stating that believers would do even greater miracles than he did. If you are a believer, he was talking about you! How does that thought affect you?

13 And I will do[728] whatever you will ask in my name,[729] so that the Father may be glorified in the Son.[730]
14 If you shall ask anything in my name,[731] I will do it.[732]

---

[728] **14:12-13.** ***"'I will do.'"*** The words "he will do" and "I will do" stand as a reminder that the ongoing work of Christ through his people in the earth is a divine-human partnership. Supernatural ministry is both something that Jesus does and something that we do, and we do it together.

[729] **14:13.** ***"'In my name.'"*** See note for 14:14.

[730] **14:13.** ***"'I will do whatever you will ask in my name, so that the Father may be glorified in the Son.'"*** Answered prayer brings the Father glory, and in 16:24, answered prayer makes our joy complete or full.

[731] **14:14.** ***"'If you shall ask anything in my name.'"*** To do anything in the name of another person is to act as their legal representative. When Jesus' disciples pray in his name, there are three significant aspects to that action:

1. They approach God's throne on the *merit* of Jesus.
2. They exercise *authority* on behalf of Jesus.
3. They obediently respond to the *mandate* of Jesus.

The phrase "in my name" occurs in 14:13-14; 14:26; 15:16; and 16:23-24, 26.

15 ¶ "If you love me, keep my commandments.
16 And I will ask the Father, and he will give you another Comforter,[733] that he may remain with you forever—[734]
17 even the Spirit of truth,[735] whom the world cannot receive, because it does not see him; neither does it know him. But you know him, for he dwells with you,[736] and he shall be in you.[737]

---

[732] **14:13-14.** ***"'I will do whatever you will ask.... I will do it.'"*** The certainty of answered prayer is a well-established biblical doctrine. Jesus expects his disciples to expect that their prayers will be answered. See 15:7, 16; and 16:23-24.

[733] **14:16.** ***"'Another Comforter.'"*** As verse 17 will make clear, the "Comforter" is the Holy Spirit. The Holy Spirit is referred to as the *parakletos,* translated "Comforter," in 14:16, 26, 15:26 and 16:7. The words, "another Comforter," suggest that the coming Holy Spirit would be just like Jesus; he would be a Comforter just like Jesus had been a Comforter. The word translated "Comforter" is *parakletos,* meaning one who has been called to a person's side as a counselor, intercessor or helper.

[734] **14:16.** ***"'That he may remain with you forever.'"*** Jesus was about to physically depart from his disciples, and he was preparing them for his departure. Between the lines, he was assuring them that, although he was about to leave, the Comforter—the Holy Spirit who was just like him—was going to come and remain with them forever. Once the Holy Spirit has been given to a person, he does not come and go. He remains. Even if the Holy Spirit's presence is not felt, he is there.

[735] **14:17.** ***"'Truth.'"*** See the note for "full of grace and truth" in 1:14.

[736] **14:17.** ***"'You know him, for he dwells with you.'"*** These disciples already knew the Holy Spirit, for Jesus had hosted his presence all the days that he had walked with them.

[737] **14:17.** ***"'He shall be in you.'"*** Something was about to change. The Holy Spirit had been *with* the disciples as he rested upon Jesus, but he was soon to be *in* them.

18 I will not leave you as orphans; I will come to you.[738]
19 In yet a little while, the world will no longer see me,
but you will see me.[739] Because I live, you will also
live.[740]
20 In that day, you will know that I am in my Father,[741]
and you are in me, and I am in you.[742]
21 He who has my commandments and keeps them, he
is the one who loves me.[743] And he who loves me shall
be loved of my Father,[744] and I will love him and will
manifest myself to him."[745]

---

[738] **14:18.** ***"'I will come to you.'"*** The words translated "I will come to you" might more literally be translated, "I am coming toward you." It is as though Jesus were saying, "It may appear that I am leaving you all alone, but I am not. I am actually coming closer to you—closer to you than I have ever been before." Jesus comes to the believer through the agency of the Holy Spirit.

[739] **14:19.** ***"'You will see me.'"*** Jesus promised that his disciples would have spiritual vision—an ability that the world would not have. With that vision, they would continue to behold him.

[740] **14:19.** ***"'Because I live, you will also live.'"*** The life of the believer is mystically bonded to the life of Jesus.

[741] **14:20.** ***"'My Father.'"*** See note for "'My Father's'" in 14:2.

[742] **14:20.** ***"'You are in me, and I am in you.'"*** These words speak of the mystical union between Jesus and his disciples.

[743] **14:21.** ***"'He who has my commandments and keeps them, he is the one who loves me.'"*** In other words, "the person who lives by my expressed desires and instructions demonstrates that he does in fact love me."

[744] **14:21.** ***"'Shall be loved of my Father.'"*** See the note for "my Father will love him" in 14:23.

[745] **14:21.** ***"'He who loves me shall be loved of my Father, and I will love him and will manifest myself to him.'"*** Jesus makes his presence known whenever

> 22 Judas (not Iscariot) said to him, "Lord, how is it that you will manifest yourself to us and not to the world?"
> 23 Jesus answered and said to him, "If anyone loves me, he will attend carefully[746] to my word,[747] and my Father[748] will love him,[749] and we will come to him and make our home beside him.[750]
> 24 He who does not love me does not keep my words. The word that you hear is not mine, but it is the Father's who sent me.
> 25 These things I have spoken to you while I am still here with you.

---

believers express their love to him. This is the glorious experience of worship: when worshipers lift love and adoration to Jesus, he showers his love and affections down on them.

[746] **14:23.** ***"'Attend carefully.'"*** These words translated from *tereo,* are often rendered as "keep." One could have the impression that Jesus is speaking of obedience; however, his concern seems to be more with guarding, treasuring, stewarding and taking care of the message, teachings or word (*logos*). Of course, obedience would be implied and understood within the responsibility to attend carefully to the word.

[747] **14:23.** ***"'If anyone loves me, he will attend carefully to my word.'"*** Love for Jesus stirs up a desire to hold all that he taught in the highest regard.

[748] **14:23.** ***"'My Father.'"*** See note for "'My Father's'" in 14:2.

[749] **14:23.** ***"'If anyone loves me,... my Father will love him.'"*** The Father already loves everyone in the world (3:16), but when he sees someone loving his Son, his affections are especially focused upon that person. The Father loves it when we love his Son, and a love for his Son includes a devotion to his Son's teachings.

[750] **14:23.** ***"'We will come to him and make our home beside him.'"*** Love for Jesus results in close fellowship with both the Father and the Son. It's like living together in the same house with God the Father and God the Son.

26 But the Comforter,[751] who is the Holy Spirit whom
the Father will send in my name,[752] he will teach you all
things and bring to your remembrance everything I
have said to you.
27 I am releasing peace[753] to you. My peace I give to
you.[754] The peace I am giving you is not like the peace
that the world gives;[755] so do not let your heart be
troubled, neither let it be afraid.[756]

---

751 **14:26.** ***"'The Comforter.'"*** The Holy Spirit is referred to as the *parakletos*, translated "Comforter," in 14:16, 26, 15:26 and 16:7. The *parakletos* is one who has been called to a person's side as a counselor, intercessor or helper.

752 **14:26.** ***"'In my name.'"*** This expression in this context signifies that the Holy Spirit would be sent representing Jesus. The phrase "in my name" occurs in 14:13-14; 14:26 (not a reference to prayer); 15:16; and 16:23-24, 26.

753 **14:27.** ***"'Peace.'"*** The biblical concept of peace conveys the idea of completeness, prosperity and wellbeing.

754 **14:27.** ***"'My peace I give to you.'"*** The peace that Jesus carried within his being was the same peace that he released to his disciples. Following Jesus' example, believers can make a significant difference in their environment by releasing their peace to others who are around them. See Matthew 10:11-13, where Jesus speaks of peace as though it were a tangible spiritual substance that can be released to others and received back to oneself.

755 **14:27.** ***"'The peace I am giving you is not like the peace that the world gives.'"*** Considering that peace is a matter of completeness, prosperity and wellbeing, the world is very limited and imperfect in its ability to deliver these blessings. Jesus imparts these blessings fully and perfectly.

756 **14:27.** ***"'So do not let your heart be troubled, neither let it be afraid.'"*** Jesus had released peace—completeness, prosperity and wellbeing—to believers; therefore, it is irrational for them to remain in a troubled and fearful state of heart. Everyone has a choice. They can either align their hearts and minds with the reality of the peace that Jesus has imparted, or they can ignore that reality and remain in

> 28 You heard how I said to you, 'I am going away, and
> I am coming to you.'[757] If you loved me, you would
> rejoice because I said, 'I go to the Father,' for my
> Father[758] is greater than I.
> 29 Now I have told you before it happens, so that when
> it does happen, you might believe.
> 30 I will not speak with you much longer, for the
> prince of this world[759] is coming, and has nothing in
> me.[760]

---

their troubled state. Jesus exhorts those who are his to not allow their hearts to remain troubled and fearful; he has released to them the peace that annihilates fear.

Philippians 4:6-7 (NIV) says, "Do not be anxious about anything, but in every situation, by prayer and petition, with thanksgiving, present your requests to God. And the peace of God, which transcends all understanding, will guard your hearts and your minds in Christ Jesus."

[757] **14:28.** ***"'I am coming to you.'"*** The word translated "to" is *pros*, which can mean "to the advantage of," "near," "by," "toward," or "with regard to"—all of which may have implications for the verse at hand. When Jesus said, "and I am coming to you," he may not have been referring to his second coming. He may have been referring to how he would once again be present with his disciples through the sending of the Holy Spirit. Although Jesus is today seated at the right hand of the Father, and although the Holy Spirit has been sent to believers as their Comforter, Teacher, Guide and so much more, Jesus is with them as well. (See John 14:21; Matthew 28:20; 1 Corinthians 5:4.) In one sense, when Jesus said, "I am going away, and I am coming to you," both the going and the coming could be two aspects of the same thing. Jesus was going to his Father, but the very act of his going to the Father would affect the arrival of the Holy Spirit, and the Spirit would sustain the presence of Jesus in the life of the believer and the church.

[758] **14:28.** ***"'My Father.'"*** See note for "'My Father's'" in 14:2.

[759] **14:30.** ***"'The prince of this world.'"*** At the beginning of human history, it might be said that the prince of the world was Adam—the one to whom God had

31 So that the world may know that I love the Father, I
am doing what he has directed me to do. Get up. Let's
be going."

given dominion over the earth (Genesis 1:26, 28). By heeding the serpent's voice (Genesis 3:1-6), Adam made himself subservient to Satan. In this way, Adam forfeited his reign, and Satan supplanted him. Thus, Satan became the prince of this world. His place as prince of this world is seen in Matthew 4:8-9 where he offered to give to Jesus all the kingdoms of the world. The mission of Jesus was to intervene through his cross-death and resurrection, resulting in the destruction of Satan's power (Hebrews 2:14 and Colossians 2:15) and making possible man's return to a position of authority—ruling and reigning together with Jesus. See 2 Timothy 2:12; Revelation 5:10; 20:6 and 22:5.

[760] **14:30.** In Revelation 12:10, Satan is called "the accuser," but here with his approach to Jesus, the accuser would find nothing in Jesus to accuse; Satan had nothing in him.

CHAPTER 15

I am the true vine,[761] and my Father[762] is the caretaker of the vineyard.[763]
2 Every branch in me that does not bear fruit he takes away, and every branch that bears fruit, he prunes[764] it, so that it may bring forth more fruit.[765]
3 You are already pruned[766] through the word that I have spoken unto you.

---

761 **15:1.** ***"'I am the true vine.'"*** In 14:31, Jesus said, "Get up. Let's be going." In 15:1, as they were getting up and preparing to leave, Jesus continued to speak with them. Here Jesus delivered the seventh of seven "I am" statements found in this Gospel: "I am the true vine." The other six statements are found in 6:35, 48; 8:12; 10:7; 10:14; 11:25; and 14:6.

762 **15:1.** ***"'My Father.'"*** Jesus openly identified himself as God's Son. See also 2:16; 5:17, 43; 6:32, 65; 8:19, 28, 38, 49, 54; 10:17-18, 25, 29, 30, 32, 37; 12:26-27; 14:2, 7, 12, 20-21, 23, 28; 15:1, 8, 10, 15, 23-24; 16:10; 18:11; 20:17, and 21.

763 **15:1.** ***"'The caretaker of the vineyard.'"*** The KJV translates "husbandman." The Greek, *georgos,* can also be translated "tiller of the soil" or "vine dresser."

764 **15:2.** ***"'Prunes.'"*** The word translated "prunes" can also be translated "cleanses." The process of pruning a vine was thought of as a cleansing of the vine to make it more suitable for bearing fruit.

765 **15:2.** ***"'Every branch that bears fruit, he prunes it, so that it may bring forth more fruit.'"*** Bill Johnsons states, "All growth is rewarded with pruning."

4 Remain in me; I also will remain in you.[767] Just as the branch cannot bear fruit by itself, unless it stays connected in[768] the vine, neither can you, unless you remain in me.

5 I am the vine; you are the branches. He who remains in me and has me living in him,[769] that person will bear much fruit, for apart from me you can produce nothing.[770]

---

[766] **15:3.** ***"'Pruned.'"*** The word translated "pruned" is usually translated "clean." See the note for "prunes" in 15:2.

[767] **15:4.** ***"'Remain in me; I also will remain in you.'"*** These words might also be translated, "Stay with me; I also will stay with you."

[768] **15:4.** ***"'Connected in.'"*** This is a paraphrased translation. The Greek text only uses the preposition, *en*.

[769] **15:4-5.** Liberty has been taken to translate the verb, *meno*, in various ways within the two verses (i.e., "stay," "remain" and "living in") to convey what is thought to be Jesus' and the Gospel writer's intended emphasis. The message here speaks of the importance of hosting and stewarding the presence of Jesus in our lives.

[770] **15.5.** ***"'Apart from me you can produce nothing.'"*** Following this imagery of the branch's relationship to the vine, clearly a detached relationship cannot be fruitful. An intellectual assent to faith in Christ will not suffice. A relationship characterized by sporadic and hurried attempts at communication with Jesus will not do either.

Here the call is for an abiding relationship. Our very life depends on Him. We cannot live without Him. We will settle for nothing less than resting in close fellowship with Him. J. Randolph Turpin and J. D. Simmons, *Friends of God: Growing in Life's Most Essential Relationship* (New Port Richey, Florida: Life Worth Living Ministries, 2006), 8.

6 If a man does not remain in me, he is thrown out as a branch that withers away. People gather such branches, throw them into the fire, and they are burned.[771]
7 If you remain in me, and if my words[772] remain in you,[773] you shall ask whatever you have in mind,[774] and it will be done unto you.[775]

---

[771] **15:6. *"'People gather such branches, throw them into the fire, and they are burned.'"*** There is little or nothing in this context that would suggest that this lesson is about the final judgment of non-believers or backsliders. Salvation does not appear to be in view here. It seems that the message is more about issues of fruitfulness. It is a summons to the branches (believers) to tend to their relationship with the Vine (Jesus). To neglect this relationship results in spiritual withering.

[772] **15:7. *"'My words.'"*** The words of Jesus are not just the words of Jesus recorded in the Bible. Yes, his words do include all that he has ever said in the past, but additionally "my words" include all that he continues to speak into the hearts of believers—even all that he is saying right now! It may help to think of the expression, "my words" (*rhemata mou*), as meaning "my declarations" or even "the sound of my voice."

Technically, any of these expressions would be suitable for this text. However, with Jesus' preceding message in 15:1-5 regarding the vital living connection between Jesus and his disciples, the living aspect of the relationship is probably best retained in the expression, "the sound of my voice." The word *rhema* speaks of that which has been uttered by a living voice. It can be any sound produced by the voice that conveys a definite meaning.

[773] **15:7. *"'If you remain in me, and if my words remain in you.'"*** A good paraphrase of these words might be, "If you have settled in and made your home in me, and if the sound of my voice has found a home inside of you,..."

[774] **15:7. *"'Whatever you have in mind.'"*** These words can also be translated, "whatever you want" or "whatever you desire."

8 In this my Father[776] is glorified,[777] in order that you may bring forth much fruit and appear on the stage of history[778] as my disciples.[779]

---

[775] **15:7. *"'It will be done unto you.'"*** This translation is actually weak. However, bringing out the meaning in its original strength reads awkwardly in translation. The expression, *genesetai humin,* is actually conveying, "It shall come into existence to you." It could almost be translated, "It will be created for you," for the language is the same as that used in 1:3 that says, "All things *came into being* through him, and apart from him not even one thing *came into existence* that has *come to be*" [emphasis mine]. The message here is that through prayer, God causes desires and thoughts to become *fulfilled* desires and thoughts, coming into actual existence in the realm in which we live. That which was imagined becomes real through prayer.

Some have erroneously said, "God promises to meet our needs, not our wants." That is not so, for this passage clearly says that God will certainly grant whatever we want or have in mind when we pray. This truth is amplified in the next verse.

The certainty of answered prayer is a well-established biblical doctrine. See 14:13-14; 15:16; and 16:23-24.

[776] **15:8. *"'My Father.'"*** See note for "'My Father'" in 15:1.

[777] **15:8. *"'In this my Father is glorified.'"*** "This" in the phrase refers back to 15:7. Although our Father delights in meeting our needs, it is not prayer for needs that is in view in 15:7. The focus is on praying desires, thoughts, ideas and dreams. The Father is especially glorified when we pray our desires, our thoughts, our ideas and our dreams, for those are the things that we carry close to the heart. When we bring those things to him, we are bringing our hearts to him, and that is what he is really after. He so desires heart-to-heart fellowship with us. He also desires to partner with us in the innovations conceived in our sanctified imaginations.

[778] **15:8. *"'Appear on the stage of history.'"*** This line is an expanded translation, based on *genesesthe* as it could be understood in this context. It may also be translated, "publicly arise." According to *Thayer's Lexicon,* the root word, *ginomai,* can in some contexts mean, "to arise," "to appear in public," "to appear in history," or "to come upon the stage."

9 As the Father has loved me, so I have loved you; [780]
continue[781] in my love.
10 If you keep my commandments, you will continue
in my love, just as I have kept my Father's[782]
commandments and continue in his love.[783]

---

[779] **15:1-8.** Consider this powerful stream of thought. Through placing a high value on the presence of Jesus and the sound of his voice (15:1-6), we become very fruitful. One of the main ways that we manifest this fruit is through praying for the things that are on our minds and the things that are burning in our hearts. Jesus promises that when we pray in the realm of our desires, those things that we desire will become reality (15:7). This is the kind of fruit that the Father wants to see! It brings him glory! It causes us to take our place on the stage of history; we become history makers! When we dare to pray within the realm of our dreams, it is then that we shine forth as disciples unto Christ (15:8)!

[780] **15:9.** ***"'As the Father has loved me, so I have loved you.'"*** Jesus loved his disciples to the same degree and in the same way that his Father loved him.

[781] **15:9.** ***"'Continue.'"*** This word is the same one translated "remain," "stay" and "living in" earlier in the chapter.

[782] **15:10.** ***"'My Father's.'"*** See note for "'My Father'" in 15:1.

[783] **15:10.** ***"'If you keep my commandments, you will continue in my love, just as I have kept my Father's commandments and continue in his love.'"*** This love does have a strong emotional quality to it, but it is also more than emotion. There is an implied covenantal relationship. There are responsibilities that accompany this love, and there is a deep desire on the part of the believer to be aligned with the heart, will and desire of Jesus—the object of the heart's affections.

11 These things I have spoken to you that my joy might remain in you and that your joy may abound.[784]
12 This is my commandment, that you love one another as I have loved you.
13 No man has greater love than this: that a man lay down his life for his friends.
14 You are my friends, if you do whatever I command you.[785]

---

[784] **15:11.** ***"'These things I have spoken to you that my joy might remain in you and that your joy may abound.'"*** Sustained overflowing joy is found in the life of the believer who has a heart and mind aligned with the will and desire of Jesus. The evidence of that alignment is an eagerness to adhere to Jesus' teachings, listen for his voice and follow his instructions. The fruit of such alignment and corresponding conduct is a sustained life of overflowing joy.

[785] **15:12-14.** The need and desire to have the almighty and merciful God as one's friend may be apparent; however, the thought that he would look to mortals who are prone to fail and yet call them friends is almost inconceivable. He called his disciples his friends.

The concept of friendship with God may initially cause one to think of benefits that the believer enjoys from this relationship; certainly he is favorably disposed toward his friends. However, the text at hand presents an aspect of this friendship that pertains more to the responsibilities that are upon the friend. A person demonstrates that he or she is one of Jesus' friends by doing what he commands. His specific command in this context is to love others as he has loved us, and he describes his love for us in these words: " No man has greater love than this: that a man lay down his life for his friends" (15:13). The idea is that when a person lays down his or her life for a friend, that person loves the way Jesus loved, and when a person loves the way Jesus loved, he or she is obeying the command of Jesus. Those who obey this command are known as his "friends." In short, we demonstrate that we are Jesus' friends by laying down our lives for our own friends.

The expression "lay down his life" does mean the surrender of a person's life unto death, but it can also figuratively mean the voluntary laying down of all that makes up one's life for the sake of preferring another person. It can mean laying down all rights to our time, talent, treasure and convenience for the sake of others. For instance, when I am laying down my life for someone, it is more important to me for that other person to eat than it is for me to eat. It is more important to me for that person to have shelter than it is for me to have shelter. It is more important to me for that person to be clothed than it is for me to be clothed.

In John 15, Jesus spoke of laying down our lives for our friends. Who are our friends? Our friends are those people with whom we have the closest relationships. Friends might even include our wives, husbands, children, fathers, mothers, brothers and sisters. Certainly in other places the Lord speaks of us loving our enemies and loving our neighbor, but here he speaks of love toward our friends.

Initially one might think, "Oh, that should be easy. I would do anything for my friends." However, the truth of the matter is that the people we usually neglect the most are those people who are the closest to us. We tend to take those people for granted. We procrastinate in our care for them and say, "Oh, they will be around tomorrow; I can do this deed of kindness for them another time." Or we might say, "I would do this deed of kindness for my friend, but right now I don't have time. That's okay because this is my friend, and my friend will understand, if I cannot get to his need right away." Can you see how your friends can easily be neglected?

Here is the point: prefer your friends above yourself in everything, and in so doing you will demonstrate that you are Jesus' friend. It works something like this: Jesus sees you treating your friend better than you would treat yourself, and he looks at you and says to his Father,

> Father, look at how my disciple is treating his friend. That is exactly the way I would treat that person. I like what I am seeing! I am attracted to that! I like to be around people who act that way! That disciple is truly my friend! I can even entrust my bride to the care of this disciple.

J. Randolph Turpin and J. D. Simmons, *Friends of the Bridegroom: Partnering with Christ in His Devotion to the Church* (New Port Richey, Florida: Life Worth Living Ministries, 2006), 24-26.

15 From this point forward, I do not call you servants, for the servant does not know what his lord does. But I have called you friends,[786] for all things that I have heard from my Father[787] I have made known to you.[788]
16 You have not chosen me, but I have chosen you and have established[789] you, that you should go and bear

---

[786] **15:15.** ***"'I have called you friends.'"*** A friend is someone to whom stewardship can be entrusted. In Jewish culture, a bridegroom would entrust the care for his bride-to-be to friends who would watch over her and provide for her until his return to take her as his bride. Jesus had this imagery in mind as he was preparing to entrust his bride—the church—to the watchful care of his disciples.

[787] **15:15.** ***"'All things I have heard from my Father'"*** The word, *para,* translated here as "from," can also be translated "by" or "near." Here Jesus speaks of all things that he has heard while being near—in close fellowship with—his Father.

"'My Father.'" See note for "'My Father'" in 15:1.

[788] **15:15.** ***"'I do not call you servants, for the servant does not know what his lord does. But I have called you friends, for all things that I have heard from my Father I have made known to you.'"*** Servants relate to Jesus on the basis of what they are told to do. Serving will always be an aspect of the Christian life; however, Jesus does not view us in a utilitarian manner—as people whose primary purpose is to do things for him. We are not just employees or errand boys. We are his friends.

Jesus describes friends as those who respond to him on the basis of revelation: what he hears from the Father, he makes known to them. He entrusts his heart to them. The life and mission of these disciples would not be dictated by a task list; they would be guided and motivated out of their heart-to-heart fellowship and friendship with Jesus.

[789] **15:16.** ***"'Established.'"*** This word carries the idea of setting something or someone in place. It can also be translated "appointed."

fruit, and that your fruit should remain,[790] so that
whatever you shall ask of the Father in my name,[791] he
may give it to you.[792]
17 These things I command you, that you love one
another.
18 If the world hates you, you know that it hated me
before it hated you.
19 If you were of the world, the world would love its
own. But you are not of the world; rather, I have
chosen you out of the world. Because of this, the world
hates you.
20 Remember the word that I said to you, 'The servant
is not greater than his lord.'[793] If they have persecuted
me, they will also persecute you. If they have kept my
saying, they will also keep yours.

---

[790] **15:16.** ***"'I have chosen you and have established you, that you should go and bear fruit, and that your fruit should remain.'"*** Jesus intends for our impact and influence upon the world to be of lasting significance.

[791] **15:16.** ***"'So that whatever you shall ask of the Father in my name.'"*** To act in the name of another is to act as their legal representative. When Jesus' disciples pray in his name, there are three significant aspects to that action:

1. They approach God's throne on the *merit* of Jesus.
2. They exercise *authority* on behalf of Jesus.
3. They obediently respond to the *mandate* of Jesus.

The phrase "in my name" occurs in 14:13-14; 14:26; 15:16; and 16:23-24, 26.

[792] **15:16.** ***"'So that whatever you shall ask of the Father in my name, he may give it to you.'"*** The certainty of answered prayer is a well-established biblical doctrine. See 14:13-14; 15:7; and 16:23-24.

[793] **15:20.** ***"'The servant is not greater than his lord.'"*** See also in 13:16.

21 But they will do all these things to you because of
my name, seeing that they do not know the one who
sent me.
22 If I had not come and spoken to them, they would
not be guilty of sin; but now they have no excuse for
their sin.
23 He who hates me hates my Father[794] also.
24 If I had not done among them the works which no
other man had ever done, they would not have had sin;
but now they have both seen and hated both me and
my Father.
25 But this is happening, that the word might be
fulfilled that is written in their law, 'They hated me
without a cause.'
26 But when the Comforter[795] has come, whom I will
send to you from the Father, even the Spirit of truth
who proceeds from the Father, he will testify of me.[796]
27 And you also will testify of me,[797] because you have
been with me from the beginning.

---

[794] **15:23.** ***"'My Father.'"*** See note for "'My Father'" in 15:1.

[795] **15:26.** ***"'Comforter.'"*** The Holy Spirit is identified as the *parakletos*, translated "Comforter," in 14:16, 26, 15:26 and 16:7. The *parakletos* is one who has been called to a person's side as a counselor, intercessor or helper.

[796] **15:26.** ***"'Even the Spirit of truth who proceeds from the Father, he will testify of me.'"*** Pentecostals and Charismatics are sometimes accused of giving too much attention to the Holy Spirit and not enough to Jesus. It is *always* appropriate to acknowledge the Holy Spirit, for he *always* testifies of Jesus.

[797] **15:27.** ***"'And you also will testify of me.'"*** When we testify of Jesus, we align with what the Holy Spirit is already doing.

CHAPTER 16

These things I have spoken to you, that you should not be offended.

2 They will put you out of the synagogues. Yes, the time is coming when whoever kills you will think that he is offering to God a sacred service.[798]

3 These things they will do to you, because they have not known the Father or me.

4 But these things I have told you, so that when the time shall come, you may remember that I told you about them. I did not tell you these things at the beginning, because I was with you.

5 But now I go my way to him who sent me, and none of you are asking me, "Where are you going?"

6 But because I have said these things to you, sorrow has filled your heart.

7 Nevertheless, I tell you the truth, it is expedient for you that I go away, for if I do not go away, the

---

[798] **16:2. *"'Sacred service.'"*** The word, *latreia,* translated here as "sacred service," was often used in reference to the service and worship of God according to the requirements of the Levitical law. Jesus' words suggest that a time was coming when the killing of his followers would be viewed as a fulfillment of law or as an act of service with which God would be pleased.

Comforter[799] will not come to you. But if I depart, I will
send him to you.[800]
8 When he has come, he will convince[801] the world of
sin, and of righteousness, and of judgment.[802]
9 Of sin, because they do not believe in me;[803]
10 Of righteousness, because I am going to my
Father,[804] and you will no longer see me;[805]

---

799 **16:7. *"'Comforter.'"*** The Holy Spirit is referred to as the *parakletos,* translated "Comforter," in 14:16, 26, 15:26 and 16:7. The *parakletos* is one who has been called to a person's side as a counselor, intercessor or helper.

800 **16:7. *"'I will send him to you.'"*** See Acts 2:33.

801 **16:8. *"'Convince.'"*** The word can also be translated "reprove" or "convict." It carries the idea of bringing something to light or exposing a matter.

802 **16:8. *"'He will convince the world of sin, and of righteousness, and of judgment."*** These words summarize what the Holy Spirit does when he moves upon the human heart. Jesus offered further explanation in the next three verses (16:9-11).

803 **16:9. *"'Of sin, because they do not believe in me.'"*** The word "sin" (*hamartia*) means "to miss the mark." When the Holy Spirit moves upon human hearts, he works to convince people who have not yet believed in Jesus that they are off of the mark. Their lives are not rightly centered. The loving work of the Spirit is to draw people to a place where they will allow their lives to become centered on Jesus.

804 **16:10. *"'My Father.'"*** Jesus openly referenced God the Father as his Father, affirming his identity as the Son of God. See also 2:16; 5:17, 43; 6:32, 65; 8:19, 28, 38, 49, 54; 10:17-18, 25, 29, 30, 32, 37; 12:26-27; 14:2, 7, 12, 20-21, 23, 28; 15:1, 8, 10, 15, 23-24; 18:11; 20:17, and 21.

805 **16:10. *"'Of righteousness, because I am going to my Father, and you will no longer see me.'"*** Jesus was going to shortly leave the earth. After his departure, the only way to behold him would be through the revelation of the Holy Spirit. With natural eyes, all that most people could see was a Jewish rabbi. However, after

11 Of judgment, because the prince of this world is judged.[806]
12 I still have many things to say to you, but you cannot bear them now.[807]
13 Yet when he, the Spirit of truth,[808] has come, he will guide you into all the truth,[809] for he will not speak of

---

Jesus' departure, he would send the Spirit, and through the Spirit, the world would behold and become convinced of the righteousness of God revealed through Jesus. Furthermore, they would become convinced through the Spirit's revelation of the marvelous fact that all who place their faith in Jesus become righteous in him.

[806] **16:11.** ***"'Of judgment, because the prince of this world is judged.'"*** The judgment in view here is not the judgment of people. It is the judgment of Satan—the prince of this world. The Holy Spirit would bring the revelation that Christ's redemptive work and his victory over Satan is complete.

[807] **16:12.** ***"'You cannot bear them now.'"*** Emotionally the disciples would not have been able to handle everything that Jesus wanted to say to them; it would have been an overload of words. They were preoccupied with their own sorrow (16:6). Furthermore, they needed further empowerment and development before they could bear the weight of the things he wanted to reveal to them.

[808] **16:13.** ***"'Truth.'"*** See the note for "full of grace and truth" in 1:14.

[809] **16:13.** ***"'He will guide you into all the truth.'"*** Given the context of what Jesus just said in 16:12, "I still have many things to say to you, but you cannot bear them now," the words, "all the truth," refer to the fullness of the "many things" that Jesus yet desired to reveal to his disciples. Jesus' guidance would continue beyond his days of physically walking the earth. He would continue to guide them through the agency of the Holy Spirit. The Holy Spirit would point the way, just as Jesus had done.

How does the Holy Spirit guide the believer into all the truth? He enables spiritual understanding, and he illuminates biblical teaching (1 Corinthians 2:6-16). He gives wisdom, understanding and revelation (Colossians 1:9 and Ephesians 1:17). He communicates through the revelatory manifestations gifts, such as the

> himself; but whatever he shall hear, that shall he speak,[810] and he will show you things to come.[811]
> 14 He will glorify me, seeing that he will take out of mine[812] and will make it known[813] to you.
> 15 Everything that the Father has belongs to me; that is why I said that he will take out of mine[814] and will make it known to you.[815]

---

word of wisdom, the word of knowledge, the discerning of spirits, prophecy, tongues and interpretation of tongues (1 Corinthians 12:8-10). He speaks through visions and dreams (Acts 2:17).

In another sense, "He will guide you into all the truth," could mean, "The Spirit will guide you into the fullness of truth—the fullness of truth as found in me! I am the truth! (14:6) The Spirit will help you to see that through me is the most perfect and complete perception of reality."

"'Truth.'" See the note for "full of grace and truth" in 1:14.

[810] **16:13.** ***"'Whatever he shall hear, that shall he speak.'"*** Just as Jesus did not speak of himself (14:10), neither would the Holy Spirit speak of himself. The Son of God was God, yet he functioned subordinate to God the Father, speaking only what he heard from the Father (12:49). Likewise, the Holy Spirit is God, yet he functions subordinate to God the Father, speaking "whatever he shall hear."

[811] **16:13.** ***"'He will show you things to come.'"*** One fulfillment of this promise is found in the giving of the prophetic gift noted in 1 Corinthians 12:10.

[812] **16:14.** ***"'He will take out of mine.'"*** "Of mine" is defined in the next verse, 16:15.

[813] **16:14.** ***"'Will make it known.'"*** These words are a translation of a verb derived from *anaggelio*, a word meaning "to announce," "to report," "to bring back news" or "to make known."

[814] **16:15.** ***"'He will take out of mine.'"*** What did Jesus mean by "mine"? What is it that belonged to Jesus? The preceding words answer the question. Everything that the Father has belongs to Jesus.

16 A little while, and you will not see me.[816] And again,
a little while, and you will see me,[817] because I go to the
Father."[818]
17 Then some of his disciples said among themselves,
"What is this that he said to us, 'A little while, and you
will not see me,' and again, 'A little while, and you will
see me,' and, 'Because I go to the Father?'"
18 Then they said, "What is this that he said, 'A little
while?' We do not know what he is saying."
19 Then Jesus knew that they wanted to ask him, and
said to them, "Do you inquire among yourselves of
that I said, 'A little while, and you will not see me,' and
again, 'A little while, and you will see me'?

---

815 **16:15.** ***"'He will take out of mine and will make it known to you.'"*** When 16:14 and 16:15 are viewed together, this message emerges: "The Spirit will take out of everything that the Father has and will make it known to you."

816 **16:16.** ***"'A little while, and you will not see me.'"*** These words foreshadow Jesus' approaching death. Very soon Jesus would be taken from his disciples and would die.

817 **16:16.** ***"'A little while, and you will see me.'"*** These words apparently foreshadow Jesus' resurrection that would follow his death. This understanding of Jesus' words seems to be reinforced by 16:20-22. However, the words that follow, "because I go to the Father," may suggest more.

818 **16:16.** ***"'A little while, and you will not see me. And again, a little while, and you will see me, because I go to the Father.'"*** In 16:29, Jesus' disciples classified these words as "veiled language."

The words, "'A little while, and you will see me, because I go to the Father,'" may suggest that Jesus' disciples would receive revelation of God's Son through the Spirit that he would send after his ascension to the Father.

20 I tell you the truth,[819] you will weep and mourn, but the world will rejoice. You will be sorrowful, but your sorrow will be turned into joy.[820]
21 A woman in labor has sorrow, seeing that her hour has come, but as soon as she has delivered the child, she no longer remembers the anguish, for joy that a child[821] has been born into the world.[822]
22 Indeed, you are sorrowful now, but I will see you again, and your heart will rejoice, and no one is taking your joy from you.[823]

---

819 **16:20. *"'I tell you the truth.'"*** The KJV translates, "Verily, verily." The Greek words here are a transliteration of the Hebrew expression, "Amen, amen." It was a way of saying, "You can be certain of what I am about to tell you."

820 **16:20. *"'Your sorrow will be turned into joy.'"*** Jesus was going to die. His disciples would "weep and mourn." At the same time, the world would "rejoice" over the death of God's Son. However, Jesus would not remain in the realm of death. He would rise victorious over death. His disciples would be reunited with him, and in this reunion, their sorrow would be turned into joy. Such joy is rooted in being *with* Jesus—being in his presence. When believers experience the presence of this victorious One, hope overtakes them, and their sorrows turn into joy.

821 **16:21. *"'Child.'"*** The word translated "child" is actually *anthropos,* a word meaning "man" or "human."

822 **16:21. *"'For joy that a child has been born into the world.'"*** This theme of anticipated joy in the context of an approaching death resonates with the words of Hebrews 12:2 (NIV) that read, "For the joy set before him he endured the cross…."

823 **16:22. *"'No one is taking your joy from you.'"*** People may affect our circumstances, but they cannot take our joy. The quality of joy is affected by the quality of our relationship with Jesus. In his presence, there is fullness of joy (Psalm 16:11).

23 In that day you will ask me for nothing. I tell you
the truth,[824] whatever you will ask the Father in my
name,[825] he will give it to you.[826]
24 Up to this time you have asked nothing in my
name.[827] Ask, and you will receive, that your joy may
be full.[828]

Pause and Reflect

1. Carefully review 16:23-24, and consider to what degree you actually believe these promises pertaining to prayer.
2. Describe how your life would change, if you were to take Jesus' words in this passage seriously.

---

[824] **16:23.** ***"'I tell you the truth.'"*** See the note for 16:20.

[825] **16:23.** ***"'In my name.'"*** To do anything in the name of another person is to act as their legal representative. When Jesus' disciples pray in his name, there are three significant aspects to that action:

1. They approach God's throne on the *merit* of Jesus.
2. They exercise *authority* on behalf of Jesus.
3. They obediently respond to the *mandate* of Jesus.

The phrase "in my name" occurs in 14:13-14; 14:26 (not a reference to prayer); 15:16; and 16:23-24, 26.

[826] **16:23.** ***"In that day you will ask me for nothing. I tell you the truth, whatever you will ask the Father in my name, he will give it to you."*** The death and resurrection of Jesus was going to result in a change of access to the Father.

[827] **16:24.** ***"'In my name.'"*** See the note for 16:23.

[828] **16:24.** ***"'Ask, and you will receive, that your joy may be full.'"*** Answered prayer makes our joy complete or full, and in 14:13, answered prayer brings glory to the Father. The certainty of answered prayer is a well-established biblical doctrine. See 14:13-14 and 15:7, 16.

25 These things I have spoken to you in veiled
language, but the time is coming, when I will no longer
speak to you in veiled language, but I will plainly tell
you about the Father.
26 At that day you will ask in my name,[829] and I am not
saying to you that I will pray to the Father for you,
27 for the Father himself loves you, because you have
loved me and have believed that I came from God.[830]
28 I came forth from the Father and have come into the
world. Again, I am leaving the world, and I am going
to the Father."[831]
29 His disciples said to him, "Behold, now you are
speaking plainly, and you are not speaking with veiled
language.[832]
30 Now we are sure[833] that you know all things and do
not need that anyone should ask you. In this we believe
that you came forth from God."

---

[829] **16:26.** ***"'In my name.'"*** See the note for 16:23.

[830] **16:27.** ***"'I came from God.'"*** These words might also mean, "I came out from my place beside God."

[831] **16:28.** ***"'I am leaving the world, and I am going to the Father.'"*** Here Jesus referred to his approaching ascension and glorification.

[832] **16:29.** ***"'You are not speaking with veiled language.'"*** Jesus' disciples felt that he previously spoke with "veiled language" in 16:16.

[833] **16:30.** ***"'Now we are sure.'"*** The disciples thought that they had already arrived at a point in the development of their understanding and faith where they could experience the fulfillment of the things that Jesus was teaching. However, Jesus' words in 16:31, "Do you now believe?" imply that they were premature in their assessment of themselves.

31 Jesus answered them, "Do you now believe?[834]
32 Attend to what I am saying:[835] the hour is coming,
yes, is now come, that you will be scattered, every man
to himself, and you will leave me alone. Yet I am not
alone, because the Father is with me.
33 These things I have spoken to you, so that in me you
may have peace. In the world you will have troubles,
but be of good cheer; I have overcome the world."[836]

---

[834] **16:31.** ***"'Do you now believe?'"*** See the note for "Now we are sure" in 16:30.

[835] **16:32.** ***"'Attend to what I am saying.'"*** The KJV translates, "Behold."

[836] **16:33.** ***"'Be of good cheer; I have overcome the world.'"*** Jesus' words, "I have overcome the world," could be interpreted in a number of ways. In one sense, he may have meant that he had *already* prevailed over every temptation and trouble he had personally encountered during his time on earth. Because Jesus set himself forth as the *example* his disciples should follow, perhaps he was teaching them that they could prevail just as he had prevailed. In keeping with this thought, Jesus' words might even be paraphrased to read, "In the world you will have troubles, but be of good cheer; *I* have overcome the world with its troubles, and *so can you*!"

In a much more intriguing sense, with great assurance he may have been speaking of his *approaching* victory over death as though it were an already accomplished fact. Let us dare to go further. Could it be that Jesus was actually speaking from the eternal perspective—positioning himself in spirit at a vantage point outside of time? Could it be that in spirit he stood on the other side of his death and resurrection, looked back at his victory from that point of view, and declared, "I have overcome the world!"

If this "outside of time" interpretation is correct, it is not the only place in John's Gospel where Jesus spoke in such a manner. He once referred to himself as "the Son of man who is in heaven" (3:13) while in body he was standing on the earth in the presence of Nicodemus. Jesus made a number of other "outside of time" references in the prayer that he prayed in chapter 17. See notes for 17:4, 11, 12, 22 and 24.

Pause and Reflect

In 16:33, Jesus said, "In the world you will have troubles, but be of good cheer; I have overcome the world." Consider the fact that he spoke these words *before* he had actually won the victory over the world, yet he said, "I *have* overcome the world." While facing his approaching death, he saw himself as already beyond the ordeal. Speaking from the vantage point of his future victory, he said, "I *have* overcome."

Jesus is our example in all things, and here he may be showing us how to deal with our own troubles. Perhaps we are to envision ourselves as already beyond whatever trouble we are facing. Perhaps we too should make declarations as though our needed victory were already an accomplished fact. For instance, a person facing financial troubles could declare, "My God has supplied all that I need." A person suffering affliction could declare, "By the stripes that Jesus took upon his body, I am healed." The weak can confess, "I am strong."

What trouble are you facing? What might your breakthrough look like beyond your ordeal? Envisioning yourself as standing at that future point in time, what might be your declaration of praise and thanksgiving at that time? Why not make that declaration now, just as Jesus confessed, "I *have* overcome!"

Whichever interpretation is accepted, because of the disciples' *spiritual union* with Jesus, his victory over the world was also their victory. Perhaps the paraphrase should read, "In the world you will have troubles, but be of good cheer; I have overcome the world with its troubles! That means that *in me you have overcome it too!*"

CHAPTER 17

Jesus spoke these words, lifted up his eyes to heaven, and said, "Father, the hour has come.[837] Glorify your Son,[838] that your Son also may glorify you.[839]
2 Seeing that you have given him authority over all flesh, that he should give eternal life[840] to as many as you have given him.[841]

---

[837] **17:1** ***"'The Hour has come.'"*** Prior to this point, Jesus had repeatedly stated that his hour had not yet come. Now, at last, it was his hour.

"'Hour.'" The word translated "hour" is *hora,* meaning "any definite time, point of time, moment." "*hora,*" *Thayer's Greek Lexicon, Blue Letter Bible,* accessed January 10, 2016, https:// www.blueletterbible.org/ lang/ lexicon/ lexicon.cfm?t= kjv&strongs= g5610. In this Gospel, when referring to the approaching hour or time for Jesus to face the crucifixion, John seems to use *hora* (2:4; 7:30; 8:20; 12:23, 27; 13:1; and 17:1) and *kairos* (7:6-8) interchangeably with little intended differentiation of meaning.

[838] **17:1.** ***"'Glorify your Son.'"*** See 17:5.

[839] **17:1.** ***"'That your Son also may glorify you.'"*** Beyond Jesus' approaching death, he would experience resurrection, ascension and glorification. Once glorified, he would send the Holy Spirit to empower the church in the continuation of his mission to "give eternal life." From his place in heaven and through his church on earth, Jesus would glorify the Father.

> 3 This is life eternal: that they might know you, the only true God, and Jesus Christ, whom you have sent.[842]
> 4 I have glorified you on the earth. I have finished the work that you gave me to do.[843]

---

[840] **17:2.** ***"'Eternal life.'"*** See also 3:15-16, 36; 4:14, 36; 5:24, 39; 6:27, 40, 47, 54, 68; 10:28; and 12:25, 50.

[841] **17:2.** ***"'As many as you have given him.'"*** See also 17:9.

[842] **17:3.** ***"'This is life eternal: that they might know you, the only true God, and Jesus Christ, whom you have sent.'"*** Eternal life is much more than perpetual longevity. It is a life qualitatively defined in terms of one's knowledge of God—an intimate relational knowledge of the Father and the Son.

[843] **17:4.** ***"'I have finished the work that you gave me to do."*** Jesus prayed these words at a point when his finished work on the cross had not yet been accomplished. Why then did he speak of his work as though it were already finished? Admittedly it requires a stretch in the imagination, but if allowable within the framework of his mission, Jesus may have in this moment positioned himself in spirit at a place outside of time. He may have been speaking from the vantage point of eternity.

The possibility of an "outside of time" interpretation has been entertained elsewhere in this commentary. See notes for 3:13 and 16:33. In other portions of Jesus' prayer in chapter 17, it appears that he spoke from the future as one who had already been glorified. He said, "I am no longer in the world" (17:11), although he was physically in the room with his disciples. Speaking in the past tense he said, "When I was with them in the world, I kept them in your name" (17:12), although he had not yet left them and was still with them in the world. There are other lines in the prayer of chapter 17 that could possibly align with this same stream of interpretation. He said, "The glory that you gave me I have given them" (17:22), although the glorification for which he prayed earlier (17:1) had not yet occurred. A similar thought continues in 17:24.

5 And now, O Father, glorify me beside your own self
with the glory that I had beside you before the world
existed.[844]
6 I have manifested your name unto the men that you
gave me out of the world. They were yours, and you
gave them to me, and they have kept your word.
7 Now they have known that all things, whatever you
have given me, are of you.
8 I have given to them the words that you gave me,
and they have received them and have known surely
that I came out from you. And they have believed that
you sent me.
9 I pray for them. I do not pray for the world, but for
them which you have given me,[845] for they are yours.[846]

---

[844] **17:5.** ***"'O Father, glorify me beside your own self with the glory that I had beside you before the world existed.'"*** The glory that Jesus had before the world came into being was the glory of face-to-face fellowship between Father and Son. Although Jesus did enjoy times of frequent communication with the Father during is earthly mission, here in this prayer, Jesus expressed his desire to return to face-to-face fellowship. See 1:1 and its corresponding footnote.

[845] **17:9.** ***"'I do not pray for the world, but for them which you have given me.'"*** Here Jesus was not disregarding the world. Rather, he was expressing particular concern for the small band of disciples that the Father had entrusted to him.

As a follower of Jesus, know that he does not view you as just one among many. He sees and cares for you individually, and you are not just part of a crowd of people that he loves in some general sense. That truth is powerfully illustrated on this occasion when Jesus took time to pray for his closest friends.

[846] **17:9.** ***"'They are yours.'"*** These disciples belonged to God the Father. Jesus recognized that the Father had entrusted to him stewardship over their lives. Herein lies a key lesson for leaders who look to Jesus as a model leader. Good leaders are

> 10 And of all mine are yours, and yours are mine; and I
> am glorified in them.[847]
> 11 Now I am no longer in the world,[848] but these are in
> the world,[849] and I am coming to you. Holy Father, keep
> in your name[850] those whom you have given me, that
> they may be one, as we are.[851]

---

faithful stewards of the people that God has entrusted to them. Such a realization causes one to be careful to treat followers as people belonging to God. If those who follow are believers, they are sons and daughters of God and should always be regarded as such. See also 17:2.

[847] **17:10.** ***"'I am glorified in them.'"*** In other words, "I am honored through their lives." To glorify Jesus through our lives is a high calling. To be affirmed by Jesus as a people who actually do glorify him is a praise that we hardly feel worthy to receive. To glorify Jesus is our highest aim.

[848] **17:11.** ***"'Now I am no longer in the world.'"*** Jesus spoke as one who was outside of time. He prayed from the vantage point of his glorification that was yet to come. Anyone in the room would have recognized that Jesus was physically present, yet in this prayer, he took his rightful place in heaven—an eternal realm not confined by the limitations of time. Regarding the possibility of an "outside of time" interpretation, see notes for 3:13; 16:33; and 17:4. Jesus may have also been speaking from the eternal perspective in 17:12, 22 and 24.

[849] **17:11.** ***"'These are in the world.'"*** While the followers of Jesus were *not* "of the world" (17:14), they *were* a people appointed to be "in the world." The world may not be the Christian's final home, but for now it is home. Believers are to live the life that Jesus has given while dwelling in this realm, influencing the world with the life of heaven. Jesus' followers are as salt and light to the world (Matthew 5:13-14). The mission to save the world must continue.

[850] **17:11.** ***"'Keep in your name.'"*** Here the Father is asked to do that which Jesus had been doing. Up to this point, Jesus had been keeping his disciples in his Father's name (17:12). A name conveys something of the character and qualities of the person represented by the name. To pray to the Father, saying, "Keep in your

12 When I was with them in the world,[852] I kept them in
your name.[853] Those that you gave me I have kept, and
none of them is lost,[854] except the son of perdition that
the Scriptures might be fulfilled.[855]
13 And now I come to you, and these things I speak in
the world, that they might have my joy fulfilled in
themselves.
14 I have given them your word, and the world has
hated them,[856] because they are not of the world, even
as I am not of the world.[857]

---

name," is a way of saying, "Preserve them by the power of all that your name represents to remain true and faithful to all that you are."

851 **17:11.** ***"'That they may be one, as we are.'"*** Jesus expected that the unity between his followers would resemble the unity he enjoyed with his Father.

852 **17:12.** ***"'When I was with them in the world.'"*** Jesus spoke of being with his disciples as though it were something in his past. He had not yet left them. He was still with them in the world. As in other places in this prayer, there is a possibility that Jesus was speaking in spirit from the vantage point of eternity. Regarding the possibility of an "outside of time" interpretation, see notes for 3:13; 16:33; and 17:4. Jesus may have also been speaking from the eternal perspective in 17:11, 22 and 24.

853 **17:12.** ***"'I kept them in your name.'"*** See the note for "keep in your name" in 17:11.

854 **17:12.** ***"'Those that you gave me I have kept, and none of them is lost.'"*** This theme occurs again in 18:9.

855 **17:12.** ***"'That the Scriptures might be fulfilled.'"*** For biblical prophecies concerning Judas' betrayal of Christ, see Psalm 41:9; 109:8; and Zechariah 11:12-13.

856 **17:14.** ***"'I have given them your word, and the world has hated them.'"*** It is Jesus' word that had separated his followers from the world. The implication is that this separation—the distinctiveness of them becoming a people devoted to the word of Christ—has stirred up the world's hatred against them.

15 I do not pray that you would take them out of the world, but that you would protect them[858] from the evil.[859]
16 They are not of the world, even as I am not of the world.[860]
17 Sanctify them through your truth; your word is truth.[861]

---

[857] **17:14.** ***"'They are not of the world, even as I am not of the world.'"*** Jesus would make this statement again in 17:16. Being united with Jesus, the world was no longer their native land. Just as Jesus' place of origin was heaven, so was his disciples' place of origin and citizenship now heaven. Jesus' followers had become aliens in the world. They were ruled by a different government—the kingdom of heaven. They had become enculturated into the life and customs of heaven. They lived by a different standard and aspired to ideals foreign to those still dominated by the fallen world's order. Although Jesus' followers would be sent to continue his mission to redeem the world, the world would esteem them as enemies. Concerning these "not of the world" disciples appointed as a people "in the world," see the note for 17:11.

[858] **17:15.** ***"'Protect them.'"*** Jesus asked the Father to protect us from evil—destructive and wicked forces or influences of every kind. If this is what Jesus asked, then this is precisely what the Father is doing: he is protecting us. We would do well to force out of our minds any thought that we are on our own in our battle against evil. If we will believe that the Father has indeed committed himself to watch over us and to keep us, then we will more likely enjoy the benefits of his care.

[859] **17:15.** ***"'The evil.'"*** These words may also be rendered, "the evil one."

[860] **17:16.** ***"'They are not of the world, even as I am not of the world.'"*** Jesus had already made this statement in 17:14.

[861] **17:17.** ***"'Sanctify them through your truth; your word is truth.'"*** When truth—God's word—is heard and received, it sanctifies. It makes holy. It separates good from evil. It sets the human heart apart for God's exclusive purposes.

18 As you have sent me into the world, even so I have
also sent them into the world.
19 And for their sakes, I sanctify myself,[862] that they
also might be truly sanctified.[863]
20 Neither do I pray for these alone, but I also pray for
them who will believe in me through their word.[864]
21 I pray that they all may be one as you, Father, are in
me and I in you;[865] that they also may be one in us[866]
that the world may believe that you have sent me.[867]

Have you heard a word from God lately? Do you sense that it somehow will not leave you? You cannot shake it. Why? It is doing something inside of you. Truth has taken on a life of its own, and it has gone to work. It is sanctifying you. It is separating light from darkness. It is changing you from the inside out.

"'Truth.'" See the note for "full of grace and truth" in 1:14.

[862] **17:19.** ***"'I sanctify myself.'"*** To sanctify means to set apart or to consecrate. Jesus set himself apart or consecrated himself as a sacrifice for the sins of the world.

[863] **17:19.** ***"'That they also might be truly sanctified.'"*** Jesus' consecrating of himself as a sacrifice for the sins of humanity would result in the sanctification of those who believe in him. Jesus willingly died for us so that we might be saved from evil and set apart as people exclusively devoted to him.

[864] **17:20.** ***"'I also pray for them who will believe in me through their word.'"*** Reader, you are mentioned in the Bible! With these words in 17:20, Jesus was praying directly for you!

[865] **17:21.** ***"'I pray that they all may be one as you, Father, are in me and I in you.'"*** Jesus wanted the unity between believers to resemble the unity that God the Father and God the Son enjoy together. See 10:30; 11:52; 17:11, 21-23.

[866] **17:21.** ***"'That they also may be one in us.'"*** The unity that Jesus desired was not just a unity between believers. God the Father and God the Son are parties in this bond. In fact, it is the presence of the Father and his Son that makes this supernatural union possible.

> 22 The glory that you gave me[868] I have given them so
> that they may be one, even as we are one:[869]
> 23 I in them, and you in me, that they may be made
> completely one, and that the world may know that you

---

[867] **17:21.** ***"'That the world may believe that you have sent me.'"*** The presence of the Father and the Son in the lives of believers combined with the unity in which Christ's followers conduct themselves would become evidence that Jesus' mission had been ordained by God.

[868] **17:22.** ***"'The glory that you gave me.'"*** It is interesting that Jesus would speak of this glory as though it had already been given to him. In 17:1, he asked the Father to give him the glory that he had once enjoyed with him prior to the incarnation, but at this point in 17:22, it had not yet been given. Why then would Jesus speak of the giving of this glory in the past tense? There is a possibility that Jesus spoke these words in spirit from the vantage point of eternity. Regarding the possibility of an "outside of time" interpretation, see notes for 3:13; 16:33; and 17:4. Jesus may have also been speaking from the eternal perspective in 17:11, 12 and 24.

The glory that was to be given to Jesus was the same glory of face-to-face communion that he had enjoyed with the Father in eternity past. See note for 17:5.

[869] **17:22.** ***"'The glory that you gave me I have given them so that they may be one, even as we are one.'"*** The "glory" in view here is the glory of face-to-face communion with the Father (1:1). Even now, Jesus draws his followers into the same relationship that he enjoys with the Father. They become participants in that communion. Being drawn into the perfection of the Father's relationship with his Son, two changes occur: believers are introduced to the glory of their own relationship with the Father, and that glory empowers them to relate to other believers in a new way—in unity.

have sent me and have loved them,[870] as you have
loved me.[871]
24 Father, I also desire that those whom you have
given me be with me where I am,[872] so that they may
see[873] my glory which you have given me, for you loved
me before the foundation of the world.[874]
25 O righteous Father, the world has not known you,
but I have known you, and these have known that you
have sent me.
26 I have declared your name unto them, and I will
continue to declare it, that the love with which you
have loved me may be in them, and I in them.[875]

---

870 **17:23. *"'That the world may know that you have sent me and have loved them.'"*** This unity is evidence that Jesus was sent by the Father and that the Father loves those who follow his Son.

871 **17:23. *"'That the world may know that you... have loved them, as you have loved me.'"*** This truth is amazing. The Father loves us, just as he loves his own Son.

872 **17:24. *"'Where I am.'"*** Where was Jesus? Jesus may have spoken these words in spirit from the vantage point of eternity. Regarding the possibility of an "outside of time" interpretation, see notes for 3:13; 16:33; and 17:4. Jesus may have also been speaking from the eternal perspective in 17:11, 12, and 22.

873 **17:24. *"'See.'"*** The KJV translates, "behold."

874 **17:24. *"'You loved me before the foundation of the world.'"*** See the note for "The Word was with God" in 1:1.

875 **17:26. *"'That the love with which you have loved me may be in them, and I in them.'"*** Jesus prayed that the same love God the Father has for the Son will be in us for the Son. In other words, Jesus prayed, "Father, I want them to love me as much as you love me." How much does the Father love his Son? How deep is that love? What is the quality of that love? What does that love look like? Whatever that love looks like, and however it may be defined, that is the same quality and depth

Pause and Reflect

1. Several places in chapter 17, Jesus speaks and prays as though he were already living on the other side of his breakthrough. If Jesus is our example, what implications does that practice hold for us as we face our troubles?
2. Chapter 17 is largely Jesus' prayer for you! What specific points in this prayer bring you personal encouragement?

---

of love that Jesus so desires to receive from us. Can the human mind even begin to comprehend this amazing truth? Jesus wants us to be passionate in our pursuit of him and in our devotion to him. This is a supernatural passion for Jesus that is just like the love that the Father has for his Son.

CHAPTER 18

The Unbelief of the Jews (18:1 – 19:42)

When Jesus had spoken these words, he went out with his disciples over the brook[876] of Kidron where there was a garden, into which he and his disciples entered.

Harmony of the Gospels			
	Matthew	**Mark**	**Luke**
Gethsemane	26:36-46	14:32-42	22:40-46

2 Judas, who betrayed him, also knew the place, for Jesus often gathered there with his disciples.

[876] **18:1. *"'Brook.'"*** The word translated, "brook," is *cheimarros,* signifying that it was a winter torrent—a seasonal stream that flowed rapidly in the winter months. Even today the Kidron is dry during most months. When Jesus and his disciples crossed the Kidron in 18:1, it was not necessarily flowing rapidly at that time, yet it still would have been called a *cheimarros* to signify that it was a seasonal stream.

3 Judas then, having received a band of men and
officers from the chief priests and Pharisees,[877] came
there with lanterns, torches and weapons.
4 Then Jesus, knowing all things that would come
upon him, went out and said to them, "Who are you
looking for?"[878]
5 They answered him, "Jesus of Nazareth."
Jesus said to them, "I am he."[879]
Judas, who betrayed him, also stood with them.
6 Then as soon as he had said to them, "I am he," they
went backward and fell to the ground.[880]
7 He asked them again, "Who are you looking for?"
And they said, "Jesus of Nazareth."
8 Jesus answered, "I have told you that I am he.
Therefore, if you are looking for me, let these men go
their way,"

---

[877] **18:3.** ***"Pharisees."*** The Pharisees were a sect noted for their strict observance of Jewish practices, adherence to oral laws and traditions, belief in an afterlife and the coming of Messiah. They are mentioned in 1:24; 3:1; 4:1; 7:32, 45-48; 8:3, 13; 9:13-16, 40; 11:46-47, 57; 12:19, 42; 18:3.

[878] **18:4.** ***"'Who are you looking for?'"*** The KJV translates, "Whom seek ye?" Jesus did not shrink back from what was awaiting him. He stepped forward, demonstrating his willingness to lay down his life.

[879] **18:5.** ***"'I am he.'"*** In English the text translates as "I am he," but in the Greek, the word "he" is not present. He actually uttered the words that once again identified him as deity: "I am."

[880] **18:6.** ***"As soon as he had said to them, 'I am he,' they went backward and fell to the ground."*** Being overwhelmed by the revelation and presence of the "I AM," the band of men and officers fell backwards to the ground. Here the sovereignty and supremacy of God's Son is vividly portrayed.

9 that the saying might be fulfilled, which he spoke,
"Out of them that you have given to me, I have not lost
anyone."[881]
10 Then Simon Peter, having a sword, drew it, struck
the high priest's servant and cut off his right ear. The
servant's name was Malchus.[882]
11 Then Jesus said to Peter, "Put your sword back into
its sheath! Shall I not drink the cup[883] my Father[884] has
given me?"[885]

---

[881] **18:9.** ***"'Out of them that you have given to me, I have not lost anyone.'"*** See 17:12.

[882] **18:10.** ***"Malchus."*** John is the only one of the four Gospel writers who provides this servant's name. Seeing that the author, John, knew the high priest (18:15), he would have easily remembered the high priest's servant's name. Later in 18:26, one of Malchus' relatives asked Peter a question, and Peter responded denying that he even knew Jesus.

[883] **18:11.** ***"'The cup.'"*** What is "the cup" that the Father had given Jesus? Was it the cup of death? Was it the cup of separation from God the Father? Some hold that it was the cup of wrath reserved for the wicked (Psalm 75:7). Isaiah 53:4-6 says,

> "Surely he has borne our griefs and carried our sorrows, yet we did esteem him stricken—smitten of God and afflicted. But he was wounded for our transgressions; he was bruised for our iniquities; the chastisement that brought us peace was upon him; and with his stripes we are healed. All we like sheep have gone astray; we have turned every one to his own way, and the Lord has laid on him the iniquity of us all."

Furthermore, 2 Corinthians 5:21 says, "For he has made him, who knew no sin, to be sin for us, that we might be made the righteousness of God in him."

[884] **18:11.** ***"'My Father.'"*** Jesus openly referenced God the Father as his Father, affirming his identity as the Son of God. See also 2:16; 5:17, 43; 6:32, 65; 8:19, 28, 38, 49, 54; 10:17-18, 25, 29, 30, 32, 37; 12:26-27; 14:2, 7, 12, 20-21, 23, 28; 15:1, 8, 10, 15, 23-24; 16:10; 20:17, and 21.

Harmony of the Gospels			
	Matthew	**Mark**	**Luke**
The Betrayal	26:47-56	14:43-52	22:47-53

12 Then the band, the captain and the officers of the
Jews took Jesus and bound him.
13 And they led him away first to Annas, for he was
father in law to Caiaphas, who was high priest that
year.[886]
14 Now Caiaphas was the one who gave counsel to the
Jews that it was expedient that one man should die for
the people.[887]

---

[885] **18:10-11.** According to Luke 22:51, at this point Jesus touched the servant's ear and healed him.

[886] **18:13.** ***"Who was high priest that year."*** These words reflect a practice imposed upon the Jews by the Romans. The Roman governor appointed high priests; they served for short periods of time and then were replaced with a successor. John Gill, *Exposition of the Bible,* accessed August 29, 2012, http:// www.biblestudytools.com/ commentaries/ gills-exposition-of-the-bible/ john-18-13.html.

[887] **18:14.** ***"Caiaphas was the one who gave counsel to the Jews that it was expedient that one man should die for the people."*** See 11:50.

15 ¶ Simon Peter followed Jesus, and so did another
disciple.[888] That disciple was known to the high priest
and went in with Jesus into the palace of the high
priest.
16 But Peter stood outside at the door. Then that other
disciple who was known to the high priest went out,
spoke to the girl keeping the door and brought Peter in.
17 Then the maid-servant in charge of the door[889] said
to Peter, "Are you not also one of this man's disciples?"
He said, "I am not."[890]
18 The servants and officers stood and warmed
themselves by a fire of coals they had made, for it was
cold. And Peter stood with them and warmed himself.

19 ¶ The high priest then asked Jesus about his
disciples and his doctrine.
20 Jesus answered him, "I spoke openly to the world. I
always taught in the synagogue and in the temple
where the Jews always assemble, and I have said
nothing in secret.

---

[888] **18:15.** ***"Another disciple."*** The reference to "another disciple" is traditionally understood to be the Gospel writer, John.

[889] **18:17.** ***"In charge of the door."*** These words can also be translated, "keeping the door."

[890] **18:17.** ***"'I am not.'"*** This denial of knowing Jesus was the first in a series of three (18:17, 25 and 27), fulfilling the words that Jesus spoke to Peter: "Before the rooster crows, you will have renounced me three times" (13:38).

21 Why do you ask me? Ask those who have heard me
what I have said to them. Certainly they know[891] what I
said."
22 When he had spoken these things, one of the officers
standing by slapped Jesus in the face, saying, "You are
answering the high priest!"[892]
23 Jesus answered him, "If I have spoken evil, tell
everyone here what I said that was so wrong.[893] But if I
have spoken honorably, why do you strike[894] me?"[895]
24 Now Annas had sent him bound to Caiaphas the
high priest.[896]

---

[891] **18:21.** ***"'Certainly they know.'"*** The NIV translates, "Surely they know," and the KJV translates, "Behold, they know." The word translated "certainly," "surely" and "behold" brings emphasis to the fact that those who heard Jesus were powerfully impacted by his teachings and were qualified to report what Jesus had actually said. Those who had heard and received his message had become credible witnesses. Jesus' work of preparing them as heralds of the Gospel was nearly complete.

[892] **18:22.** ***"'You are answering the high priest!'"*** The officer's remark was the equivalent to saying, "How dare you talk to the high priest like that!"

[893] **18:23.** ***"'Tell everyone here what I said that was so wrong.'"*** This statement is a paraphrase of words more literally translated as "bear witness of the evil."

[894] **18:23.** ***"'Strike.'"*** The word translated here as "strike" actually signifies treatment more severe than striking. The word, *dero,* speaks of beating and thrashing. In some contexts, it is a word used for the skinning of an animal.

[895] **18:23.** ***"'Why do you strike me?'"*** The question, "Why do you strike me?" probes into the motives of the unreceptive and resistant heart—motivations that are disproportionate to any perceived offense. The question should cause even an unbelieving reader to ponder, "What is the *real* reason for my distance, my unresponsiveness and even my hostility toward Jesus?"

25 And Simon Peter stood and warmed himself. Then
they said to him, "Aren't you also one of his disciples?"
He denied it and said, "I am not."[897]
26 One of the servants of the high priest—a relative of
the man whose ear Peter cut off—said, "Didn't I see
you in the garden with him?"
27 Peter then denied again, and immediately the
rooster crowed.[898]

Harmony of the Gospels			
	Matthew	**Mark**	**Luke**
Before Annas, Caiaphas and the Sanhedrin. Peter's Denial	26:57-58; 26:69-75	14:53-54; 14:66-72	22:54-65

28 ¶ Then they led Jesus from Caiaphas to the Roman
Praetorium,[899] and it was yet early. They[900] did not enter

---

[896] **18:24. *"Now Annas had sent him bound to Caiaphas the high priest."*** John's Gospel does not provide the details of Jesus' trial before Caiaphas. See Matthew 26:57-58; 26:69-75; Mark 14:53-54; 14:66-72; and Luke 22:54-65.

[897] **18:25. *"'I am not.'"*** This denial of knowing Jesus was the second in a series of three (18:17, 25 and 27), fulfilling the words that Jesus spoke to Peter: "Before the rooster crows, you will have renounced me three times" (13:38).

[898] **18:27. *"Peter then denied again, and immediately the rooster crowed."*** This denial of knowing Jesus was the third in a series of three (18:17, 25 and 27), fulfilling the words that Jesus spoke to Peter in 13:38. The other Gospels show that Peter went out and wept after the rooster crowed.

[899] **18:28. *"Praetorium."*** The KJV translates, "judgment hall." The Latin word is used in the body of this text due to the fact that the *Praetorium* was more than just a judgment hall; it was the Roman headquarters in the city.

into the *Praetorium* so that they would not be defiled,
but might be fit to eat the Passover.[901]

Harmony of the Gospels			
	Matthew	**Mark**	**Luke**
Christ before Pilate	27:1-2; 27:11-14	15:1-5	23:1-6
Judas' Suicide	27:3-10		
Jesus before Herod			23:7-12

29 Pilate then went out unto them and said, "What
accusation do you bring against this man?"

Harmony of the Gospels			
	Matthew	**Mark**	**Luke**
Accusations and Condemnations	27:15-26	15:6-15	23:13-25

30 They answered and said to him, "If he were not an
evildoer, we would not have delivered him up unto
you."
31 Then Pilate said unto them, "You take him and
judge him according to your law."

---

[900] **18:28. *"They."*** Here "they" signifies the Jews who were escorting Jesus and accompanying him as he was being taken to the *Praetorium*.

[901] **18:28. *"But might be fit to eat the Passover."*** This rendering has been borrowed from the Amplified version. From the perspective of these Jews, the breaking of religious tradition would have been more defiling than plotting the execution of God's son. In other places, John repeatedly refers to Passover, highlighting its significance in the telling of the Gospel story. See 2:13, 23; 6:4; 11:55; 12:1; 13:1; 18:39; and 19:14.

The Jews therefore said to him, "It is not lawful for us
to put any man to death,"[902]
32 that the saying of Jesus might be fulfilled which he
spoke signifying what death he should die.[903]
33 Then Pilate entered into the *Praetorium* again, called
Jesus and said to him, "Are you the King of the Jews?"
34 Jesus answered him, "Are you saying this thing of
yourself, or did others tell it to you of me?"[904]

---

[902] **18:31.** ***"The Jews therefore said to him, 'It is not lawful for us to put any man to death.'"*** Why did the Jews say that it was not lawful for them to put any man to death? Didn't their own law authorize them to stone people for serious violations, such as adultery and blasphemy? Yes, they were authorized to do so by Jewish law, but they were restrained from doing so by recently imposed Roman regulations. These Jewish leaders might have also been stretching the truth when they said, "it is not lawful for us to put any man to death," taking advantage of Pilate's ignorance of Jewish laws and customs. Their objective here was to gain Roman support for an execution. Without Roman backing, a Jewish execution of Jesus could cause a tumult among his followers, whereas an execution authorized by Pilate would suppress any potential uprising.

[903] **18:32.** ***"What death he should die."*** The Jews typically carried out capital punishment by stoning. The Romans carried out capital punishment by crucifixion. The insistence of these Jews that the Romans carry out the execution would lead to the fulfilling of John 3:14; 8:28; 12:32 and 34—the Son of God would be "lifted up," indicating execution by crucifixion. The Jews wanted Jesus' death to be by crucifixion, for that was the most humiliating mode of execution of that time. In their thinking, a crucifixion would clearly mark Jesus as one who was accursed, for Deuteronomy 21:23 states, "Cursed is every one that hangs on a tree." See also Galatians 3:13.

[904] **18:34.** ***"'Are you saying this thing of yourself, or did others tell it to you of me?'"*** In effect, Jesus is saying to Pilate, "Are you asking this question because this is something that you are truly concerned about, or are you asking this solely on the basis of what you are hearing from these Jews?"

35 Pilate answered, "Am I a Jew? Your own nation and
the chief priests have delivered you unto me. What
have you done?"
36 Jesus answered, "My kingdom is not of this world.
If my kingdom were of this world, then my servants
would fight[905] so that I should not be delivered to the
Jews. But now, my kingdom is not from this place."
37 Then Pilate said to him, "So, are you not then a
king?"
Jesus answered, "You are saying that I am a king. For
this purpose I was born, and for this purpose I came
into the world,[906] that I should bear witness to the
truth.[907] Everyone who is of the truth hears my voice.
38 Pilate said to him, "What is truth?"[908]
When he had said this, he went out again unto the
Jews, and he said to them, "I find in him no fault at all.

---

[905] **18:36.** ***"'If my kingdom were of this world, then my servants would fight.'"*** The kingdom of Christ is not advanced through war, revolution, political alliances or any battle against flesh and blood. See 2 Corinthians 10:4 and Ephesians 6:10-18. In the Bible, the terms "kingdom of Christ," "kingdom of heaven" and "kingdom of God" are references to the same kingdom.

[906] **18:37.** ***"'For this purpose I was born, and for this purpose I came into the world.'"*** The two occurrences of "for this purpose" in this verse are more literally translated "into this."

[907] **18:37.** ***"'Truth.'"*** See the note for "full of grace and truth" in 1:14.

[908] **18:38.** ***"'What is truth?'"*** Pilate's question sits on the page without a written answer. The reader is left to ponder the question. This commentary leaves the reader to ponder the question as well.

39 But you have a custom that I should release unto
you one at the Passover.[909] Therefore, do you want me
to release to you the King of the Jews?"
40 Then they all cried again, saying, "Not this man, but
Barabbas." Yet Barabbas was a robber.

---

[909] **18:39.** ***"'Passover.'"*** John's repeated reference to the Passover highlights the significance that it held for the telling of the Gospel story. See 2:13, 23; 6:4; 11:55; 12:1; 13:1; 18:28; and 19:14.

CHAPTER 19

Then Pilate took Jesus and flogged him.[910]
2 And the soldiers braided a wreath of thorns[911]
and placed it on his head. And[912] they threw
upon[913] him a purple robe

---

[910] **19:1. *"Pilate took Jesus and flogged him."*** Whips used for flogging or scourging consisted of cords or straps with sharp pieces of metal or bone attached. There was no justifiable reason for Jesus to be flogged or scourged.

[911] **19:2. *"Wreath of thorns."*** The KJV translates "wreath" as "crown." The crown of thorns is a reminder of the thorns that infested the ground following the fall of man (Genesis 3:17-19). The thorns represent the curse. Jesus took the curse resulting from man's sin upon himself (Galatians 3:13) and died the cross-death in man's stead.

[912] **19:2. *"And."*** Here and in many other places in this narrative, to the English reader, the conjunction, *kai* (translated in most places as "and" and occasionally as "even"), seems to be overused. However, most instances of its use have been retained in the body of this text to preserve the intended sense of swift movement—one thing quickly leading to the next thing.

[913] **19:2. *"They threw upon him."*** The KJV translates, "put on," but *periebalon* (from *periballo*) carries the imagery of a garment being thrown upon or around a person. The word, *periballo,* is constructed from *peri,* meaning "around," and *ballo,* meaning, "to throw." In this context the use of the word contributes to the overall image of disrespect and mockery.

3 and said, "Hail, King of the Jews!"[914] And they
slapped him in the face.

Harmony of the Gospels			
	Matthew	**Mark**	**Luke**
Treatment by the Soldiers	27:27-31	15:16-20	23:36-37

4 Then Pilate went out again and said to them, "Look, I
am bringing him out to you that you may know that I
find not even one fault in him."[915]
5 Then Jesus came out, wearing the wreath of thorns
and the purple robe. And Pilate said to them, "Behold
the man!"[916]

---

[914] **19:1-2.** These were acts of mockery: placing the crown of thorns on Jesus' head, casting the purple robe upon his shoulders, and crying, "Hail, king of the Jews!"

[915] **19:4.** ***"' Look, I am bringing him out to you that you may know that I find not even one fault in him.'"*** Pilate thought that presenting a humiliated and beaten Jesus to the mob would be enough to satisfy them. He had been impressed by Jesus' meekness, and he hoped that the crowd would be affected in the same way. There was nothing about this falsely accused man that would even hint at a need for further punishment.

[916] **19:5.** ***"Behold the man!"*** In other words, "Here he is! Look at him!" It is in this moment that we should pause with worshipful hearts and behold this man in a way that Pilate never intended. Fix your gaze upon him. Do you realize who this is that you are gazing upon? Are you grasping the significance of what is going on here? Behold the Son of God, and realize that in these moments God was making him who had no sin to be sin for us, "that we might be made the righteousness of God in him" (2 Corinthians 5:21). "Behold the man," for he is the Lamb of God—the one of whom John the Baptist spoke when he proclaimed, "Behold, the Lamb of God who carries away the sin of the world!" (1:29)

6 When the chief priests and officers saw him, they
cried out, saying, "Crucify him! Crucify him!"
Pilate said to them, "You take him, and crucify him, for
I find no fault in him."
7 The Jews answered him, "We have a law, and by our
law he ought to die,[917] because he declared himself to
be the Son of God."

---

[917] **19:7.** ***"'By our law he ought to die.'"*** The law to which the chief priests and officers referred could have been Deuteronomy 18:20 (NIV), which says, "But a prophet who presumes to speak in my name anything I have not commanded, or a prophet who speaks in the name of other gods, is to be put to death." They could have also been thinking of Deuteronomy 13:1-5 (NIV):

> If a prophet, or one who foretells by dreams, appears among you and announces to you a sign or wonder, and if the sign or wonder spoken of takes place, and the prophet says, "Let us follow other gods" (gods you have not known) "and let us worship them," you must not listen to the words of that prophet or dreamer. The Lord your God is testing you to find out whether you love him with all your heart and with all your soul. It is the Lord your God you must follow, and him you must revere. Keep his commands and obey him; serve him and hold fast to him. That prophet or dreamer must be put to death for inciting rebellion against the Lord your God, who brought you out of Egypt and redeemed you from the land of slavery. That prophet or dreamer tried to turn you from the way the Lord your God commanded you to follow. You must purge the evil from among you.

If these are the passages the Jewish authorities had in mind, the inaccuracy of their accusation is apparent. Jesus spoke only what his Father commanded (12:49), and he never spoke "in the name of other gods." Neither had he called for the following of "other gods." See also the law requiring the execution of blasphemers in Leviticus 24:16.

8 ¶ When Pilate heard that saying, he was rather afraid.[918]
9 And he went again into the *Praetorium* and said to Jesus, "Where are you from?" But Jesus gave him no answer.
10 Then Pilate said to him, "Do you not speak to me? Do you not know that I have power to crucify you, and I have power to release you?"
11 Jesus answered, "You possess no authority at all against me, if it is not given to you from above. Therefore, the one who delivered me to you has the greater sin."[919]
12 Out of regard for what Jesus had said,[920] Pilate sought to release him, yet the Jews cried out, saying, "If

---

[918] **19:8. *"When Pilate heard that saying, he was rather afraid."*** The words of the Jews in 19:7 combined with the warning from Pilate's wife's dream in Matthew 27:19 caused Pilate to be fearful.

[919] **19:11. *"'The one who delivered me to you has the greater sin.'"*** Was the "one who delivered" Jesus to Pilate a reference to Judas or Caiaphas? Both had sinned against the light of grace and revelation. Caiaphas had knowledge of the Scriptures predicting the arrival of the Messiah, and Judas had an unprecedented relational knowledge of God's Son. Whether the "one who delivered" was Judas or Caiaphas, both were guiltier than Pilate, for they had sinned against a great light that had left them without excuse.

[920] **19:12. *"Out of regard for what Jesus had said."*** These words are a paraphrase of *ek toutou,* literally translated, "out of this." That which follows in verse 12 flows "out of" that which precedes in verse 11. The KJV translates, "And from thenceforth." In the Greek there is no conjunction that would suggest the inclusion of the word, "and," in the translation.

you ever release this man, you are not Caesar's friend.
Whoever makes himself a king speaks against Caesar."

13 ¶ When Pilate heard that saying, he brought Jesus
out and sat down in the judgment seat[921] in a place that
is called the Pavement, but in the Hebrew, Gabbatha.[922]
14 It was the day of preparation for the Passover,[923] and
about the sixth hour,[924] and he said to the Jews, "Behold
your king!"[925]
15 But they cried out, "Away with him! Away with
him! Crucify him!"

---

[921] **19:13. *"Judgment seat."*** The word translated here is *bema*. Actually, the *bema* was the raised platform upon which the seat was placed.

[922] **19:13. *"Gabbatha."*** This word is the Hebrew equivalent of "Pavement," and it is found only one other place in the entire Bible—2 Kings 16:17. In that passage, King Ahaz removed the laver from its base and placed it on a *pavement* of stones. This Jewish leader, Ahaz, had been dominated by a Gentile leader, and this act was his token of surrender to apostasy. Conversely, Pilate, a Gentile leader, had been dominated by Jewish leaders, and in the text at hand, he joins with them in the rejection of the Messiah. This observation is suggested by Arthur W. Pink, *Exposition of the Gospel of John* (Grand Rapids, Michigan: Zondervan, 1968), 1038.

[923] **19:14. *"Passover."*** John's repeated reference to the Passover highlights the significance that it held for the telling of the Gospel story. See 2:13, 23; 6:4; 11:55; 12:1; 13:1; and 18:28, 39.

[924] **19:14. *"The sixth hour."*** Here time is represented according to the Roman measurement, placing the time at about 6:00 a.m.

[925] **19:14. *"'Behold your king!'"*** Pilate did not actually believe Jesus to be the king of the Jews. His declaration, "Behold your king!" was said with the intent to mock them.

Pilate said to them, "Shall I crucify your king?" The chief priests answered, "We have no king but Caesar."[926]
16 Then he delivered him to them to be crucified. And they took Jesus, and led him away.
17 And bearing his cross[927] he went out into the place called "the place of the skull," which is called in Hebrew, "Golgotha,"
18 where they crucified him and two others with him—one on each side and Jesus in the middle.[928]

19 ¶ Pilate wrote a title and put it on the cross. And the inscription was "JESUS OF NAZARETH[929] THE KING OF THE JEWS."[930]

---

926 **19:15.** ***"'We have no king but Caesar.'"*** These Jews were speaking hypocritically. They had no desire to honor Caesar; they hated him.

927 **19:17.** ***"Bearing his cross."*** Jesus may have carried only the horizontal cross-beam section of the cross.

928 **19:18.** ***"They crucified him and two others with him—one on each side and Jesus in the middle."*** Jesus' crucifixion between two thieves calls to mind Isaiah's prophecy: "He was numbered with the transgressors" (Isaiah 53:12).

929 **19:19.** ***"'JESUS OF NAZARETH.'"*** Nazareth was a tiny frontier community that was not known for anything important. Remember Nathanael's question in 1:46: "Can anything good come out of Nazareth?" Craig S. Keener notes that members of the Judean elite were especially unimpressed with Jesus' rural Galilean origins (7:41-42, 52). When Pilate referenced Nazareth in the inscription on Jesus' cross, he may have intended it to be part of his mockery against the Jews. Craig S. Keener, "Can Anything Good Come out of Nazareth?" *Bible Odyssey*, accessed January 5, 2016, http:// www.bibleodyssey.org/ places/ related-articles/ can-anything-good-come-out-of-nazareth.aspx.

20 Then many of the Jews read this title, for the place
where Jesus was crucified was near the city, and it was
written in Hebrew, Greek, and Latin.[931]
21 Then the chief priests of the Jews said to Pilate, "Do
not write, 'The King of the Jews,' but that he said, 'I am
King of the Jews.'"
22 Pilate answered, "What I have written I have
written."

23 ¶ Then the soldiers, when they had crucified Jesus,
took his garments and made four parts—to every
soldier a part. They also took his tunic, but the tunic
was seamless, woven as one piece from top to
bottom.[932]
24 Then they said to one another, "Let's not tear it but
cast lots for it to determine whose it shall be," that the
scripture might be fulfilled, which said, "They divided

---

930 **19:19.** ***"'JESUS OF NAZARETH THE KING OF THE JEWS.'"*** Pilate's intention with the posting of this title was to mock and irritate the Jews. He did not realize that the words he had posted in derision comprised an accurate and powerful declaration of Jesus' true identity.

931 **19:20.** ***"It was written in Hebrew, Greek and Latin."*** The title on the cross was written in three languages so that anyone walking by would be able to read it.

932 **19:23.** ***"The tunic was seamless, woven as one piece from top to bottom."*** This description of Jesus' tunic is similar to Josephus' description of priestly garments. Josephus, *Antiquities of the Jews*, Book 3, Chapter 7, Section 4, accessed January 29, 2016, http:// www.earlyjewishwritings.com/ text/ josephus/ant3.html. Concerning the priesthood of Jesus, see Hebrews 7:23-28; 9:11-14; and 10:10-14.

my garments among them, and they cast lots for my clothes."[933] The soldiers certainly did these things.[934]

Harmony of the Gospels			
	Matthew	**Mark**	**Luke**
The Crucifixion	27:32-38	15:21-28	23:26-34

25 ¶ There by the cross of Jesus stood his mother, his mother's sister—Mary the wife of Cleophas, and Mary of Magdala.[935]
26 Then when Jesus saw his mother and the disciple whom he loved[936] standing by, he said to his mother, "Woman, behold your son."

---

[933] **19:24.** ***"That the scripture might be fulfilled, which said, 'They divided my garments among them, and they cast lots for my clothes.'"*** Regarding the fulfillment of the scripture, see Psalm 22:18.

[934] **19:24.** ***"The soldiers certainly did these things."*** The author gives emphasis to what has been described to indicate his certainty of the details. He was an eyewitness.

[935] **19:25.** ***"Mary of Magdala."*** According to Mark 16:9, Jesus had cast seven demons out of Mary of Magdala.

[936] **19:26.** ***"The disciple whom he loved."*** In John's Gospel, there are five direct references to a disciple whom Jesus loved (13:23; 19:26; 20:2; 21:7; and 21:20). Many scholars believe that this disciple is the Apostle John, the author of this Gospel. It is unlikely that John was elevating himself above his peers or implying that Jesus had a lesser love for the other disciples. He repeatedly referenced the love of Jesus because he had been so profoundly impacted by Jesus' love. In fact, John is now known as the Apostle of love, due to his emphasis on love found in the body of biblical literature attributed to him.

27 After that he said to the disciple, "Behold your
mother." And from that hour that disciple took her into
his own home.[937]

Harmony of the Gospels			
	Matthew	**Mark**	**Luke**
Mockings	27:39-44	15:29-32	23:35-39
The Repentant Criminal			23:40-43

28 ¶ After this,[938] knowing that all things were now
accomplished, that the scripture might be fulfilled,
Jesus said, "I am thirsty."
29 A vessel was lying there full of vinegar, and they
filled a sponge with vinegar, put it on a stalk of hyssop,
and put it to his mouth.
30 Then when Jesus had received the vinegar, he said,
"It is finished,"[939] and he bowed his head and gave up
the spirit.[940]

---

[937] **19:27. *"From that hour that disciple took her into his own home."*** The word "home" does not appear in the original text. The meaning here is that this disciple took responsibility for Mary, as though she were his own mother, just as Jesus had requested.

[938] **19:28. *"After this."*** It is estimated that approximately three hours passed between 19:27 and 19:28.

[939] **19:30. *"'It was finished.'"*** The long reign of sin over the earth was finally over. God's plan for redemption had been accomplished. The wages of sin is death (Romans 6:23), and that payment had been paid in full.

[940] **19:30. *"He bowed his head and gave up the spirit."*** His spirit was not *taken* from his body. He voluntarily "gave up" or released his spirit. Jesus was in full control.

Harmony of the Gospels			
	Matthew	**Mark**	**Luke**
Darkness and Other Signs	27:45-53	15:33-38	23:44-45
The Bystanders	27:54-56	15:39-41	23:47-49

31 Since it was the day of preparation,[941] so that the
bodies would not remain upon the cross[942] on the
Sabbath—for that Sabbath was a very important one,[943]
the Jews asked Pilate that their legs might be broken[944]
and that they might be taken away.
32 Then the soldiers came and broke the legs of the first
one and of the other one who was crucified with him.

---

[941] **19:31.** ***"The day of preparation."*** It was a day designated as a time to prepare for the Passover (19:14).

[942] **19:31.** ***"So that the bodies would not remain upon the cross."*** It was the Roman custom to leave the bodies of the executed on their crosses for an extended period of time until they were devoured by birds of prey. "John 19:31-37," *Benson Commentary, Bible Hub,* accessed January 30, 2016, http:// biblehub.com/ commentaries/ john/ 19-31.htm

[943] **19:31.** ***"That Sabbath was a very important one."*** It was the first day of unleavened bread, and it was also an ordinary Sabbath. With both occurring on the same day, this Sabbath was regarding as a "high day"—a very important Sabbath. Many regarded it as the most solemn season of the Jewish year. "John 19:31-42," *Jamieson-Fausset-Brown Bible Commentary, Bible Hub,* accessed January 30, 2016, http:// biblehub.com/ commentaries/ john/ 19-31.htm.

[944] **19:31.** ***"That their legs might be broken."*** It was difficult for criminals to breathe as they hung on the cross. However, by applying pressure against the spike holding their feet, with their legs they were able to raise themselves up to inhale. But once their legs were broken, it became impossible for them to breathe in this manner. Consequently, they died more quickly.

33 But when they came to Jesus and saw that he was
already dead, they did not break his legs.
34 But one of the soldiers pierced his side with a spear,
and immediately, out came blood and water.[945]
35 The one who saw it has given testimony,[946] and his
testimony is true. He knows that what he says is true,
that you may believe.[947]
36 For these things were done, that the scripture might
be fulfilled, "Not one of his bones will be broken."[948]
37 Again another scripture says, "They shall look on
him whom they have pierced."[949]

---

[945] **19:34.** ***"Out came blood and water."*** All doubt that Jesus actually died is removed at this point in the narrative. A flow of blood and a water-like liquid would have occurred with the piercing of any person in the region of the heart. Some commentators say that the blood signified atonement or justification and the water signified sanctification or purification. However, it is likely that the only significance intended here was to indicate that Jesus was truly dead.

[946] **19:35.** ***"The one who saw it has given testimony."*** The Gospel writer, John, is here referring to himself. For other references to the testimony theme, see 3:11, 3:32-33; 5:31, 34, 36; 8:13-14, 17; 12:18; and 21:24. The author's words on the page are like the signature of a medical examiner on a death certificate, certifying that all evidence points to only one conclusion: the person in question is dead.

[947] **19:35.** ***"That you may believe."*** For the writer, the certainty of Jesus' death was important to establish, because his death was essential to redemption and the faith of believers. His death was the fulfillment of numerous prophecies, including Genesis 3:15; Daniel 9:26; Isaiah 53:1-12; and Zechariah 12:10.

[948] **19:36.** ***"'Not one of his bones will be broken.'"*** The references supporting the scripture quotation are Exodus 12:46, Numbers 9:12 and Psalm 34:20.

[949] **19:37.** ***"'They shall look on him whom they have pierced.'"*** See Zechariah 12:10.

38 ¶ After these things, Joseph of Arimathaea,[950] being a disciple of Jesus (but secretly because of fear of the Jews[951]), asked Pilate that he might be permitted to take away Jesus' body, and Pilate gave him permission. Then he came and took away the body of Jesus.

---

[950] **19:38.** ***"Joseph of Arimathaea."*** He is mentioned in all four Gospels. Mark 15:43 indicates that he was a member of the Sanhedrin and that he had been "searching for the kingdom of God." Matthew 27:57 indicates that he was a rich man.

[951] **19:38.** ***"Because of fear of the Jews."*** In at least five places in this Gospel, behavior was motivated out of fear of the Jews:

1. The first occurrence is in 7:13 where people were afraid to speak openly of Jesus because of their fear of the Jews.
2. The second is in 9:22 where the parents of a man healed from blindness were afraid to testify concerning their son's healing.
3. The third is in 12:42 where many of the chief Jewish rulers who believed in Jesus did not openly confess him "because of the Pharisees;" they feared that they might be put out of the synagogue.
4. The fourth is here in 19:38 where Joseph of Arimathaea was secretive regarding his allegiance to Jesus because of his fear of the Jews.
5. The fifth is in 20:19 following Jesus' resurrection; at that time, the disciples assembled secretly behind closed doors because they feared the Jews.

39 Nicodemus,[952] who first came to Jesus by night, also
came bringing a mixture of myrrh and aloes, about
seventy-five pounds[953] in weight.
40 Then they took the body of Jesus and wound it in
linen cloths with the spices, according to the burial
customs of the Jews.
41 In the place where he was crucified, there was a
garden, and in the garden there was a new tomb,[954] in
which no one had yet been placed.
42 There they laid Jesus because of the preparation day
of the Jews, seeing that the tomb was nearby.[955]

Harmony of the Gospels			
	Matthew	**Mark**	**Luke**
Jesus' Burial	27:57-61	15:42-47	23:50-56
The Guard of the Tomb	27:62-66; 28:11-15		

[952] **19:39.** ***"Nicodemus."*** Nicodemus appears the third time. He appears a total of three times in John's Gospel: 3:1-21; 7:45-51; and 19:39-42.

[953] **19:39.** ***"Seventy-five pounds."*** The KJV translates, "an hundred pound." In the Greek, the word translated "pound" is *litra,* which is a Roman measurement equal to about 11½ ounces or 327 grams. See the footnote on 19:39 in *The Holy Bible, English Standard Version* (Wheaton, Illinois: Good News Publishers, 2001).

[954] **19:41.** ***"A new tomb."*** According to Matthew 27:60, this tomb was Joseph of Arimathaea's own tomb that he had cut out of the rock.

[955] **19:42.** After placing Jesus in the tomb, Joseph of Arimathaea rolled a large stone in front of its entrance (Matthew 27:60).

CHAPTER 20

The Victory of Christ (20:1 – 21:25)

On the first day of the week, early in the morning while it was still dark, Mary of Magdala came to the tomb,[956] and she saw that the stone had been taken away from the tomb.
2 Then she ran and came to Simon Peter and to the other disciple whom Jesus loved,[957] and she said to them, "They have taken away the Lord out of the tomb, and we do not know where they have laid him."

---

[956] **20:1. *"Mary of Magdala came to the tomb."*** According to Mark 16:1, Mary of Magdala was accompanied by "Mary, the mother of James" and Salome. In Mark's account, the three women went to the tomb with sweet spices to anoint him. Luke's account suggests that a fourth woman named Joanna might have been with them as well (Luke 24:10).

[957] **20:2. *"The other disciple whom Jesus loved."*** In John's Gospel, there are five direct references to a disciple whom Jesus loved (13:23; 19:26; 20:2; 21:7; and 21:20). Many scholars believe that this disciple is the Apostle John, the author of this Gospel. It is unlikely that John was elevating himself above his peers or implying that Jesus had a lesser love for the other disciples. He repeatedly referenced the love of Jesus because he had been so profoundly impacted by Jesus' love. In fact, John is now known as the Apostle of love, due to his emphasis on love found in the body of biblical literature attributed to him.

3 Peter then went out, and the other disciple, and they
came to the tomb.
4 The two of them raced together, and the other
disciple ran more swiftly than Peter, and he came first
to the tomb.
5 And stooping down and looking in, he saw the linen
cloths[958] lying there, yet he did not go in.
6 Then Simon Peter came following him, and he
entered the tomb and beheld[959] the linen cloths lying
there
7 and the burial cloth that had been on his head, not
lying with the linen cloths but wrapped together in a
place by itself.[960]
8 Then the other disciple also entered—the one who
came first to the tomb, and he saw and believed.[961]

---

[958] **20:5.** ***"Linen cloths."*** Strips of linen cloth were used for wrapping the dead.

[959] **20:6.** ***"Beheld."*** The word translated "beheld" in the KJV carries the idea that Peter looked at the linen cloths with great interest, considering the significance of these items lying there.

[960] **20:7.** ***"Wrapped together in a place by itself."*** The scene did not have the appearance that one might expect from a grave robbery. There are two possibilities with the given description. Jesus' resurrected body may have passed through the cloths without disturbing them, causing the material to collapse in place with the head cloth remaining in the position of the head separated from the other wrappings. The other possibility is that Jesus or an angel may have folded the head cloth and laid it aside to give a visual indication that what had occurred was intentional and by design.

[961] **20:8.** ***"He saw and believed."*** With these words, the reader is drawn into the presence of the eyewitness and is invited to behold the same scene that he beheld.

9 For they did not yet know the scripture, that it was
necessary for him to rise from the dead.[962]
10 Then they returned to the other disciples.

11 ¶ But Mary[963] stood outside at the tomb crying, and
as she cried, she stooped down and looked into the
tomb.
12 And she saw two angels in white seated where the
body of Jesus had been, one at the head and the other
at the feet.
13 And they said to her, "Woman, why are you
crying?"
She said to them, "They have taken away my Lord, and
I do not know where they have placed him."
14 When she had said these things, she turned around
and saw Jesus standing there, and did not perceive that
it was Jesus.[964]

What John saw affected him to the core of his being. The writer's hope is that all who read his account would also be brought to faith (20:31).

[962] **20:9.** ***"They did not yet know the scripture, that it was necessary for him to rise from the dead."*** Although the death and resurrection of Jesus had been foretold, the Jews did not typically live with a view that the Messiah would die and then come back to life. The biblical support for what was transpiring would be understood later. See Job 19:25-27; Psalm 16:9-10; Zechariah 12:10; Isaiah 26:19-21; 53:10-12; Hosea 6:1-2.

[963] **20:11.** ***"Mary."*** Verses 20:1 and 20:18 indicate that this Mary is Mary of Magdala.

[964] **20:14.** ***"She... did not perceive that it was Jesus."*** It appears that in his post-resurrection form, Jesus was able to cloak his identity. His resurrected body

15 Jesus said to her, "Woman, why are you crying? Who are you looking for?"
She, supposing him to be the gardener, said to him, "Sir, if you have carried him away, tell me where you have placed him, and I will take him."
16 Jesus said to her, "Mary."
She turned herself and said to him, "Rabboni!"[965] which is to say, "Teacher."
17 Jesus said to her, "Do not cling to me, for I have not yet ascended to my Father,[966] but go to my brothers[967]

---

evidently had abilities that transcended his natural body. After his resurrection, he was unrecognizable on at least two other occasions. See Luke 24:16 and John 21:4.

[965] **20:16.** ***"'Rabboni.'"*** This word is Aramaic for "teacher."

[966] **20:17.** ***"'Do not cling to me, for I have not yet ascended to my Father.'"*** In the surprise and excitement of the moment, Mary's thought might have been, "So, you are not going to leave us after all!" With Jesus' response, he was saying to her, "Mary, do not cling to me as though I am here to stay. I will not be remaining physically present with you. I will be ascending to my Father."

"'My Father.'" Jesus openly referenced God the Father as his Father, affirming his identity as the Son of God. See also 2:16; 5:17, 43; 6:32, 65; 8:19, 28, 38, 49, 54; 10:17-18, 25, 29, 30, 32, 37; 12:26-27; 14:2, 7, 12, 20-21, 23, 28; 15:1, 8, 10, 15, 23-24; 16:10; 18:11; 20:17 and 21.

[967] **20:17.** ***"'My brothers.'"*** This expression appears to be a reference to Jesus' disciples and not his biological brothers. For the first time in John's Gospel, Jesus spoke of his disciples in this manner. The cross-death and resurrection had established a new kind of relationship between the Lord and his disciples. Over the course of Jesus' journey with them, this progression was evident: first they related to him as *servants*, then they were his *friends*, (15:15) and here he calls them *brothers*.

and say to them, 'I ascend to my Father and your
Father; and to my God and your God.'"[968]
18 Mary of Magdala came and told the disciples that
she had seen the Lord, and that he had spoken these
things to her.

Proposed Summary of the Resurrection Sequence
1. Early in the morning while it was still dark, Mary Magdala, Mary the mother of James, Salome and possibly Joanna set out to the tomb with spices.[969]
2. While the women were on their way to the tomb, the sun broke over the horizon.[970]
3. While on their way to the tomb, it occurred to the women that moving the stone might be problematic.[971]

---

[968] **20:17.** ***"'Go to my brothers and say to them, 'I ascend to my Father and your Father; and to my God and your God.'"*** The death and resurrection of Jesus had secured for his disciples a personal identity in relationship with God that had not been previously known. Not only was it true that God was Jesus' Father; now God was also the disciples' Father. The expressions, "my Father and your Father," and "my God and your God," carry a sense of a new intimacy in the relationship. When these expressions are viewed together with his reference to his disciples as brothers, it is clear that he is emphasizing the fact that a new family had just been created. (Hints that Jesus had come to create a new spiritual family are found in 3:3, 7; 20:17; and 21:23.) No doubt, this conversation was an emotional moment for both Jesus and Mary.

[969] Matthew 28:1; Mark 16:1; Luke 24:1, 10; John 20:1.

[970] Mark 16:2.

[971] Mark 16:3.

4. Before the women arrived at the tomb, there was a violent earthquake. An angel came down from heaven, rolled back the stone and sat on it. The guards shook and became like dead men.[972]
5. Before the women arrived, apparently the angel who had sat on the stone disappeared.
6. The women arrived and saw that the stone had been rolled away.[973]
7. The women entered the tomb, wondering what had happened to the body of Jesus.[974]

---

972 Matthew 28:2-4.

973 Mark 16:4; Luke 24:2; John 20:1.

974 Mark 16:5; Luke 24:3-4.

975 John 20:2.

976 Matthew 28:5-7; Mark 16:5-7; Luke 24:4-7.

977 Matthew 28:8.

978 Matthew 28:9-10.

979 Luke 24:9-11.

980 Luke 24:12; John 20:3.

981 John 20:4.

982 Luke 24:12; John 20:5.

983 John 20:6-8.

984 John 20:10-11.

985 John 20:11-13.

986 John 20:14-17.

987 John 20:18.

8. While the other women remained at the tomb, evidently Mary of Magdala ran to tell Peter and John that the body of Jesus had been taken.[975]
9. After Mary of Magdala had left the tomb, two men or angels appeared to the remaining women telling them that Jesus had risen.[976]
10. The women ran from the tomb to tell the other disciples.[977]
11. While the women were on their way back to the other disciples, Jesus appeared to them.[978]
12. The women reported to the Eleven apostles what they had seen and heard. If Mary of Magdala heard their report, evidently she did not immediately believe that Jesus had risen.[979]
13. Peter and John ran to the tomb.[980]
14. John was the first to arrive at the tomb, but he did not go in.[981]
15. Peter arrived at the tomb. Both Peter and John bent over looking into the tomb, wondering what had happened.[982]
16. Peter entered the tomb first, and then John followed.[983]
17. Mary of Magdala followed Peter and John back to the tomb, in all likelihood, hoping that the report of the other women was true. A few other disciples may have accompanied her.
18. Peter, John and perhaps a few other disciples returned to the place where they had been staying, but Mary of Magdala stayed outside of the tomb crying. She had not yet seen the risen Lord.[984]
19. Mary of Magdala bent over, looked into the tomb and saw two angels. They began to converse with her.[985]

20. Mary turned around and saw a man she thought to be the gardener, but then she discovered that it was Jesus.[986]
21. Mary of Magdala returned to the other disciples to tell them that she had seen Jesus.[987]

Harmony of the Gospels			
	Matthew	**Mark**	**Luke**
The Resurrection	28:1-10	16:1-11	24:1-12
Disciples Going to Emmaus		16:12-13	24:13-35

19 ¶ Then the same day at evening, being the first day
of the week, when the doors were shut where the
disciples were assembled for fear of the Jews,[988] Jesus

---

[988] **20:19.** ***"For fear of the Jews."*** In at least five places in this Gospel, behavior was motivated out of fear of the Jews:

1. The first occurrence is in 7:13 where people were afraid to speak openly of Jesus because of their fear of the Jews.
2. The second is in 9:22 where the parents of a man healed from blindness were afraid to testify concerning their son's healing.
3. The third is in 12:42 where many of the chief Jewish rulers who believed in Jesus did not openly confess him "because of the Pharisees;" they feared that they might be put out of the synagogue.
4. The fourth is in 19:38 where Joseph of Arimathaea was secretive regarding his allegiance to Jesus because of his fear of the Jews.
5. The fifth is here in 20:19 following Jesus' resurrection; at that time, the disciples assembled secretly behind closed doors because they feared the Jews.

came and stood in the midst, and said to them, "Peace be to you."

20 Having said this, he showed them his hands and his side. Then the disciples rejoiced when they saw and knew that this was the Lord.[989]

21 Then Jesus said to them again, "Peace be to you. Just as[990] my Father[991] has commissioned[992] me, in the same way,[993] I am sending you."[994]

---

[989] **20:19-20.** Here and in other places in this narrative, a phrase by phrase study almost robs the text of its impact; it slows down the movement too much. The events and emotions represented here move swiftly from one high to the next high. Imagine this sequence:

1. The risen Jesus suddenly and supernaturally appears in a locked room. Everyone is startled!
2. A second later, Jesus says, "Peace to you!"
3. With the adrenaline from the surprise still pumping though their veins, Jesus then shows them his hands and his side. For a few moments their eyes are riveted on him. Thus far, probably no more than fifteen seconds has passed. They have seen the physical proof of his wounds. They do not launch an in-depth investigation; in a split second they make their assessment. There is no doubt; this is Jesus!
4. They go wild with rejoicing!

In 20:20, the KJV translates the final portion of this verse as "Then were the disciples glad, when they saw the Lord." The word translated "saw" comes from *eido,* a word that speaks of perception—both seeing and knowing. Thus we see the reason for offering the translation that reads, "Then the disciples rejoiced when *they saw and knew that this was the Lord."*

[990] **20:21. *"'Just as.'"*** The translation, "just as," is from the word *kathos,* a word meaning, "even as," "in the same proportion as," or "in the same degree that."

[991] **20:21. *"'My Father.'"*** See note for 20:17.

22 When he had said this, he breathed on them, and
said to them, "Receive[995] the Holy Spirit!"
23 Whoever's sins you forgive, they are forgiven,[996] and
whoever's sins you retain, they are retained."

24 ¶ But Thomas, one of the twelve, called Didymus,[997]
was not with them when Jesus came.[998]
25 Therefore, the other disciples said to him, "We have
seen the Lord."

---

[992] **20:21. *"'Has commissioned.'"*** This word, *apestalken,* is derived from *apostello.* The KJV translates, "hath sent."

[993] **20:21. *"'In the same way.'"*** The word, *kago,* is here translated, "in the same way." It can also be translated, "in the same manner." The KJV translates, "even so."

[994] **20:21. *"'Just as my Father has commissioned me, in the same way, I am sending you.'"*** The commission that Jesus has given his disciples is an extension and continuation of the commission that God the Father gave to Jesus.

[995] **20:22. *"'Receive the Holy Spirit!'"*** The word "receive" is from *lambano,* meaning "I take," "I receive what is given," or "I get." Receiving is not a passive exercise. It is an intentional taking of that which is given. In a sense, Jesus is saying, "Take the Holy Spirit!" or "Be getting the Holy Spirit!"

[996] **20:23. *"'Whoever's sins you forgive, they are forgiven.'"*** The Greek conveys the idea of sin being sent away from the person that the believer forgives.

[997] **20:24. *"Thomas, one of the twelve, called Didymus."*** Both names, Thomas (Hebrew) and Didymus (Greek), mean "twin." The fact that Thomas is singled out by his Greek name implies that he may have been known among the Gentile recipients of this Gospel. Reference to his Greek name is also made in 11:16 and 21:2.

[998] **20:24. *"Thomas... was not with them when Jesus came."*** He may have had a good reason for being away, but look at what Thomas missed by being absent. Every moment in fellowship with other believers is to be cherished. One never knows what divine surprise may await those who gather in Jesus' name.

But he said to them, "Unless I see in his hands the print
of the nails, put my finger into the print of the nails,
and thrust my hand into his side, I will not believe."

26 ¶ After eight days, again his disciples were inside,
and Thomas was with them. Then Jesus came, the
doors being shut, and stood in the midst, and he said,
"Peace be to you."[999]
27 Then he said to Thomas, "Reach here with your
finger, and see my hands; and reach here with your
hand, thrust it into my side, and no longer be
unbelieving, but believing."[1000]
28 Thomas answered and said to him, "My Lord and
my God."[1001]

---

[999] **20:26.** ***"Then Jesus came, the doors being shut, and stood in the midst, and he said, 'Peace be to you.'"*** This moment was a replay of 20:19. The only difference this time was that Thomas was present. Jesus showed up in the middle of Thomas' doubt and unbelief. Here is a picture of God's great love. Jesus did not say, "Sorry Thomas. You should have been here when I showed up. You missed out." No, Jesus came a second time, apparently for the sole purpose of blessing Thomas with the same joyful visitation that the other disciples had enjoyed.

[1000] **20:27.** ***"'Reach here with your finger, and see my hands; and reach here with your hand, thrust it into my side, and no longer be unbelieving, but believing.'"*** Phrase for phrase Jesus countered everything Thomas had said eight days earlier (20:25). Jesus had known Thomas' every thought, feeling and word.

[1001] **20:28.** ***"'My Lord and my God.'"*** Thomas was overtaken by Jesus' appearing and the tangible proof that he was alive. But could it be that his response of faith was actually due to the fact that Jesus cared enough to come a second time just for him? When Thomas heard the sound of Jesus' voice, it left no doubt that the Son of God knew him intimately (20:27) and was not willing to leave him in his unbelief.

29 Jesus said to him, "Thomas, because you have seen me, you have believed. Happy are they who have not seen, and yet have believed."[1002]

Harmony of the Gospels			
	Matthew	**Mark**	**Luke**
Appearances in Jerusalem		16:14-18	24:36-49

30 ¶ And truly Jesus did many other miraculous signs in the sight of his disciples that are not written in this book.
31 But these are written that you might believe[1003] that Jesus is the Christ, the Son of God, and that by believing you may have life in his name.[1004]

Only God was worthy of these words, "My Lord and my God." Jesus accepted this worship from Thomas. He wanted his disciples to know him as Lord and God.

[1002] **20:29.** ***"'Happy are they who have not seen, and yet have believed.'"*** Reader, with these words, Jesus is talking about you! Here Jesus speaks a blessing to all who read this account and to all hearers of the Gospel.

[1003] **20:31.** ***"These are written that you might believe."*** The word translated "that you might believe" can be understood in two ways. If taken as the aorist subjunctive, then this statement means, "that you might begin believing." If taken as the present subjunctive, then it means, "that you might go on believing." The content and context of this Gospel suggests the latter. *The Full Life Study Bible* (Grand Rapids, Michigan: Zondervan Publishing House, 1990), 182.

Miraculous signs (20:30) and believing (20:31) stand together. Miracles affect the hearts and minds of people, causing them to believe upon Jesus (2:11, 23; 4:48, 53; 7:31; 10:37-38; 11:15, 45, 48; 12:11; and 14:11). The writer is confident that just by reading this record of Jesus' miracles, people will be brought to faith.

[1004] **20:30-31.** These two verses state the purpose of John's Gospel.

Chapter 21

After these things Jesus showed himself again to the disciples at the Sea of Tiberias.[1005] He showed himself in this manner:
2 There were together Simon Peter, Thomas (also called Didymus),[1006] Nathanael (of Cana in Galilee), the sons of Zebedee,[1007] and two other disciples.
3 Simon Peter said to them, "I am going fishing."[1008]
They said to him, "We will also come with you." They went out and immediately stepped up into a boat, and that night they caught nothing.[1009]

1005 **21:1.** ***"The Sea of Tiberias."*** This body of water was also known as the Sea of Galilee and the Sea of Gennesaret.

1006 **21:2.** ***"Thomas (also called Didymus)."*** Both the name Thomas (Hebrew) and the name Didymus (Greek) mean "twin." The fact that Thomas is singled out by the Greek form of his name implies that he may have been known among the Gentile recipients of this Gospel. Reference to his Greek name is also made in 11:16 and 20:24.

1007 **21:2.** ***"The sons of Zebedee."*** The words, *hoi tou zebedaiou,* literally mean "the ones of Zebedee, but here they are understood as meaning, "the sons of Zebedee." Two of Jesus' disciples, James and John, were sons of Zebedee.

1008 **21:3.** ***"'I am going fishing.'"*** Feeling that he had failed in his ability to be a good disciple, Peter reverted back to that which was familiar. It was as though he were thinking, "I may not be a good disciple, but I am a good fisherman."

4 But when morning was dawning,[1010] Jesus stood on the shore,[1011] but the disciples did not know that it was Jesus.[1012]
5 Then Jesus said to them, "Children,[1013] do you have any meat?"
They answered him, "No."
6 And he said to them, "Cast the net on the right side of the boat,[1014] and you will find.[1015]" Then they cast their

---

1009 **21:3.** ***"They caught nothing."*** Their former way of life was no longer productive.

1010 **21:4.** ***"But when morning was dawning."*** The phrase, *proias de ede genomenes,* is translated, "But when the morning was now come," in the KJV. When read together with the preceding verse, a dramatic picture is painted: in the very moment that these disciples had given up, the morning began to dawn.

1011 **21:4.** ***"Jesus stood on the shore."*** As this account unfolds, it becomes apparent that Jesus came for Peter's sake. Jesus came and stood in Peter's world. He showed up in the middle of Peter's shame and sense of failure.

1012 **21:4.** ***"The disciples did not know that it was Jesus."*** It seems that in his post-resurrection form, Jesus was able to cloak his identity. His resurrected body evidently had abilities that transcended his natural body. After his resurrection, he was unrecognizable on at least two other occasions. See Luke 24:16 and John 20:14.

1013 **21:5.** ***"'Children.'"*** The word, *paidion,* translated in the KJV as "children," literally means "little children" or "little boys." While it is true that some of these disciples may have been teenagers at this time, it is unlikely that Jesus was implying that they were young in age. The word, *paidion,* can also be used as a term of endearment in reference to people of any age; such is the more likely intent with the expression in this context.

1014 **21:6.** ***"'Cast the net on the right side of the boat.'"*** This was the second time Jesus had given these fishermen a directive that would result in a miraculous catch. The first time was in Luke 5:4 at the beginning of his journey with them. Here near the end of his time on earth, he repeated the miracle that was to follow. It appears

net, and they were not able to draw it because of the
large number of fish.
7 Then the disciple whom Jesus loved[1016] said to Peter,
"It is the Lord."[1017] Now when Simon Peter heard that it
was the Lord,[1018] he wrapped his fishermen's coat

---

that he was intentionally setting Peter up with a reminder of that day when Jesus called him and his companions to become fishers of men (Luke 5:10).

1015 **21:6. *"'You will find.'"*** The word, *heuresete,* derived from *heurisko,* conveys the idea of finding that for which one has been searching.

1016 **21:7. *"The disciple whom Jesus loved."*** In John's Gospel, there are five direct references to a disciple whom Jesus loved (13:23; 19:26; 20:2; 21:7; and 21:20). Many scholars believe that this disciple is the Apostle John, the author of this Gospel. It is unlikely that John was elevating himself above his peers or implying that Jesus had a lesser love for the other disciples. He repeatedly referenced the love of Jesus because he had been so profoundly impacted by Jesus' love. In fact, John is now known as the Apostle of love, due to his emphasis on love found in the body of biblical literature attributed to him.

1017 **21:7. *"'It is the Lord.'"*** It was not Jesus' appearance or the sound of his voice that convinced John that this was the Lord speaking to them. The *miracle* revealed the identity of the man standing on the shore. Miracles awaken the human heart to the reality and presence of Jesus.

1018 **21:7. *"When Simon Peter heard that it was the Lord."*** Peter witnessed the same miracle that John had witnessed, but apparently Peter did not recognize the miraculous nature of what had just occurred. Perhaps he thought it random coincidence that heeding the stranger's advice shouted from the shore would produce such a bountiful catch. He did not realize that the stranger was Jesus until John said, "It is the Lord." Often the Lord's amazing works go unnoticed until someone of faith speaks up and says, "It is the Lord."

around him, (for he was unclothed[1019]) and jumped into
the water.[1020]
8 The other disciples came in a small boat (for they
were not far from land—about two hundred cubits[1021])
dragging the net of fish.
9 As soon then as they stepped onto the land, they saw
a heap of burning coals there,[1022] and fish[1023] lying on it,
and bread.
10 Jesus said to them, "Bring some of the fish that you
have just caught."
11 Simon Peter stepped up, and drew the net to land
full of large fish—one hundred fifty-three—and there
were so many, yet the net was not torn.

[1019] **21:7.** ***"Unclothed."*** The KJV translates *gymnos* as "naked." In that day, a person could remove their outer garments and still be wearing undergarments, and yet they would have been considered naked.

[1020] **21:7.** ***"Jumped into the water."*** A more literal translation would be "did cast himself into the sea." The context suggests that Peter jumped into the water to swim to the shore.

[1021] **21:8.** ***"Two hundred cubits."*** The NIV translates, "a hundred yards."

[1022] **21:9.** ***"They saw a heap of burning coals there."*** Here the word, *keimenen*, meaning, "lying," is translated as "there" in the KJV.

[1023] **21:9.** ***"Fish."*** The word here is *opsarion* and not the usual Greek word for fish, *ichthus*. The word, *ichthus*, was the most common word for "fish," but *opsarion* was a trade term used for fish. Some scholars point out that only someone who was familiar with the fishing trade would have used this word. This observation supports the authenticity of the claim that John the son of Zebedee (a fisherman) was the author of this Gospel. A. N. Wilson, *Jesus: A Life* (New York: W. W. Norton and Company, 2004), 49.

12 Jesus said to them, "Come here! Eat breakfast!" Yet
none of the disciples dared to ask him, "Who are you?"
knowing that it was the Lord.
13 Jesus then came and took the bread, and he gave it
to them, and the fish likewise.
14 This was now the third time that Jesus showed
himself to his disciples,[1024] being raised from the dead.

15 ¶ When they had then eaten breakfast, Jesus said to
Simon Peter, "Simon, son of Jonah, do you love[1025] me
more than these?"[1026]

[1024] **21:14.** ***"This was now the third time that Jesus showed himself to his disciples."*** Jesus' two previous post-resurrection appearances are recorded in 20:19 and 20:26.

[1025] **21:15.** ***"'Do you love me?'"*** Jesus had already confronted Thomas' doubt and unbelief (20:26-29). Here he confronted Peter's shame and sense of failure.

When Jesus asked Simon Peter, "Do you love me?" he used the word *agape.* This word stands in apparent contrast to *phileo,* the word that Simon used in his response in the same verse. Jesus will use *agape* again in 21:16, but then in 21:17, he will use the word, *phileo,* when he questions Simon. It appears that *agape* and *phileo* are being used interchangeably here with no substantial contrasts of meaning intended.

[1026] **21:15.** ***"'Do you love me more than these?'"*** Various interpretations of this question have been offered. The following paraphrases represent the possible variations in meaning:

1. "Do you love me more than you love these men—your companions?"
2. "Do you love me more than these other disciples love me?"
3. "Do you love me more than you love these things—the fish, the nets and the boat (signifying Peter's previous occupation as a fisherman)?"

He said to him, "Yes, Lord; you know that I love[1027]
you."
He said to him, "Feed my lambs."
16 He said to him again the second time, "Simon, son
of Jonah, do you love me?"
He said to him, "Yes, Lord; you know that I love you."
He said to him, "Feed my sheep."
17 He said to him the third time,[1028] "Simon, son of
Jonah, do you love me?"
Peter was grieved because he said to him the third
time, "Do you love me?"

The first option does not seem likely. The second or third are more probable. If Jesus meant the second, "Do you love me more than these other disciples love me?" he could have been confronting the overconfidence that Peter had once had in his ability to love Jesus more than anyone else (Matthew 26:33; Mark 14:29). If Jesus meant the third, "Do you love me more than you love these things—the fish, the nets and the boat?" he could have been reminding Peter of the initial motivations that compelled him to forsake his trade as a fisherman for the sake of becoming a follower of Christ and a fisher of men. Given the overall context of this incident, the third interpretation appears to be the most relevant one.

[1027] **21:15. *"'Yes, Lord; you know that I love you.'"*** Simon uses the word, *phileo,* for love. Jesus was not asking about *phileo;* he was asking about *agape*. Simon Peter was evading the question.

[1028] **21:17. *"He said to him the third time."*** In 13:38, Jesus said to Peter, "Before the rooster crows, you will have renounced me three times." In 18:17-27, Peter did in fact renounce Jesus three times. Here in 21:15-17, Jesus gave Peter an opportunity to redeem himself. For each of the three times that Peter denied knowing the Lord, Jesus gave him an opportunity to profess his love for the Lord. By encountering Peter in this manner, Jesus removed Peter's shame, demonstrated his great love for him, and restored his confidence that Jesus still fully accepted him.

And he said to him, "Lord, you know all things; you
know that I love you."
Jesus said to him, "Feed my sheep.
18 I tell you the truth,[1029] when you were younger, you
dressed yourself and walked to where you wanted to
go, but when you are old, you will stretch out your
hands, and someone else will dress you, and carry[1030]
you to where you do not want to go."
19 This he spoke signifying by what kind of death Peter
would glorify God,[1031] and saying this, he then said to
him, "Follow me."[1032]
20 Then Peter, turning around, saw the disciple whom
Jesus loved[1033] following—the one who also leaned on

[1029] **21:18.** ***"'I tell you the truth.'"*** The KJV translates, "Verily, verily." The Greek words here are a transliteration of the Hebrew expression, "Amen, amen." It was a way of saying, "You can be certain of what I am about to tell you."

[1030] **21:18.** ***"'Carry.'"*** This word, *phero,* in some contexts conveys the idea of being carried with force or speed.

[1031] **21:19.** ***"This he spoke signifying by what kind of death Peter would glorify God."*** Traditionally it is held that Peter was executed in Rome by crucifixion, thus fulfilling Jesus' prophecy.

[1032] **21:19.** ***"'Follow me.'"*** In 13:37, Peter said, "Lord, why can't I follow you now? I will lay down my life for your sake." Here Jesus gives Peter another opportunity to follow him—even unto death.

[1033] **21:20.** ***"The disciple whom Jesus loved."*** It is traditionally held that this disciple is John, the writer of this Gospel. See the note for "the disciple whom Jesus loved" in 21:7.

his chest at the dinner[1034] and said, "Lord, who is going to betray you?"
21 Peter seeing him said to Jesus, "Lord, what about him?"
22 Jesus said to him, "If I should want him to remain until I come, what is that to you? You follow me!"
23 For this reason, the saying went out to the brothers,[1035] that this disciple would not die, yet Jesus did not say to him, "He will not die," but rather, "If ever I want him to remain until I come, what is that to you?"

Harmony of the Gospels			
	Matthew	Mark	Luke
Instructions at the Mountain in Galilee[1036]	28:16-20		

24 This is the disciple testifying concerning these things,[1037] and the one writing these things, and we know that his testimony[1038] is true.

[1034] **21:20.** ***"The one who also leaned on his chest at the dinner."*** See 13:25.

[1035] **21:23.** ***"The brothers."*** Followers of Jesus are part of a new family, and they are referred to as brothers. Hints that Jesus had come to create a new spiritual family are found in 3:3, 7; 20:17; and 21:23.

[1036] Other than his words at his ascension, these words in Matthew 28:16-20 comprise the final recorded conversation that Jesus had with his disciples. Acts 1:3 (NIV) states, "After his death Jesus showed the apostles a lot of convincing evidence that he was alive. For 40 days he appeared to them and talked with them about the kingdom of God."

25 Yet there are also many other things that Jesus did, which, if every one of them could be written down, I suppose that not even the world itself could contain the books that should be written. Amen.

Harmony of the Gospels			
	Matthew	**Mark**	**Luke**
The Ascension		16:19-20	24:50-53[1039]

[1037] **21:24.** ***"This is the disciple testifying concerning these things, and the one writing these things."*** These words establish the authorship of this Gospel. The author was the disciple to whom Jesus and Peter referred in the preceding verses—"the disciple whom Jesus loved" (21:20). It is traditionally held that the author is John, one of the sons of Zebedee. In 21:2, it is noted that the sons of Zebedee were present on this occasion.

[1038] **21:24.** ***"Testimony."*** See 3:11, 3:32-33; 5:31, 34, 36; 8:13-14, 17; 12:18 and 19:35.

[1039] ***Luke 24:50-53.*** Luke's expanded account of Jesus' ascension is found in Acts 1:6-11.

Pause and Reflect

1. John's Gospel testifies of evidences demonstrating the truth concerning Jesus' nature and identity. Having reviewed this body of testimony, who is Jesus to you?
2. This Gospel should be read and studied with a heart of worship. Having reached the end of this study, what do you now want to express to Jesus in worship and adoration? Declare back to him who you have discovered him to be.
3. What has the Father spoken to you as you have worked your way through these pages? What has he done in your life? Take time to write down what you have heard and what you have experienced.
4. Finally, in response to all that the Father has said, write a letter back to him, and include in that letter your words of praise and adoration for the Son of God.

And truly Jesus did many other miraculous signs
in the sight of his disciples that are not written in this book.
But these are written that you might believe
that Jesus is the Christ, the Son of God,
and that by believing you may have life in his name.
(John 20:30-31)

Paperback: 90 pages
Language: English
ISBN-10: 1460995341
ISBN-13: 978-1460995341
Product Dimensions: 8 x 5 x 0.2 inches

Available in both Paperback and Kindle formats.

For ordering information, visit DeclarationPress.com.

101 Prayer Models

J. Randolph Turpin, Jr.

This book is both personal and missional. It is a practical resource to help Christians jump-start their personal prayer lives. It is a concise collection of ideas to help small groups and churches mobilize for the ministry of prayer. It is for anyone seeking to link the power of prayer with the fulfillment of the Great Commission.

101 Prayer Models is a catalog of models designed to involve everyone. Presented as a set of annotated lists, the models are arranged in four categories: personal and family models, small group models, congregational models and evangelistic models.

The author, Dr. J. Randolph (Randy) Turpin, has been training congregants, pastors and students for the ministry of prayer for over twenty years. For a number of those years, he produced various hardcopy handouts listing ways to cultivate a culture of prayer among God's people. In February of 2011 he decided to compile those lists and make them available as a published booklet—*101 Prayer Models*.

Dr. Turpin serves as president of Valor Christian College in Columbus, Ohio. Previously he served as lead pastor of Royal Ridge Church of God in Scarborough, Maine. He also served as an adjunct faculty member with the Pentecostal Theological Seminary teaching subjects related to leadership, ministerial practice and prayer. He is an ordained bishop in the Church of God (Cleveland, Tennessee) and has earned a B.A. degree in Biblical Studies from Lee University and M.Div. and D.Min. degrees from the Pentecostal Theological Seminary.

Randy's calling to minister to leaders has taken him to South America, Africa, Asia and various training venues in North America. He and his wife, Kerry, have devoted their lives to promoting prayer, spiritual renewal and the Spirit-empowered life.

Paperback: 150 pages
Language: English
Product Dimensions: 8 x 10 inches

For ordering information, visit DeclarationPress.com.

Prayer Strategy

A Planning Workbook

J. Randolph Turpin, Jr.

This workbook is designed to help ministry teams develop the ministry of prayer in local churches and ministry organizations. It is formatted as a retreat guide, but it can also be used in other settings. The process is presented in three parts: pre-retreat, retreat and post-retreat.

Part One, Pre-retreat, provides a guide for an initial orientation meeting, a personal prayer inventory and a congregational assessment instrument.

Part Two, Retreat, directs the team through four steps of a five-step planning process: (1) assess, (2) set goals, (3) plan a course of action and (4) agree and celebrate—a covenant-making step. Integrated with these steps is a process for the shared discernment of God's will.

Part Three, Post-retreat, fulfills the final step in the five-step process: work the plan. Through a series of follow-through meetings combined with work conducted between meetings, the team pursues the goals set during the planning retreat.

Dr. Turpin serves as president of Valor Christian College in Columbus, Ohio. Previously he served as lead pastor of Royal Ridge Church of God in Scarborough, Maine. He also served as an adjunct faculty member with the Pentecostal Theological Seminary teaching subjects related to leadership, ministerial practice and prayer. He is an ordained bishop in the Church of God (Cleveland, Tennessee) and has earned a B.A. degree in Biblical Studies from Lee University and M.Div. and D.Min. degrees from the Pentecostal Theological Seminary.

Randy's calling to minister to leaders has taken him to South America, Africa, Asia and various training venues in North America. He and his wife, Kerry, have devoted their lives to promoting prayer, spiritual renewal and the Spirit-empowered life.

For more, go to
DeclarationPress.com

www.ingramcontent.com/pod-product-compliance
Lightning Source LLC
Chambersburg PA
CBHW080526090426
42733CB00015B/2502
9780692635346